THE *CURS*-ED NET

A Biblical Reality of the UFO & Abduction Phenomenon.

By:

Byron LeBeau & Richard Stout

Copyright © 2007 by Byron LeBeau & Richard Stout

THE CURS-ED NET
by Byron LeBeau & Richard Stout

Printed in the United States of America

ISBN 978-1-60477-149-7

All rights reserved solely by the author. The author guarantees all contents are original and do not infringe upon the legal rights of any other person or work. No part of this book may be reproduced in any form without the permission of the author. The views expressed in this book are not necessarily those of the publisher.

Bible quotations are taken from:

King James Version. Copyright © 1985 by Thomas Nelson, Inc.

New International Version. Copyright © 2002 by Zondervan.

New King James Version. Copyright © 1982 by Thomas Nelson, Inc.

www.xulonpress.com

CONTENTS:

DEDICATION... ix

FOREWORD:
  by Greg Messina... xi

INTRODUCTION:
  A Nutshell of The *Curs*-ed Net xvii

PART I: THE BITE

CHAPTER ONE:
  The Bite of the Serpent 27

CHAPTER TWO:
  Cattle Mutilations Sustain Demonic Hybrids....................39

CHAPTER THREE:
  Unmasking the UFO Facade 43

CHAPTER FOUR:
  Breaking Through the *Curs*-ed Net 49

CHAPTER FIVE:
  Satanic Hosts of Deception 55

CHAPTER SIX:
  Light Dwellings of the Stellar Order 63

THE CURS-ED NET

CHAPTER SEVEN:
    Domiciles of the Fallen Angels 73

CHAPTER EIGHT:
    Of the Dew – Olive Oil & Various Flowers...........................81

CHAPTER NINE:
    Show & Tell...91

CHAPTER TEN:
    The Original Agenda of the Supernatural Powers............107

CHAPTER ELEVEN:
    Missing Time 117

PART II: THE CODE

CHAPTER TWELVE:
    Breaking the Scriptural Code within Prophecy 125

CHAPTER THIRTEEN:
    The Abduction Phenomenon within Joel & Revelation....145

CHAPTER FOURTEEN:
    The Swarming Locusts 157

CHAPTER FIFTEEN:
    The Cutting Locusts..175

CHAPTER SIXTEEN:
    The Hopping Locusts...179

CHAPTER SEVENTEEN:
    The Destroying Locusts 183

PART III: SPIRITUAL FREEDOM

CHAPTER EIGHTEEN:
  The *Curs*-ed Net...189

CHAPTER NINETEEN:
  Symbols of the Net's Beasts...233

CHAPTER TWENTY:
  Conclusions of the Co-authors...265

DEDICATION

Without the assistance of the Father, Son and Holy Spirit, these inspired writings contained within this present work would not have been possible. To those people who, with a true heart, seek **the Truth** surrounding the UFO and abduction phenomena, there is an unconditional promise by God in Psalm 91 that He will deliver you from this deceptive trap.

> *You will not fear the terror of night,*
> *nor the arrow that flies by day;*
> *nor the pestilence that stalks in the darkness,*
> *nor the plague that destroys at midday.*
> *-Psalm 91:5-6 NIV*

Foreword

I had the opportunity to meet Byron (Brian) and Richard in May of 2005 while working on my own documentary regarding the paranormal. I had always taken an interest in this area when I was younger and during my studies at film school I met someone who had an interesting UFO encounter. His experience was unlike any kind of "ghost" story I ever heard and it compelled me to dig deeper into the UFO phenomenon. After graduating film school I focused on a story of an alleged UFO crash that happened not too far from where I grew up. It was during this time when I realized this documentary I was working on became more than just an interest.

I had interviewed a number of people involved with investigating the crash and others in the vicinity that had just experienced the unexplainable and were searching for answers like myself. Brian was one of the first two that I was able to interview and when I first contacted him I knew off the bat I was dealing with a scholar. He is someone who is extremely knowledgeable in the field of UFO culture and writes essays on the internet pertaining to the paranormal. Brian is one of the many people that investigated the alleged crash site in one of Long Island's largest county parks back in November of 1992. I figured if anyone would be able to give me information on what happened over 12 years ago, it would be him. I must have been on the phone with Brian for seven hours the first time I spoke with him. It was getting to be that time for me to tell him politely, "this is great stuff Brian, but save it for the interview." I needed him fresh

THE CURS-ED NET

and alert in the morning and get myself some sleep. At least he was someone easy to get a hold of.

Richard was not so easy to reach. His address was listed but the phone number was disconnected so I had only one option of getting in touch with him. I figured I would take the chance of walking up to his house and greeting him, not knowing what to expect, given this guy's history of seeing UFO's, moth-man, reptilian men and alien beings. Was this guy crazy, was he someone looking for publicity or was he on heavy drugs? Either way, I knew he had a compelling story to tell, so I was anxious to hear it whether I came out of his house alive or not. Sure enough, Richard was at the door; it was as if he were expecting me.

Rich was not part of the investigation of the crash site. He did however help co-found and run the UFO organization that Brian was a part of after Rich had left. Amazingly, the two were part of the same network and never crossed paths. Rich left the organization for a very important reason and this will become clear why he did by the end of this Foreword. He was someone I found to be just the opposite of what I was expecting. This man was calm, articulate, and extremely polite and above all, a born-again Christian, and not at all what I had envisioned a UFO enthusiast (or Ufologist,) as they call themselves.

While filling Rich in on my semi-professional project, he asked me an important question ∾ a question with an answer that I soon realized would change the course of my documentary and even my own life. He asked, "You know who is behind all this UFO & alien stuff, right?" I replied with a simple, "No...who?" He gave me a smirk and said, "Satan, that's who." Surprisingly my first reaction was not to run out of there with pen and notepad in hand. No! My initial thought was that this guy had been through some traumatic experiences in his life and needed to turn to religion for it. After all, it's too easy to blame this on the Devil, right? So I just went along with it and listened to what he had to say. [*My dear brothers, take note of this: Everyone should be quick to listen, slow to speak and slow to become angry... James 1:19 NIV*]

And I can assure you that every word that came from his mouth was a seed being planted by the Holy Spirit, and that seed fell on good soil with me.

THE CURS-ED NET

Something just struck the right chord with me that day, because I knew Rich was telling me the truth. He mentioned he had been going through much turmoil for over 5 years since being involved with investigating the UFO phenomenon and other areas of the occult and paranormal. It was when it became so unbearable with images he would see in his room at night, pin-spots of light, shadows running around, red glowing orbs and severe headaches and pains in his neck that he took action. Did he take medication prescribed by a psychiatrist, you may ask? No! Rich called out to the heavenly Father, the Creator of the heavens and earth and said, "What must I do to have your one true Son come into my heart?" Rich has prayed to God many times before, but this was the first time he did it with a sincere heart, calling upon the Father for His Son Jesus.

It was at that point when he described to me what felt like a weight in his chest lift up out of him, and to this day Richard has not experienced any more of the traumatic grievances that almost led him to committing suicide. Here this down-to-earth individual who is married and a father of two is explaining to me what you would think only happens in the movies. "The Lord Jesus took the evil out of me; and I'm growing with Him every day." [*You, dear children, are from God and have overcome them, because the one who is in you is greater than the one who is in the world. 1 John 4:4 NIV*]

There was something unique about this man that I did not see in others when interviewing them about the paranormal, which led me to wanting to hear more of what he had to say. It's one thing to say a person is rectifying the problem by seeing a psychiatrist, reading self-help books, meditating or doing Yoga techniques. But this man tells me Jesus was able to take this stuff OUT OF HIM! I don't know about you, but that's pretty amazing to me, especially when you hear the name Jesus, all people think about these days would be the going to church or religion class. It's as if there is some kind of branding or brain washing going on in today's society and making the King look like the enemy. I wonder where that could be coming from, or from whom that is coming from?

So I found myself visiting Rich on a consistent basis to hear more of what he had to say. As my visits increased Rich would point out various key words in the Bible that he thought closely pertained to

xiii

UFO eyewitness accounts and abduction cases. Whether one believes in UFOs or not, their beliefs don't change reality folks! This is a very real phenomenon and if you do your research like I have, you will soon take notice to the many cases that have occurred throughout history; it is no laughing matter! With Rich's research it all started with one simple key word in Scripture: starry hosts. From there he would be led to another key word and then another, and another. He would find these key words and reference them with Bible dictionaries, English dictionaries and Biblical concordance charts.

It became clear to me that this man has been given a gift. Rich was popping out key words left and right and referencing them with eyewitness accounts that even theologians, Biblical scholars and top Ufologists in the field haven't mentioned in their studies. [*But God chose the foolish things of the world to shame the wise; God chose the weak things of the world to shame the strong. He chose the lowly things of this world and the despised things—and the things that are not—to nullify the things that are, so that no one may boast before him. 1 Corinthians 1:27-29 NIV*]

Since Rich had left the UFO organization that Brian had been a part of prior to the alleged crash, I had introduced the two of them and Brian was astounded by the knowledge Rich had attained. Rich gleefully responded, "It's not coming from me, but from the Holy Spirit."

I am happy to have met Brian and Rich, but more importantly I am enthralled to have God put me on a path that bears much spiritual fruit. For without Him I would not be in the position that I am in now. I am dedicated to serving the Lord and growing with Jesus everyday. My hope and prayer is to help others out there who are involved with the paranormal and/or the occult, and take them away from the fruitless deeds of darkness that serve no real purpose in our lives ~~ and to show them the power that Jesus has over any form of evil. [*Have nothing to do with the fruitless deeds of darkness, but rather expose them. Ephesians 5:11*]

If the majority truly understood the power of the Holy Spirit and what Jesus can do in our lives (as all authority in heaven and on earth has been given to Him,) one wouldn't bother turning to other areas of spirituality.

I warn the readers now that the writings in this book are a mixture of both theology and prophecy. Do not be quick to pre-judge as it contains vital information regarding true events that will take place in the very near future. The information will get heavy at times and may be somewhat difficult to follow for those who have not experienced anything involving the UFO phenomenon, but - if it is not for you, please pass it onto a friend or colleague who may benefit from this book. It is for our own good and spiritual well being that one recognizes the importance and true essence of this material.

For those Christians out there who may believe this to be heresy or sacrilegious, I can assure you it is not. The Holy Spirit is alive and active in today's churches and people are prophesying and speaking in tongues all the time. If you are at odds with this, I suggest you do some research of your own on the web or pray on it. A lot of the disbelief today is due in part to the evil one and the only one who can deliver you from the spirit of doubt is the Holy Spirit so long as you ask. These writings are NOT to be added to Scripture or act as a supplement to Scripture. It is simply decoding the Holy Bible by inspiration through the Holy Spirit to give us all a better understanding of the origin of evil that is so prevalent today, and how to counteract the evil by calling upon the Lord Jesus who is also very alive and active today.

I can attest to the fact this is all coming from God as many things have occurred in my own life that can only be summed up in one word: supernatural. Within only two years of meeting Brian and Richard, I have put my documentary on a halt, I've come to serving the Lord Jesus with all my heart, formed a ministry with my two brothers in Christ (Brian & Rich) and have been on the radio several times to explain the devastating effects the Devil can have on an individual, and all this from someone who had done poorly on tests and had to stay behind in religion class as a Roman Catholic.

God has certainly touched my life in extraordinary ways and it is my hope and prayer that others out there come to the understanding that the world can have a personal relationship with the Creator of the heavens and earth. Yes, you! He wants to have a personal relationship with us, where we just need to allow for Him to come into our lives as He will not force that relationship on us or it would be a

THE CURS-ED NET

rape of love. The evil one (Satan) wants to control us, he wants us to think everything is alright when it isn't, and he wants us to believe there are space brothers out there in the universe because he knows our thoughts and knows we will fall for it. [...*He is filled with fury, because he knows that his time is short." Revelation 12:12 NIV*]

Please, please, please...don't fall for the lies! Come and get to know our King and Savior, Jesus the Christ.

[*Jesus answered, "I am the way and the truth and the life. No one comes to the Father except through me. John 14:6 NIV*]

God Bless in Jesus' Holy name,
Gregory Messina

P.S.: For any updated information on the material found in this book please go to:
TheCursedNet.com or RevelationVII.com.

Some of the proceeds of this book will assist in our ministry and we thank you for your support.

For I am persuaded that neither death nor life, nor angels nor principalities nor powers, nor things present nor things to come, nor height nor depth, nor any other created thing, shall be able to separate us from the love of God which is in Christ Jesus our Lord. –Romans 8:38-39 (NKJV.)

INTRODUCTION

When Richard Stout & I first envisioned our concepts, based on the *Ethiopian Book of Enoch*, chapter 68, it took the form of an eleven-part **Internet** group of writings that we had entitled, *The Bite of the Serpent*. Subsequently, Richard had found that two writings in the Old Testament (Joel & Revelation,) actually complimented & supplemented the information penned in what became these eleven chapters in this present work, and it was entitled, ***Breaking the Scriptural Code within Prophecy***. This same group of writings is presently represented as chapters 12 through 17. We began to see that all the dots were not completely connected, so the last two parts of our **Internet** group became known as THE *CURS*~ED NET, which we decided would make an excellent title for the whole thesis: namely, that the Fallen Angels (as told via the above-cited Book of Enoch,) were indeed caught-up in their own ***curs*-ed net**, having been judged and found wanting, and now they were bent & determined on incorporating mankind within the **same** cursed net, perhaps being jealous of what they had lost, and what we were still able to receive: i.e., ***becoming inheritors of God's kingdom as His children.***

This is what was the foundation of the present work. **Chapter One** starts off with the examination of ENOCH 68:18; this very important verse shows (at least to the authors of this treatise,) that Enoch was acutely aware of the ***demonic*** abduction phenomenon, in all of its specific detail, and was showing the fruits and effects of what had transpired after the ***Fallen Angels*** transgressed against the laws of God (via the sin of presumption,) as well as via the sin of lust. This chapter will also discuss the difference between the Nephilim & the Nophelim, and how certain evangelists were well aware of these things, and also well aware of *The Book of Enoch*, especially saints Jude, Peter, Matthew, Paul, Luke, John, Daniel, as well as the author of the *Book of Revelation.*

Chapter Two shows how the cattle mutilation phenomenon is part of the 'alien' hybrid situation where — not aliens — but *demons* are infecting **the bite of the serpent** upon unsuspecting female humans, and are using these procedures as part of their overall devilish plan to thwart God Himself — if they could! The evil forces seem to be intent on increasing their stock while diminishing the stock of human beings.

Chapter Three reflects how Richard, by using key word analysis of the Holy Scriptures (via various concordances and dictionaries,) comes to an understanding of what St. Jude really meant by the expression, wandering stars, and how they were related to the fallen angels as those who transgressed the laws of God. These dark angels are also responsible for the *facade* of the UFO phenomenon, masking their demonic intentions as part of their overall evil plan, but do so in a way as to lure mankind to think these fallen angels/demons are simply the product of some types of extra-terrestrial race(s.)

Chapter Four demonstrates how Richard breaks through the deception of the above-mentioned FAÇADE (hence the title of said chapter,) — and how he did it — vis-à-vis **by praying to Jesus**, which resulted in a real transformation that allowed the "heavy weight of evil spirits" to leave him for good! This is a powerful chapter that should somehow add some "bite" to the overall thesis being presented!

Chapter Five (Satanic Hosts of Deception) goes into the details of **Satan's Seed**, that involves both scorpions as *Grays*, (which is the label given to three to four foot beings with big black eyes and grayish-type bodies,) and how these evil spirits are *not* ET, but rather the **same** culprits that Jesus talked about in the New Testament (as unclean spirits,) which He gave the power to His disciples to cast out! [Incidentally, there is an interesting link to Fr. Gabriele Amorth's

"SATAN'S SMOKE," which discusses an exorcist who actually identifies these same two types of demons, i.e., the scorpion (as in above) & the serpent (as *Reptilian,*) which will be examined thoroughly throughout the presentation.] How these **Grays & Reptilians** beings interact within this **demonic** phenomenon is also shown.

Chapter Six (Light Dwellings of the Stellar Order...) identifies the 200 fallen angels and how their number is determined using both *The Book of Enoch*, as well as *The Book of the Secrets of Enoch*, where Satan himself is in charge of the legions of demons and fallen angels. Richard makes connections to what we are seeing today in Ufology, and I show how these so-called Ufological events are nothing more than part of the *façade side-show* being put on by the demonic forces to distract us into believing the ET hypothesis instead of focusing on the true evil — the fallen angels in pursuit of trapping mankind, both in body & soul!

Chapter Seven (Domiciles of the Fallen Angels,) actually identifies the who-what & where of the demonic abduction phenomenon, using II ENOCH 5 (the *Slavonic* version,) as a clue to the "treasure houses of the snow!" Richard uses scriptural deduction to show how these "mother ships" actually store those things necessary for the ongoing demonic abduction phenomenon which is posing as the "alien" abduction phenomenon...and ostensibly fooling many people who take just a casual notice to the things that are going on; meanwhile, *hybrids* are, in fact, being produced — hybrids that contain demonic strains within them, which again reflects how these demonic beings are transgressing the laws of God continuously, *as in the days of Noah*. [I add some data from Ufology *(the study of UFOs and related phenomena,)* to support the strongly felt convictions that Richard is presenting in his *three-part* thesis.] After reading the comprehensive details, you may be prompted into actually reading the full text of both I ENOCH I & II ENOCH, both of which can be done free online by doing a simple *Google search*.

Chapter Eight (Of the Dew – Olive Oil & Various Flowers) uses as its source (II ENOCH 6,) that delves into some of Richard's speculations about the power sources of supernatural beings that can be interfaced with in our third dimensional reality. According to Richard, much of this energy revolves around "hydro-electric" power, which

THE CURS-ED NET

can be easily attained via the super abilities of the demons' ships traversing both air and sea. A discussion of so-called "port holes" (portals) also enters into the discussion, and its links to Ufology are cited by me, since Ufology may just be an extension of the spiritual dynamics under consideration, which may, in fact, be being *blurred with a sprinkle or two of pure unadulterated obfuscation,* <u>yet</u> is part of the underpinnings of this present thesis! (Religious activity must be viewed very carefully within this mix since there may be more than one *façade sideshow* going on here also, most likely because *the trickster, Satan, plus his minions,* are hard at work trying to deceive mankind in as many disguises as possible.)

SHOW & TELL (as **Chapter Nine**) is a special & important chapter that actually gets to the core of *paranormal activity,* showing quite clearly how it is part & parcel of the demonic dynamics being passed off as a UFO FAÇADE SIDE SHOW — but more insidiously, it details how the dark forces go about massaging *mediums* to do their bidding (since it is rather the *familiar spirits* who <u>know things</u>, but pretend as to appear like they are "simply" dead people, thus playing a *"sting"* on the unsuspecting & gullible.) This is a controversial topic (that may not be accepted by all readers,) yet the **Bible** does point out, time and again, that heeding mediums (along with following the influences of astrology,) are <u>**forbidden**</u> by God for mankind to entertain — since the "entertainment" is a deadly poison that can entreat man away from God — to both physical and spiritual death! THIS IS NOTHING TO FOOL AROUND WITH, yet many people seem to be in denial about the truth of these things! This is a *must read* chapter! These mediums fall into a category called *receivers,* which are the third group used by the fallen angels/demons, the other two being categorized by Richard as being *donors,* who supply the parts needed for the hybridization program, and *hosts,* who are the unlucky females 'chosen' for the initial stages of developing the embryo before it is extracted as a fetus, to be tampered with by these same dark forces.

Chapter Ten (The Original Agenda of the Supernatural Powers) concerns Richard exposing the full intent of I ENOCH 15, and just who these <u>*Giants*</u> were, and just what their spirits are all about after their death, as in <u>*unclean spirits*</u>! This chapter will fill in some of

THE CURS-ED NET

the postulations of the aforementioned SHOW & TELL. It will also enumerate some of the evil functions of the fallen angels (which, in turn, will throw some light on how man got and utilized this information that was spun by the demonic forces so that mankind would *honor & serve* these same presumptuous dark and deadly forces!

MISSING TIME (the name of **Chapter Eleven**) which ends *The Bite of the Serpent* part of the book,) examines the key words of Enoch 68:18 regarding the "blow & stroke'" of the bite of the serpent. I add some interesting cases from Ufology to back up this part of the demonic abduction phenomenon, while exploring the nature of lies incumbent within this dark side of Ufology.

The second group of ideas in this three-part book can be found in **PART TWO**, and itself is divided into six chapters. The purpose of **Chapter Twelve** is to make one aware of both the original curse of Canaan, as well as to explore what certain prophets (such as Zacharia & Joel) may have **coded** within the borders of their prophetic statements about what we fashionably term the "alien abduction phenomenon." I found Richard's explanation about Zacharia's *Flying Scroll* most intriguing; the timeframe of THE GREAT FLOOD also put this thesis in a certain perspective. How *the Giants* of Enoch 15 & Genesis 6:4 fit into this curse is also very important to the whole of the thesis concerning the demonic abduction phenomenon, and how hybrids developed from this same dynamic, showing quite clearly how the *demonic* abduction phenomenon holds sway over the **ET** hypothesis (in the opinion of both Richard & myself.) There is also a reference to the timeframe analysis by Craig Winn, which makes for interesting Biblical speculation, especially as to how it relates to the endgame of Zacharia's 15 by 30 flying scroll, *the Tribulation period,* as well as the end-plan of the same dark forces under discussion throughout this treatise. Concepts like the story behind *Satan's Seed* as well as Steven Quayle's **empirical data** about historical GIANTS, make this chapter a compelling read!

Chapter Thirteen analyzes very interesting parallels among Joel 1-2, Revelation 9, and Enoch 68. *Locusts* are shown by Richard to be part of Satan's symbolic network, and also can be illustrated to be the same type of demons — doing the same type of things as can be shown happens within the "alien" abduction phenomenon.

xxi

I cited a book by Kim Carlsberg called ***BEYOND MY WILDEST DREAMS*** that seems to reflect the dark side of demonic activity, posing as ET shenanigans....

THE SWARMING LOCUSTS introduces the next four chapters (**14** through **17**) that leads up to an exploration of the differences of the soul from the spirit, thus becoming another compelling read! It is designed to show the dynamics about how the demons and fallen angels are part of the ongoing judgments, as seen through the light of scripture, which is also reflected by the suggested data in Ufology. The soul vs. spirit discussion at the end of this chapter puts into focus some of the more sensitive issues facing Ufology, especially when it comes to the stated experiences of Whitley Strieber, as commented on by Texe Marrs. Is there some kind of a transcendental link among the fallen angels of old, a goddess worshipped by ancient peoples, and what Ted Rice had to endure in today's world, all entwined in the reality-net (***curs-ed net***) of demonic activity? By reading this particular chapter, you may be able to judge better for yourself what is ***really*** happening, and what is potentially being presented in an obfuscated form.

Chapter Fifteen revolves around the second of four types of locusts that were mentioned in Revelation 9, namely, ***the cutting locusts***! The symbolism directly relates to the demonic abduction phenomenon, where those (demons) who take the "embryo/fetus" representing those who "bite" as in the serpent, *diminishing* the embryo, which is echoed in verse 18 of the 68th chapter of *Enoch*. (How did Enoch know about these very technical aspects of the "alien" abduction phenomenon so long ago, ***unless, of course, he were a true prophet***?!

Chapter Sixteen (THE HOPPING LOCUSTS) symbolizes the UFO portion of this demonic dynamic, as alluded to in a previous chapter (**Six.**) They can move (hop) from one dimension to another — which not so coincidentally is a facility reported on in the UFO phenomenon. From a spiritual point of view, it would not be surprising either, since St. Paul had indicated in his epistle to the Ephesians that the spiritual hierarchy of wickedness comes from ***on high*** (6:12.)

Chapter Seventeen (THE DESTROYING LOCUSTS) shows how this deadly phenomenon of UFOs can lead you down the

THE CURS-ED NET

rabbit hole to spiritual oblivion; I have a link to my web page called **RELIANCE** in this chapter that explains (from my own testimony) just how easily this seduction can ingratiate itself with the unwary. Although Richard's *testimonial* within **Chapter Four** is certainly more dramatic, the *more subtle* testimony that I bear witness to could eventually have been just as potentially deadly. I invite everyone who reads this book to also "click on" this particular Internet web page, *and I invite the reader to take the time to review the other Internet links, since (like the other book & article sources,) provide an interesting group of "back-up" material that hopefully reinforces the three-part thesis being presented.* A solid faith should have no fear of what is within **TOTAL REALITY** that — per force – will itself throw a light on the *false reality* we are presently being bombarded with.

The last of the three-part series concerns the two-part extended essay called, "THE *CURS*-ED NET." Part One (as **Chapter Eighteen**,) revolves around the warning not to honor or serve the sun, the moon, or *any* star, as per Deuteronomy 4:19. Ample evidence is provided that the wily fallen angels, using their aforementioned knowledge of astronomy and astrology (as per *Enoch* 8,) try to get mankind to honor and serve them by using the stars as their councilors and guides…and this is the reason why it was forbidden by **The Bible**, since it leads one away from relying upon the one true Father of all! A comprehensive review of the key words behind the constellations of the **zodiac**, plus the constellation of **Orion**, should leave no doubt about how this *curs*-ed net is trying to bind mankind to the dark side! Some ideas from Ufology are also thrown into the mix (such as those who hail from the brilliant star of *Rigel*, which just happens to be a part of the Orion system, and how the *facade* of Ufology is used to weave the demons' unsuspecting plan of ingratiating themselves with mankind by spinning fables about their so-called needs, and how we can help in their collective endeavors. You have to hand it to these demons – as in *giving the devil his due* — that they are very imaginative with spinning yarns that we are supposed to accept as gospel! The gullibility factor, especially for those with no Biblical anchor, runs very high, from what I can surmise.

xxiii

THE CURS-ED NET

Part Two (as **Chapter Nineteen**) focuses on the symbolism of the two beasts of Job, chapters 40 & 41, namely, the **Behemoth & the Leviathan**, which should not be too much of a surprise. It also incorporates an understanding of the full dynamics of our present UFO-ALIEN ABDUCTION PHENOMENON! The *Behemoth* represents the "earthbound" demons, while the *Leviathan* incorporates the fallen angels operating in and around the sea, the atmosphere, and near space! Their costumes are many and varied, and their UFO ships are very colorful, but all for one purpose: to present a convincing **FACADE** for their evil purpose, which is to incorporate us into their *curs*-ed net!

Richard ends (as part of the concluding chapter) with a heartfelt plea to pay attention to Psalm 91, (as he did,) since the answer to defeating the mighty beasts of the mighty men (fallen angels,) is simply to rely on the one true Father of All, and His only-begotten Son, Jesus, who will do battle for us, and *__all we need to do__* is but to rely and call upon the Father and the Son! If we do not do this, the power of the beast can and will overcome us! THIS IS THE MAJOR MESSAGE OF HOLY SCRIPTURE ~~ LOUD AND CLEAR!

I end the treatise by drawing the reader's attention to *The Mystery of Orion*, which was a curious show that was put on in the mid-1990s, concerning researchers Robert Bouval & Graham Hancock, among others. The long and short of this tale was to show that certain constellations and stars (like **Orion & Sirius**,) were ensconced in *The Great Pyramid* in Egypt, with two shafts (of this very pyramid) pointing to the god of resurrection (Osiris) within the belt of ORION, and the other shaft pointing to his consort, (Isis,) represented by the dog star, SIRIUS. The latter goddess (also known as Ishtar,) is none other than the queen of heaven that Jeremiah had warned the Jewish people about (7:18-21.) Bouval immortalizes the timeframe of this honoring as 10,500 B.C.E., based on some computer references regarding the belt of Orion and the alignments of the three pyramids at Giza. It all sounds good until one realizes the implications and then overlays this present three-part thesis that hopefully will give one the insight to connect the spiritual dots to an otherwise ufological or historical level of understanding. The intent of this honoring and serving (as in the case of Pharaoh,) was

THE CURS-ED NET

to hitch *your* star to Osiris's star, so one could wander together in Osiris's constellation of Orion, or, as I would put it, allow oneself to be ensconced within THE *CURS*-ED NET!

I hope you take the time to read all of the three-part thesis within these twenty chapters, so as to better spiritually arm yourselves in the ensuing battles that lie ahead, and thus avoid being stung & poisoned by ***The Lord of the Stings,*** which would allow one to fall into his deadly NET, another victim (statistic) to be consumed by the deadly spider (similar to what almost happened to *Frodo* in The Lord of the Rings.) Sometimes art echoes real life.

CHAPTER ONE:

THE BITE OF THE SERPENT

[*An introduction to Richard Stout by* **co-author** *Byron LeBeau*:]

The below is an analysis of Enoch 68:17-18, as it relates – *not to* the "alien abduction phenomenon" but rather to the *demonic abduction phenomenon*. The presentation had been put together by a man named Richard Stout (a self-professed "alien abduction" experiencer,) who also, being saved by the Holy Spirit, feels now inclined to give the viewer his insight into the above-captioned verses of ENOCH, using a Greek dictionary; all other references, if noted, will simply be their general meaning (GM) in one form or another. If you wish to correspond with Richard about the below or any other chapter about this present work, please email Greg Messina at greg@revelationvii.com and he will forward your correspondence accordingly.

[marginal note: How to contact Richard Stout]

AN INTRODUCTION TO THIS SENSITIVE MATERIAL

First of all, what do verses 17 & 18 of chapter 68 of ENOCH say?

V.17 " The name of the fifth (Fallen Angel) is Kasyade; he discovered to the children of men every wicked stroke of spirits and of demons."

V.18 "The stroke of the embryo in the womb, to diminish it; the stroke of the spirit by the bite of the serpent, and the stroke which is

THE CURS-ED NET

given at midday by the offspring of the serpent, the name of which is Tabaet."

All of the words in italics will be thoroughly reviewed in Richard's analysis of these very interesting and intriguing verses by Enoch, after Richard presents his general idea as to what is going on here, and how (via his own experience,) he feels he has come to an understanding of the meaning of these words, and therefore — perhaps — a KEY to the understanding of what has been called, loosely, *the alien abduction phenomenon.*

Allow me to make a few observations about this intriguing subject. First of all, it is important to realize the meaning of two words, one *nephilim,* and the other (which will be the meaning that is being referred to in verse 18,) *nophelim.* Nephilim is used in the passive tense as those who were thrown down and therefore - per force - must have preceded GENESIS 6:4; on the other hand, nophelim is the active tense, as in those who came down of their own accord, so that the **watchers** referred to in ENOCH 68:18, are the same ones referred to in GEN 6:4 — or the Fallen Angels who lusted after the daughters of men. After reading the full *Book of Enoch,* I formed the opinion that the original NEFILIM had committed a <u>different</u> sin against the ALMIGHTY: one of **presumption** — and that is the reason they had lost their "first estate." There seems to be some evidence of this "secret judgment" against this sin of presumption, where the wicked angels were acting "like Lords," especially if you go to the 67th chapter of the *Book of Enoch.* [Incidentally, the "SECOND FALL" (of LUST) is shown as distinct from "THE FIRST FALL of PRESUMPTION" if you go to *the Book of the Secrets of Enoch,"* (18:3) where certain angels called **grigori** (who were later identified as the so-called Nophelim,) came down from their place in the SECOND HEAVEN, unto the daughters of men; their prince, Satanil, was being held in the FIFTH HEAVEN.

What is really intriguing to me (and the reason I wanted Richard to read the *Book of Enoch,* is the fact that in the canonical Epistle of Jude, Jude actually refers to Enoch as one who prophesies; the <u>problem</u> is that Enoch did *not* prophesy in the canonical Old Testament, but was merely referred to in GENESIS 5; however, he did prophesy in the *Book of Enoch,* which the ROMAN CATHOLIC

CHURCH has (for some reason) dismissed as non-canonical — yet — it is this **very book** that throws a mighty light on the characteristics of the Fallen Angels, what their names were, and why they were contended with by the Holy Angels who did "not lose their first estate." In this same amazing epistle of Jude, he also identifies the "men" as these same Fallen Angels, who were subsequently referred to as "wandering stars" (JUDE, v. 13) that Richard will also analyze below.

If the below analysis is in any way valid, I contend (speaking as a Ufologist of forty some odd years,) that we (collectively) have to re-examine our understanding concerning the UFO phenomenon (and related alien abduction phenomenon,) and perhaps admit that the combined phenomena are rooted in *a more spiritual dynamic and/ or framework* as indicated in the combined Old & New Testaments, with *Enoch, perhaps,* serving as the proper prologue to same, since an understanding of his work would make more understandable the heretofore *baffling verse (GENESIS 6:4,)* as is presently understood in certain religious quarters. It would also go a long way in our more comprehensive understanding of the equally *baffling details surrounding the UFO & alien abduction phenomenon,* which we are trying to comprehend in today's society.

All I can ask anyone reading this is to be patiently open-minded, and hold on to your collective hats, since the details of *Enoch (as analyzed by Richard,)* should open up new vistas of understanding when it comes to UFOs as well as the fruits of this mystery. Occasionally, I may interject a parenthetical remark amidst the notes of Richard, and they will be thusly noted by the "{{ }}" indicators; this will be done to confirm what Richard is surmising while analyzing the selected verses within *the Book of Enoch,* as well as related scripture. Since Richard is both a Biblical student, as well as an *experiencer in the world of the strange & unusual,* the viewer may find his insights *stimulating,* to say the least.

THE GENERAL IDEAS OF RICHARD

{{His source material is basically, *VINE'S COMPLETE EXPOSITROY DICTIONARY OF OLD & NEW TESTAMENT*

WORDS, published by THOMAS NELSON, INC., NASHVILLE, TN, 1996.}}

I, Richard, believe that the *Book of Enoch,* chapter 68, verse 18, explains in some detail, about the (alien) abduction scenario, and by the use of the tools of certain key words (decoded from Greek,) and sometimes Latin, Hebrew, etc., plus the general meanings, all chosen with my experience and knowledge of the phenomenon, I will try to demonstrate how it accurately brings ALL THE KEY WORDS AND MEANINGS HERE TOGETHER in such a way as to relate the story of the **abduction phenomenon,** including why it was done, and more importantly, who's doing it!

They apparently merge together to reveal the truth as to the whole abduction sequence, including the hybrids, which, I believe, are being used for specific purposes, and also created for future use, specifically as an army for the ANTICHRIST.

When a person (or persons) are abducted, whether it be day or night, inside or outside, they are unexpectedly and suddenly struck with a blow ~~ a stroke ~~ a violation, done, physically by force. This always seems to happen when the victim is involved with a sighting (UFO) or usually alone in a house or car. They are immediately put into a trance- whether awake or not. They are then rendered immovable, and transported out of their natural state of mind.

They are abducted for a specific reason — a specific use, all mostly intended for medical examination, to determine which person has the best to offer ~~ each person offering that specific tissue, etc., which could best be used for their ABDUCTORS' needs.

THE "CHOSEN" PEOPLE

Abductees fall into three categories: *Hosts—donors—receivers. Hosts* would be chosen females for implantation & procreating hybrids, medically examined for "host" use. *Donors* would be medically examined people who have met the grade, having a special tissue etc. in chosen parts of their bodies for use as to engraft into the "sperm" which is also chosen from males whose sperm has been tested and found to be useful in its capacity to mix with the DNA tissue, taken from the chosen abductees. (This is referred to as the

THE CURS-ED NET

human abductee tissue donors.) *Receivers* would be those people who claim to receive special abilities, such as visions, etc.

Now *implants* are surgically planted devices placed under the skin. These implants are used for tagging an abductee, chosen for use because of a special source of tissue, etc. Their possession is needed for the *Evil Ones'* procreation of their own hybrids. These implants are placed at specific locations, (in each of the donors' bodies,) exactly where the tissue is to be found, which is not the same in every abductee. These implants then monitor the substances needed to tell the life, function & useful condition of said tissue for use if needed at any time; implants also tell the location of the donor when needed to be found; by extension, it shows the location of the tissue needed. It monitors the condition of a person if that person dies, or gets a disease that threatens the needed tissue; at this point, the implant would be medically extracted, and sometimes they just seem to dissolve!

BACKGROUND to ENOCH, verse 17

The name of the fifth (fallen angel) is Kasyade. He "discovered to the children of men every wicked stroke of spirit and demons."

Now, according to Richard, armed with his Greek dictionary, the word discover means to reveal, and wicked means bad or evil (and by extension — injurious.) (*Satan* is mentioned as the *Evil One*; note MATT 13:38 & 5:37 as well as EPHESIANS 6:16)

Stroke is a sudden occurrence or attack, as paralysis. Paralysis is the inability to move or function; total stoppage or severe impairment of activity. {{If this is the meaning of *stroke*, then it becomes fairly obvious in the alien abduction literature what may be going on here in this verse.}}

Spirit is a supernatural being as in angel or demon; according to ENOCH, stars are used figuratively as angels & also as **Watchers**, the *holy* watchers as well as the *unholy* watchers. In Greek, 'phantasma' is rendered "spirit"; also see 'apparition.'

Apparition is Greek for phantom or phantasm, which is "to appear." According to Richard, then, those ghostly light images may appear as humans, "Grays," Reptilians, or others.

THE CURS-ED NET

Phantom was shown to be something elusive or delusive, or an image that appears only in the mind as illusion.

Demon (or a demon) in the New Testament denotes "an evil spirit" as used in MATT 8:31, and mistranslated as devils. Acting under Satan, (according to REV 16:13-14. demons are permitted to afflict with bodily disease; also LUKE 13:16. {{This concept of causing disease is important and will be addressed again.}}

ENOCH 68:18 *analyzed*

What is "the stroke of the embryo in the womb"? According to Richard, the embryo becomes an offspring — the offspring of the serpent, which must be the evil spirits or "children of the Nophelim" since they came into being illicitly as per GEN 6:4; {{remember, as explained before, the original nophelim *chose to come down* unto the daughters of men: THEY WERE NOT CAST DOWN as were the Nephilim! Therefore, the serpent must represent the stars or *unholy* watchers that somehow could act within that same serpent (as perhaps as had transpired in the Garden of Eden; there is actually an *unholy* angel who is named in ENOCH for being responsible for doing just that, which will be mentioned later when we discuss chapter eight of ENOCH.}}

When the Nophelim died, (being earthbound,) they became the *offspring* or evil spirits, who today would be the **prime suspects in doing today's implants!** Now the word *stroke* means to inflict a blow, but also means to penetrate or enter one's mind or to remove or separate as if with a blow. *Strike* (GM) is to wound by biting, especially of a snake; to afflict suddenly. *Blow* can also mean to lay or deposit eggs in. The Greek word for blow is "hupo" which means "under;" it indicates repression or trance state. 'Repression' further means to exclude from the conscious mind, as in the unconscious exclusion of painful impulses or fears from the conscious mind. (A person remembers only under hypnosis.) {{Is not this how most abductees recall traumatic alien abduction events, as enumerated by hands-on researchers such as John Mack (now deceased,) David Jacobs & Budd Hopkins, once the victim(s) undergo hypnosis? It is important to note that not all victims need to have hypnosis to recall abductions; the late Karla Turner would be a prime example, showing that what happens to some abductees *is remembered in real time.}}*

According to the Greek, with the word *trance*, it says to see "amaze," and when we come to *amaze*, we find that it is connected to a root that signifies "to render immovable" and frequently associated with terror! *Trance* is a condition in which ordinary consciousness and the perception of natural circumstances were withheld, and the soul was susceptible; furthermore as a noun, it means a hypnotic, cataleptic, or ecstatic state or detachment from one's physical surroundings.

Embryo (as noun) and with respect to human beings, is the product of a conception from implantation through the eighth week of development. On the other hand, a *fetus* is the unborn young from the end of the eighth week after conception to the moment of birth — as distinguished from the earlier embryo. {{You may note that — according to the alien abduction literature, the *embryo*/fetus seems to be taken at some point in the first trimester, so could ENOCH be alluding to this illicit stealing from the female *host* so many years ago — a phenomenon that continues to this very day?}}

Diminish is Greek for defect, or a lessening, decreasing or loss! As a verb, it means to detract from the authority of, as of Fallen Angels. Furthermore, *loss* (as a noun) is the condition of being deprived of something; *deprived* (as verb) means "to take" something away from or "to remove" and in Latin, "to rob"!

Strike means to fall; it also says to see *smite*, which in Greek (metaphorically) is the infliction of disease by an angel. (Richard notes that in chapter 85 [of Enoch] "the stars fell from heaven — i.e., the *unholy* watchers; also "angels"; and JUDE 13 refers to them as "wandering stars;" in Greek, they are referred to as *deceitful* angels.) {{This is the same reference I had made in my introduction to this subject, where the "men" of JUDE, were, in fact, the **unholy angels or wandering stars.** What did Jude know about all these connections, and there were at least nine other canonical sources, including Peter, James, Matthew, Paul, Timothy, Luke, John, Daniel, & Revelation that quote ENOCH **almost word for word**; this can be found in a book called *FORBIDDEN MYSTERIES OF ENOCH*, in a section called "Biblical Parallels to the Book of Enoch," and makes one

THE CURS-ED NET

(like me) really wonder how come this *Ethiopian* Enochian book was not considered worthy enough to be considered canonical?}}

Now the word *disease* in Greek means "to have badly" which is "to be ill or in an evil case." *Case* idiomatically, interestingly enough, means "to make one's own" {{which, of course, the abductors of the embryo "stealing," seemingly do, in effect!}}

Bite (from the Greek 'dekno') has the idea of rendering with reproaches, and metaphorically, of wounding the soul. {{Is this, then, what THE BITE OF THE SERPENT is all about? It certainly would have us look at the "alien abduction phenomenon" in a possibly new & different light!}}

Richard would now have us look at the word *wander* as in JUDE 13's reference to the wandering stars as angels — the unholy watchers talked about in ENOCH. The word "wander" is Greek (planao) that means "deceit." So THE BITE OF THE SERPENT could mean the deceit or deception of the unholy angels. {{No matter how you look at this curious phrase, it does strongly suggest that the Fallen Ones & their progeny are up to *no good*, especially when it comes to interfering with the daughters of men, both way back when, and *maybe* even to this very day!}} To add insult to injury, the word *deceit* can also be linked to "the deceiver" which is also one of the titles of the devil; cf. REV 12:9.

The word *serpent* in verse 18 is mentioned twice, so let's look at its fuller meaning. A characteristic of the *serpent* (as alluded to in scripture) is *evil*. The general aspects of its evil character are intimated in the Lord's rhetorical question as in MATT 7:10 AND LUKE 11:11. Its characteristic is concentrated as the *arch-adversary* of God and man. This is metaphorically described as the *serpent* both in 2 COR 11:3 & REV 12:9. Furthermore, *serpent* in Greek is "herpeton" which means a reptile. {{And remember, too, all of these sources seemed to be very familiar with the *Book of Enoch* (in possibly a copy that had subsequently been lost to history.)}}

THE NAME OF THE OFFSPRING

This name is given as "Tabeat" at the end of verse 18, and it means *male* or *strong*. *Strong* is a Greek adjective that also means *mighty*; this has been cited regarding the angels in REV 5:2, 10:1,

THE CURS-ED NET

& 18:21. *Male* in Greek (arseo) or (arreo) is translated as *men* in the plural,{{which, if you recall, was the same link that JUDE had given to the word "men" in his epistle, but these "men" were *unholy* angels if you read the epistle (and footnotes) carefully, and it is only one chapter long!}}

As to the phrase, "the stroke is to be given in the midday..." Richard alludes to the famous Psalm 91:5-6, which uses this same word of "midday" in reference to evil striking at man:

"You will not fear the terror of night, nor the arrow that flies by day, nor the pestilence that stalks in the darkness, nor the plague that destroys at **midday**." {{Richard will refer again to this important verse in his concluding remarks, at the end of the book.}}

Now the word *plague* in Greek is (mastix) which metaphorically refers to "disease" by an angel. (Remember, it was mentioned before, that the word *strike*, which is repeated three times in verse 18 as "the stroke" — also means *smite*, which metaphorically means the infliction of a disease by an angel, {{so the meaning begins to emerge more clearly, perhaps, and all these STRIKES *spell* TROUBLE to the children of men!}}

Preliminary comments by Byron LeBeau

Richard has done other analysis that will be explored in the next chapter, yet I believe that the above examination of the key phrases (in both verse 17 & 18,) seems to point to an interesting tentative *conjecture*, no matter how vague it may seem at first glance, and this current examination is only the tip of the iceberg, just so that the viewer can get the gist of this amazing thesis from a "non-scholarly approach," but yet analyzed by one who had experienced the *other side* (i.e., the *curs*-ed net,) and was determined to find its root, and escape! I applaud his ostensibly successful effort (as will be explained in chapter four,) and am fully cooperating with his spiritual sojourn by **co-authoring** his troubled *yet hopeful* journey.

If we can agree with ST. JUDE that ENOCH was a prophet, then perhaps his chapter 68:17-18 were a **coded prophecy** where Enoch himself was prophesying that our current "alien abduction phenomenon" really should have been called THE *DEMONIC* ABDUCTION PHENOMENON.

THE CURS-ED NET

If you are not convinced that this may be the case, then — perhaps — after we examine the second part of this three-part series of this multi-layered thesis, Richard will have nailed down his case for aliens as being none other than the demons that infest and infect our current reality, even as I pen these words.

A *NUTSHELL* OF THE PRECEEDING IDEAS CONTAINED within the *ETHIOPIAN ENOCH, (*Chapter 68:17-18):

It is being *revealed* that the *Evil One* who is *Satan* suddenly attacks his victims with a paralysis (*stroke*) and these *spirits* are identified as the Fallen Ones (Nophelim) who had transgressed the commandments of God. They come in *apparitions* — being elusive, and are linked to the same *evil spirits* as noted in the New Testament, (sometimes called "**unclean spirits.**")

Verse 18 continues by noting that the *embryos* become the offspring of the Nophelim, and these evil spirits are doing implants (perhaps to this very day, and may be *the grays* we see reflected in Ufology.) This *stroke* **penetrates** the victims' minds and may deposit eggs, while the victims are in a *trance state*, and the same victims are left with a *repressed memory* (that ostensibly can be mostly retrieved by hypnosis, with some exceptions.)

This *trance* leaves the victims **immobilized**, while the womb is *diminished*, i.e., robbed of its embryo due to the *disease of the Fallen Angels* who are also the "deceitful angels of old — or spiritual robbers!" This *disease* is **evil** because the perpetrators are stealing to make the product (illicitly done) *their own property*!

The bite of the serpent wounds the soul because of this process, which, as stated before, is FORBIDDEN BY THE ALMIGHTY!!! Yet, the evil spirits (GRAYS) continuously transgress the *laws of God* & the will of the Father. These *serpents* can be referred to as (walking) REPTILES! "Tabeat" was one of them, depicted as a strong *mighty man* (remembering that Jude called "men" fallen angels in his own epistle.)

SPECIAL NOTE: If you want to read a link from a researcher who has REALLY taken a "bite" out OF *the serpent*, exposing these Reptilian Overlords for what they truly are (*despicable*), then you must read James Bartley; in my opinion, he probably knows as much

THE CURS-ED NET

or more about this subject than any other researcher out there, especially among the UFO *crowd.* GO TO the following Internet link: *[handwritten: James Bartley's website]*
http://www.alienlovebite.com/on_the_march_revised.html

CAVEAT ON ABOVE: Regardless of how well James characterizes these reptilian beings, trying to fight them may not be such a wise idea unless we are armed with the **reliance upon the Father of All, as well as Jesus Christ,** since it is a spiritual war (where the reptilians do reflect the darkness *and temporary power* of the fallen angels,) and therefore must ultimately be made null & void by their maker; all we can do is **not be a part of** their evil ways, and reflect this "armor" by being holy, pure, and showing kindness to all.

I emphasized this concept in the second part of **THE CURS-ED NET** (chapter 20.) Having said that, it is also important not to view things that happen in the UFO field in black & white. James Bartley has also highlighted other deceptions going on (such as the **MILAB** phenomenon, which demands our attention and discernment. A good article on this subject, a subject that is a sub-set of the evil dark Reptilian dynamics being perpetrated upon humanity can be found at

[handwritten: James Bartley's website]

http://www.alienlovebite.com/bartley4.htm

END NOTES:

Vine's Complete Expository Dictionary of Old and
New Testament Words:
Publisher: Thomas Nelson, Inc. ©1996
Used by permission of Thomas Nelson, Inc

CHAPTER TWO:

CATTLE MUTILATIONS SUSTAIN DEMONIC HYBRIDS

The below analysis reflects the ongoing notes of Richard, and his attempt to show how "alien" abductions and the present phenomenon of cattle mutilations are useful contributors to the creation of hybrids, which seems to be the end product of what was alluded to in Chapter One, especially as analyzed regarding **ENOCH** 68:18. Richard's interpretations will be put in parenthesis, while any comments of Byron LeBeau will be continually set off as such: {{ }} *The ongoing storyline is a reflection of Richard's many notes on the various aspects of the UFO & 'ALIEN' ABDUCTION PHENOMENON.*

Again, Richard connects certain key meanings from the general meanings (GM) as well as some key Greek roots (as per *VINE'S COMPLETE EXPOSITORY DICTIONARY.)* Richard starts with the idea of *seizing*, which (among its meanings) has to do with putting one in possession of something. (This possession could mean implantation.)

'Seize' also can mean "to overwhelm" or affect deeply in mind or emotion. (TRANCE STATE?) These words are also interconnected to some of the descriptions that Richard had applied to 68:18 (of Chapter One), i.e., stroke—afflict—repress—seize—control—effect—appear—amaze—abduct.

CATTLE MUTILATIONS

The first meaning of mutilate is "to deprive of a limb or essential part;" interestingly enough, *essential* relates to, or being a dysfunction or a disease of an unknown cause. (Remember — the disease by an angel, derived from the word "SMITE" as in an unknown cause.)

'Deprive' also means "to cut" as in (GR. 'aphaireo') where we come to the word 'butcher.' Oddly enough, the word comes from the OLD FRENCH ~ ~'bouchier' which means — of all things — **"HE GOAT!"** (*HE-GOAT* in Hebrew is used for *SATYR, with an understanding that it is tied to the demon creatures of some sort; cf. Willmington's Guide to the Bible.* (Could these creatures be in any way connected to the present reports of *mothman* (a la John Keel) — *chupacabra – Big Foot* and/or aliens?) {{My sneaking suspicion is that *all* of the above are "alien-connected" from their original source, i.e., *the Fallen Angels & their equally fallen and soulless progeny.* There **_definitely_** seems to be a connection between things "paranormal" and the demonic fruit it seems to produce. I will actually show some data from my own life that may tend to beck this up when I discuss my web page *RELIANCE,* in the chapter relating to THE *CURS*-ED NET.}} Richard seems left with the speculation that the word 'cut' as a *stroke* or *strike* can be linked to the Greek word, 'kope' (slaughter or the key word *strike* which also means to "remove or separate" or "to deprive of essential parts,") so it would fit in with the whole idea of mutilating as we had discussed in Chapter One. NOTE: *Cattle* in Greek means "whatever is fed or nourished."

HYBRIDS

Among the meanings of *to hybridize* includes "to produce and preserve desirable traits in a stock, or "to engender." It further means "to procreate," which stems from the Greek work 'genos' (beget,) but it also denotes "an untimely birth" from the Greek 'ektitrosko' (to miscarry,) {{which, not so coincidentally, is the same *footnoted* word for 68:18, as to the diminishing of the embryo of the womb!}} An untimely birth also means an improper time; the word improper also means abnormal, and the meaning of abnormal is the alteration

THE CURS-ED NET

of obsolete. The word obsolete (biol) means imperfectly developed, especially in comparison with other individuals or related species.

(*Richard asks:* Does not then 'miscarry' also have the idea of "abducted"[?]) {{As suggested in Chapter One, I do not think this is a stretch to arrive at this tentative hypothesis, especially in light of today's so-called "alien" abduction phenomenon, where the fruit of these bitter experiences is far from being — *how shall I say* — purely angelic.}}

In closing, it seems that Enoch certainly had the gift of prophecy, (as mentioned by St. Jude,) a prophecy that <u>*only now*</u> seems to be capable of being seen for what it is: THE STEALING (TRANSGRESSION) by THE FALLEN ONES (and their minions) FOR THE PURPOSE OF INCREASING THEIR OWN STOCK, WHILE DIMINISHING THE STOCK OF THE HUMAN RACE, as well as *misusing* the cattle we were put in charge of (as per **THE BOOK OF GENESIS.**) THESE TRANSGRESSORS ARE "like stars out of their season" — wandering in their misbegotten orbits! *Only evil can come of their fruit as in* **the Bite of the** Serpent.

END NOTES:

Vine's Complete Expository Dictionary of Old and
New Testament Words:
Publisher: Thomas Nelson, Inc. ©1996
Used by permission of Thomas Nelson, Inc

CHAPTER THREE:

UNMASKING THE UFO FAÇADE

*SPECIAL NOTE from Byron LeBeau: I have decided to print the full notes of Richard for this part (without any editing or synthesis other than minor punctuations, spellings, so that the reader may see just how this **co-author** goes about "flushing out" (via general meanings (GM) as well as Vine's Greek dictionary,) the pertinent nouns, verbs and adjectives that reflect an overall connection (at least from the author's point of view) of Fallen "alien" Angels as they "bite" "smite" & "stroke" the alien abduction phenomenon as wandering stars, which heretofore have been hypnotizing the reader into a **parallax view** of the real truth of **demonology**.*

INTRODUCTION to WANDERING STARS

The meaning of the word *star* in reference to 'wandering stars': Stars are used figuratively as 'angels' in ENOCH (*Ethiopian* version of chapters 1-101;) it is also reflected in Jude 13 & the Book of Revelation.

Angels (stars) are used metaphorically as real stars as far as this meaning in *Vine's*. (Jude 13 uses the expression *wandering stars,*) as if the "stars" really intended for light & guidance became the means for deceit by irregular movements (UFOs) which itself is only a *façade of varying lights to mask the malevolence behind it.*

'Wander' in Greek = "deceit" and 'stars' = "angels" (reflected in both ENOCH & THE BIBLE,) *therefore* wandering stars are, in

43

THE CURS-ED NET

fact, *deceitful angels!* [The following is a "page by page" description of the process Richard uses to deduce the salient ideas:]

PAGE ONE: 'Wander' = Greek (planao) for that which we see in deceit; 'deceit' Greek (apate) which gives a false impression, whether by appearance, statement or influence. (Dalos) is Greek for primarily a "bait" or "snare." (Phrenapatao) in Greek literature = "to deceive in one's mind." (Dolioo) in Greek = to "lure."(Pagis) in Greek = "snare" or a "trap." This is used metaphorically as allurements to evil by the "devil," as in 1TIMOTHY 3:7 & 2:26 *(2 Tim. 2:26)*

PAGE TWO: 'Deceit' is a noun (GM) = the act or practice of deceiving (whereas) 'deceive' as verb = to cause to believe what is not true. 'Ensnarte' is Latin (de-,de-t capere,) which means "to seize" (abduct?) 'Seize' as a verb = to grasp suddenly and forcibly; to have a sudden overwhelming effect on; to overwhelm physically; kidnap. 'Kidnap' as a verb = "to seize & detain."

PAGE THREE: 'Abduct' as a verb = "to carry off by force or kidnap." 'Cause' as a noun = "the producer of an effect, result or consequence." (Producer originator (of deception) is a title of Satan "the deceiver" as per REV 12:9.) (Akuroo) is Greek for 'effect' = "to render void" and (Katarargeo) = "to reduce to inactivity; to render useless." (What about to render immovable and to abduct under trance!)

PAGE FOUR: 'Produce' is a verb = to bring forth, exhibit; to yield (produce offspring;) to create by physical or mental effort; to cause to occur or exist. (In reference to #3 above of the meaning for "produce" — supernaturally transcending the material order or brought forth into existence (as in *the UFO phenomenon!*) 'Void' as a verb = to take out (such as the contents of — like a fetus?) to empty; ineffective, useless (or to render immovable through trance!)

PAGE FIVE: 'Yield' is a verb = to give forth as if by a natural process, especially by cultivation. 'Cultivate' is a verb = to improve & prepare; to promote the growth of; to nurture. (COMMENT: "improve" = more highly developed —"prepare" = selection of the best donor needs physically for implantation! 'Nurture' = the best means of proteins made available through cattle mutilations.) {{It has been shown that the blood of cattle can be used in human transfusion in emergency situations, so this might allow for yet another part of this *baffling* mystery via aliens, i.e., *the demons and henchmen of the New World Order, who themselves may have "given themselves over to the forces of darkness!"*}} 'Prepare' is a verb = to make ready beforehand for a specific purpose; to make by combining various elements. (That which is implanted.)

PAGE SIX: 'Prepare' = to make ready beforehand for a specific purpose. (COMMENT: This is why abductions to find the right donor through medical examination & testing [is that] which is contributed by chosen people to be used in the mixtures for implantations.) {{This truly looks like a *devil's brew* that adds the serpent seed within the contour of humanity so that the hybrid truly has a **demonic element** if Richard is correct.}} 'Prepare' also means to make by combining various elements. 'Occur' (as verb) = to take place, come about; to be found to exist or appear. 'Exist' is a verb = to have actual being; to continue to be; to be present under certain circumstances or in a specified area.

PAGE SEVEN: 'Nurture' is a noun = sustenance (food;) environmental influences and conditions acting on an organism; to nourish or feed; to develop. (COMMENT: 'Sustenance' = cattle's protein blood; "influences" of evil spiritual realm of influences; "nourish & feed" = *the reason for the cattle mutilations* while 'develop' = a highly developed hybrid.) {{The reader is enjoined to read the recently published book, ***RAECHEL'S EYES***, which is an alleged true account of how "alien hybrids" are nurtured *socially*; I got the feeling that the book was really about *demonic* activity, and when you read how & why they dispose of Raechel for "the sin" of just trying to be <u>compassionate</u>, it may add a little exclamation point to what is being stated here!}} Richard ends this PAGE with a statement:

book: Rachel's Eyes

"The UFO phenomenon was created by Satan and controlled by evil spirits and fallen angels to make us believe aliens exist when they **do not!** This is a deception {{a **parallax** view?}} to hide the real truth going on behind the scenes via the evil of creating hybrids!

PAGE EIGHT: *Wandering stars = deceitful angels.* (Satyrs are figurative of angels, as in *The Book of Enoch*, chapters 1-105, and also in **THE HOLY BIBLE**, as in Job 38:7; REV 8:10-11 & 9:1-2. 'Deceit' is a Greek adjective signifying "wandering" or leading "astray;" it also means seducing (1 TIM 4:1,) as in seducing (spirits)

45

THE CURS-ED NET

and used as a noun, it denotes an "imposter" or "one engaged in a deception." 'Deceit' as a Greek noun (Apate) = that which gives a false impression, whether by appearance, statement or influence.

PAGE NINE: 'Impression' = an effect, a feeling, or an image retained as a consequence of an experience; a remembrance. (COMMENT by Richard as an *abductee*/experiencer: Often, through hypnosis, you remember the horrible images retained in your mind by these experiences.) The Greek (Eidos) = "image" which is a shape or form as appearance, but not necessarily based on reality; (Skia) is Greek for a *shadowed* form or resemblance. 'Shadow' = a phantom or ghost.

PAGE TEN: 'Consequence' = something that logically or naturally follows from an action or condition as in a played out event. 'Appearance' (from the Greek (phaino) = "to become evident to appear." (This is the same reference in Greek that MATT 14:26 exhibits, as well as MARK 6:49.) 'Appariton' is a ghostly figure, a specter; a sudden or unusual sight; the act of appearing.

PAGE ELEVEN: 'Deceit' in literature = to deceive in one's mind or to deceive by "fancies." This is a mental faculty through which whims, visions, and fantasies are summoned up. As far as "consequence" goes, it leads to "remembrance" as the Greek word (mnemoneuo) that signifies "to call to mind." (Hupomimnesko) = to cause to remember. (Hupo) for 'under' implies "suggestion." 'Suggestion' = the process by which a thought or mental image leads to another."

PAGE TWELVE: *Look on back*: (COMMENT) The evil ones & evil spirits induce the person's mind through suggestion of what *they* would like you to remember, so while under hypnosis, tell the story the way your mind was given it. {{This may very unfortunately be the case in our real world of nuts & bolts, but Karla Turner had indicated in her short treatise on the matter, (**ABDUCTIONS IN A GINGERBREAD HOUSE**) that a good psychologist may break through this deceptive technique by going to "layer three" of hypnosis; Barbara Bartholic would be <u>*such a person*</u> that the now deceased Dr. Turner had in mind, when she made this statement; this story by Turner can be found on the Internet by doing a 'GOOGLE' search.}}

THE CURS-ED NET

RETURNING TO RICHARD'S COMMENTS: (I believe that the story given to each person that was abducted is personal, but contributes all the familiar characters, surroundings, and events which also take place for everyone else. If you can tell the person who put you under this story and tell him or her exactly what you are seeing and how it can be described, then isn't it the same as if you actually were awake when all of this happened? How come you have to be *put under* to remember it if your eyes were open to see the event take place? Would you not be awake and in control of your senses at this time?

PAGE THIRTEEN: "Phantom/phantasm" = something having no physical reality but apparently seen; an illusory mental image; in Platonic philosophy, objective reality as perceived and distorted by the five senses. 'Phantasma-gory' as noun = a fantastic sequence of haphazard associative imagery; a constant changing scene composed of numerous elements; the art of creating supernatural illusions. 'Supernatural' = of or relating to the immediate exercise of divine power; miraculous.

PAGE FOURTEEN: Now 'miraculous' is an adjective of the nature of a miracle; 'preternatural' = out of or being beyond the normal course of nature, differing from the natural; transcending the natural or material order. 'Transcend' as a verb = to pass beyond the limit of. (COMMENT: Through supernatural powers, the evil ones & Satan take whatever God has created for their use, i.e. deceiving mankind, and then, by transcending the material order, they change the molecular structure of said order. {{This may be the reason why certain UFOs are reported to change shapes, merge and even split up and disappear, as observed by many people over time.}}

PAGE FIFTEEN: (SUMMARY COMMENT: These materials are used to make them work specifically for their (the evil ones') use so as to make them look real in our world, i.e., that the phenomenon is real, and that these substances and materials are *not* from this world *when, in fact, they are*! They are *simply* supernaturally changed by transcending the material order, and how? For the very simple reason that *fallen angels and demons have these kinds of powers!* In effect, they push the materials beyond their natural structure {{*like a super-magic show,* and therefore there are nothing but ***props of deception***. Michael Heiser called such a show, ***THE FACADE*** in his own novel that addresses these same issues of **aliens as** *demons*; it was quite an insightful "novel" that seemed to *hit the nail on the head when it came to identifying the real culprits behind the UFO & ALIEN ABDUCTION phenomenon,* and is **highly recommended** by this co-author.}}

Many of these **UFO** objects *are real,* and can be touched and felt, but are ***not exactly*** what they appear to be. {Remember St. Paul even said that we wrestle with beings that ***are not flesh & blood.)*** Hybrids, posing as aliens, are part and parcel of this deception. Remember ~~ we are being {{"had" ***big-time***}} through supernatural powers, so, in effect, *anything goes!*

{{AS you peruse these notes above, you will see that *Fallen Angels* have many skills — probably beyond the expertise of *any* professional magician, since they have been at it for a very long time, and seem to do it with a deceptive gusto, where the average human would be no match for their skullduggery, unless skilled in heightened awareness, and more importantly, protected from above.}}

END NOTES:

Vine's Complete Expository Dictionary of Old and
New Testament Words:
Publisher: Thomas Nelson, Inc. ©1996
Used by permission of Thomas Nelson, Inc

CHAPTER FOUR:

BREAKING THROUGH THE CURS-ED NET

(Observations and a TESTIMONIAL by *co-author* Richard.)

{{After having listened to Richard for some months, I was convinced of his **sincerity** that seemed to ooze from every pore. It is in this spirit, feeling the same passion for getting to the core of the so-called UFO and related phenomena, that I present to you Richard's key ideas and TESTIMONIAL regarding **the Bite of the Serpent** as part of an ongoing series.

INTRODUCTION by Richard: Thousands of years ago, there were many cults & religions whose followers worshipped the heavenly hosts. These were the Sun, Moon, Stars, Planets, etc. This then, in my opinion, is one of the ways Satan was able to receive worship by people believing that these heavenly hosts were truly gods.

Satan deceived these people because they did not know *the true God*. Today, "starry host" now comes to mean one thing, i.e., the UFO phenomenon. We are to open our minds & hearts to the following information so we are not deceived. The UFO phenomenon is a **cloak of deception** used for Satan's benefit.

 "What is the "starry host"?
ANSWER: It is the light characteristics of UFOs!
EXAMPLES: "Starry" (adj.) that means

THE CURS-ED NET

1. Shining like a star
2. Shaped like a star
3. Illuminated of or coming from the stars

Star (GK) [A quote from *VINE'S* yields the following: "Of certain false teachers described as 'wandering stars' (Jude 13,) are cited as if the *stars* intended for light and guidance became the means of deceit by irregular movements!

Richard feels that it sure does sound like objects resembling stars at great distances, which are controlled by deceitful angels for *more* deceitful purposes, where the *stars* move at irregular angles with these same movements that reflect the same phenomenon we see in UFOs.

Shine means to emit light—reflect light—to be immediately apparent (appear) & to aim or cast a beam or glow of light.

Illuminate means to provide or brighten with light—to decorate with light—to adorn with designs of or brilliant colors of light— to expose or to reveal by radiation (where light is electromagnetic radiation) & to provide intellectual or spiritual enlightenment and understanding.

This last derivation explains many abductees' claims where they receive special powers from their contact event. **This is a deception**! These people are being used by the evil ones, not knowing themselves that they are. (Cf. Cor. 11:14-15, showing Satan as an angel of "light" or a false appearance of Christ, with his evil agents as angels.) **I know** *because it happened to me*, Richard; in fact, it happened several times. Now that I am truly with Christ, not one sighting or event by evil has appeared to me – going on twelve years now! {{Richard had marked off from the time these *dark forces* left him, which coincides with about 1994.}}

TESTIMONIAL

Through my beloved relationship with the Lord, I've prayed to know about that suffering and years of torment, with every imaginable event involving the UFO phenomenon that had plagued me day after day. Eventually then, in desperation, and feeling like *ending it all,* I called upon the heavenly Father, and crying said: What do I have to do to find your real son? You see, I was being deceived

THE CURS-ED NET

by Satan before this who himself had posed as an angel of light to me. I thought he (Satan) was Christ, but that was a deception – a false image! Through the blessed mercy of the *true* Son of God, my spirit was led to believe. I was being deceived because the way my relationship is now with the true Christ, there is a *definite* differ- ence. Through deception, I just could never understand what was happening, but when it came to the *real* Christ, all of a sudden (in time) love—peace — joy & truth began to show themselves, which was something *I never had experienced through the false Christ!*

Afterwards, I prayed to the Father. **He immediately lifted this weight out of my chest.** I know now that what was lifted out of me was **the evil spirits**! Soon after this, the next day — no more experiences with *any* of the UFO stuff that I had been accustomed to. It ALL stopped — and I mean *all of it!* It included things like seeing objects periodically, *Grays*, Reptilians, out-of-body experi- ences, visions, headaches, frequencies ringing in the ear, voices, noises in the house, false angels, balls of light, nose bleeds, etc. *To say the least*, by discovering the true Christ, all of this went away for good!

So I prayed day after day to know the truth about all of this, and after twelve years **THE HOLY SPIRIT** showed me through these *key words* that I have been writing about (in these aforementioned parts of *The Bite of the Serpent series (which now is appearing in the book you are reading*,) and showed me all of what is really happening!

How this book came about

DON'T TAKE MY WORD FOR IT. SEE ITS FOUNDATION OF TRUTH ~~ THE BIBLE! Continuing on…

Shine is a Greek verb "to cause to appear." In Greek (perias- trapto) is "to flash around, to shine round about." So these afore- mentioned keys words about "lights" (to me) show something that I *now* describe as UFOs. Look at the below list and picture the char- acteristics of these lights: emitting lights—glowing—decorations of lights—brilliant colored lights—radiation –suddenly appearing— lights flashing around (the object lights going on and off) & lights moving round about.

Shine is (GK) "to appear" while *appear* is to come into exis- tence, and *appearance* = the outward aspect of.

THE CURS-ED NET

Aspect = "mien" or an appearance from a specific vantage point; a way in which something is also "viewed by the mind."

Mien (as noun) is an appearance "bearing", especially as it reveals an inner state of mind (such as a suggestion?); alteration, influence by appearance!

Bear (as verb) = to exert pressure, force or influence on, to overwhelm, to effect.

Color (from illuminate, as noun) = the characteristics of light by which the individual is made aware of an object or objects or light sources described in terms of dominant wavelength; to give a distinctive character (of which UFOs certainly have;) to exert influence on, affect; primary colors whose mixtures may be subjective.

Dominant (as adj.) = exercising the most influence or control over.

Subjective (as adj.) = proceeding from or taking place within a person's mind such as to be unaffected by the external world. (When put in a trance, you are totally absent in mind from the outside world.) It also means particular to a given person ("chosen") personal; psychological existing only within the experiencer's mind or (influence through light & color!)

Let's look at the word *color* in Greek; here it says to see the word 'cloak,' {{written as "cloke" by Richard, which in Greek = (epikalumma,) which is a covering, a means of hiding, a pretext, a cloke for wickedness.}} See *deceit*.

Pretext (as noun) = an effort or strategy intended to conceal something; in Latin (to disguise.)

Wickedness (GK) = (kakia) which is evil.

You see how *in the Greek*, color explains it as an instrument for deceit, to influence people through lights and brilliant colors, & to set in our minds through deception in believing we are seeing something *not of this world'* — when indeed, it itself is being used as a prop for deception.

UFOs and the related phenomena are created to deceive us into believing we are being visited by other races of beings not of this world. Where else would we expect them to come from? The whole UFO agenda accomplishes all of its deceptions, which are just clokes {{cloaks}} to hide Satan's real intentions. When we see aliens

THE CURS-ED NET

---

doing abductions, medical examinations, & cattle mutilations, we just don't understand what the meaning behind all of this is. Years of research, both by governments and private people/organizations, have resulted in *no concrete answers!* **HOW COME?!?**

BUT

When we use God's specific words, decoded meanings in Greek, Hebrew, Latin, and the general meanings, we may perceive the sensible truth emerge to explain what all these UFO-related events are, and what is being done deceivingly behind our backs, so to speak. Just open your hearts and minds. Pray about what you are reading. *Let God guide your spirit to the truth!*

(NOTE): The primary colors are red, yellow, blue & green, as well as the achromatic pair of black & white. These are most often seen and used colors of lights on UFOs.

{{This ends Richard's im*passioned* TESTIMONIAL & observations for *the bite of the serpent portion of* **THE *CURS*-ED NET**, but it does not end his complete observations about the *starry host* (i.e., *the hosts of deception*) and more very specific references to scripture about to be exposed in the next chapter, that will go even further in identifying **SATAN—the serpents—and the scorpions under his sway** as *the Prince of this world*.

END NOTES:

Vine's Complete Expository Dictionary of Old and
New Testament Words:
Publisher: Thomas Nelson, Inc. ©1996
Used by permission of Thomas Nelson, Inc

CHAPTER FIVE:

SATANIC HOSTS OF DECEPTION
(SATAN'S SERPENTS & SCORPIONS)

{{The below information by *former abductee*/experiencer, Richard, zeroes in on the potential culprits of the heretofore UFO enigma, and squarely points the finger at the demons that Jesus talked about in the New Testament, namely, *serpents & scorpions*. Coincidentally, there will also be cited a **seasoned** exorcist priest, who will, not so coincidentally, finger the same culprits as he discusses the latest doings in the ROMAN CATHOLIC CHURCH as it pertains to the rite of exorcism, and how this rite is being ~~ perhaps ~~ **mitigated!**}}

Richard starts this new chapter by focusing on the word ***host*** that is one who furnishes facilities and resources for a function or an event. A *facility* is something created to serve a particular function such as for the UFO phenomenon.)

Resources are assets available for an event and describe what is available and used to support the event or function, as in (deceptive phenomenon.) The created assets are deceiving *props* and all that is needed by Satan. It is *fashioned* by him *supernaturally* via the transcending of the material order to convince the world that alien races exist. It is being used as a "cloke (cloak) of deception" for Satan's use and the use of the evil spirits (demons) for their own agenda. When people look at outer space, and say we can't be the only ones

THE CURS-ED NET

here, there's got to be other life out there, then Satan has *already got you hooked with all of his props, etc.*

It makes his job so much easier, because we might feel that there should be life out there; however, we did not create the universe — God did! So why don't we ask Him if there's life out there. If you believe God's word as reflected in the Bible, don't you think God would have told us if there is, especially if that alien life was coming to give *so many so much torment*? {{I take the *larger* view on this issue: **Since no one can say for sure that there isn't many forms of life "out there," then — perhaps – what is the *real dynamic* has more to do with the <u>preparation for the "meeting" of these other forms</u> when the *appropriate time has come, i.e.,* after we (as God's children) have truly been <u>elected into His company,</u> and at that blessed point, *all the rest will be revealed to us!*** This would solve the knotty problem of "out there" as well as solve the problem of "going out there" once the "course" of the Bible has been *__passed!__* <u>The other issue is a mystery:</u> *Grace (and not earning credit) is an intimate part of this "course dynamic" (if we take St. Paul seriously,) so it is not like a karmic debt overcome that brings on this blessed event.* Now that I have totally confused everyone, let's continue.}}

God fashioned Man in *God's* own image. Why then would He create an evil alien race to dominate us from every aspect? *Ask yourself:* If there is life out there, pertinent to us, God should have told us in the Bible, shouldn't He have? So then, if He remained mute on the subject, what are we dealing with? [Note: For those who are familiar with the *Book of Enoch,* He did *not* remain mute on the subject, and that, of course, is another reason for connecting the dots of this book, so that you will be *acutely* aware of what you are up against in our *third dimensional* reality.]

CLUES TO THE "HOST"

Host (as in the GK. (Xenos) means "stranger," coming from 'strange;' *strange* means "foreign or alien." *Alien* as in the (GK (allotrios) "is the belonging to another, not of one's own & an enemy." *Enemy as in the* (GK (echthros) means "hateful or hated." This hate is akin to (ektos) which means "outside," and in the active

an intelligent and a fair comment

56

THE CURS-ED NET

sense, "hostile." Used as a noun, an *enemy* adversary is equated to the devil; cf. MATT 13:39 & LUKE 10:19. *Outside,* as a noun, is "an outward aspect or appearance." *Aspect,* also as noun, is "a way that something is viewed by the mind."

As we continue with these linkages of words, *strange* means "out of the ordinary — not previously known — differing from the normal — not of one's own locality or environment & characteristic of another place." *Ordinary* means "commonly encountered" (while UFOs are not!) *Outward* has a Greek note with it: The phrase *en to, phanero* in (LIT) refers to "in the open" & "manifest" which is rendered as outwardly. (In the KJV, 2 Cor.10:7, there is a reference to "outward appearance." (Keep in mind where the word *appearance* leads us, further on in this analysis.)

Viewed (in our mind) comes from "aspect." *View* (as noun) means "an individual and personal perception; an effect having an ability to be perceived as real to the mind, chosen specifically in use to each individual." (The supernatural fashioning of the creatures or objects result in the overall effect, *so intense* that our minds perceive them to be real. It has chosen each event as personal to each individual.)

Vision (as noun) is "unusual competence in discernment or perception — a mental image & the experience of seeing a supernatural being." (*Supernatural being* is to mean *not of* flesh & blood, but a created image by supernatural beings.

Shine from the Greek (phaino) means "to cause to appear." *Cause* (as noun) means "the producer of an effect, result or consequence; to cause for a reason; therefore (the UFO phenomenon is created for deception as a "cloke" of hiding.)

Consequence (as noun) means a relation of the result to its cause (where the effect is supernaturally executed as real so we believe it to be real; the result is: *WE BELIEVE IT*!)

KEY WORD

Appear (phaino) in the active voice means "to shine," whereas in the passive voice, it means "to be brought forth into light, and lastly, to become evident; to appear." Now *appear* as in the Greek (anaphaino) means "to appear *suddenly*" *while* (phaneroo) in the active voice, "to manifest," from the word *outward. Manifest* (GK

57

THE CURS-ED NET

'phaneros') is "to open to sight; visible," and comes from the root ('phan') that signifies *shining*.

DRAWING ON ABOVE, RICHARD MAKES THE FOLLOWING OBSERVATION:

In order for something to appear *suddenly'* — to become visible (open to sight,) the appearance means the "instance of coming into sight" or to come into existence; *instance* means "occurring immediately or at once," so then for these images to appear suddenly, wouldn't they have to be *invisible* to begin with, or at least created by a force that is invisible, effected instantly? AND — if these images appeared suddenly, then how could they be of living matter, i.e., flesh and blood? To follow this logic, let's see where the word *spirit* goes....

Spirit (a noun) means "a supernatural being as in angel or demon;" it is a being inhabiting or embodying a particular place, object or natural or unnatural phenomenon. (Do the demons inhabit *hybrids*? Do they inhabit created false images manifested to the point that they can be *felt*? Do you know that because you can touch something, *it doesn't necessarily mean* that it is a real creature or an animate object as it appears to be? REMEMBER: The use of supernatural powers creates a dynamic where *anything goes!* If you are creating a deceptive phenomenon, you will make it *look* real, and use all of the support characters needed. {{To me, this is reminiscent of *virtual reality* where, once put into an **altered state,** everything flows from that naturally, *yet* it is still virtual reality *and not true reality*! Anyone familiar with the sophisticated tricks used in MIND CONTROL would not see Richard's argument as being *too far fetched!*}}

BACK TO RICHARD & "SPIRIT"

This is a Greek word (*pneuma*) that denotes the "wind," akin to (pneo) which means "to breathe; blow; also breath." The spirit is then like the wind — *invisible* (as in *evil spirits!*) *Spirit as in the* GK (phantasma,) is reflected in both MATT 14:26 & MARK 6:49 of the KJV,) which is equivalent to the word *apparition*; this latter word means "a phantom, a phantasm" from (phaino) which means "to appear; appearance."

THE CURS-ED NET

Phantom/phantasm = something having no physical reality but apparently seen, as in an illusory mental image & (in Platonic philo) objective reality as perceived and distorted by the five senses.

SNAKES & SCORPIONS UNMASKED

In the Gospel of Luke (10:19) of the *NIV LIFE & SPIRIT BIBLE,* Christ is speaking:

"I have given you authority to trample on snakes and scorpions, and to overcome all the power of the enemy; and nothing will harm you."

In a note in this same Bible, relating to the above **snakes & scorpions,** they both are terms representing the most **dangerous** forces of spiritual evil. {{If you go to the below *Internet* link, about an exorcist who confronts both types, and could even recognize them by the look in their eyes, you will see that this is no joke, but actually **real** phenomenon that exists and has been documented; go to: *internet page* ✳

http://www.speroforum.com/site/article.asp?id=2879

Incidentally, Richard notes that the word *enemy* from LUKE 10:19, also is used as one of the titles of Satan; the same holds true for MATT 13:39.}}

Snake (as noun) means "any of numerous scaly, legless, and sometimes venomous reptiles of the suborder *serpents. Serpent* also happens to be another title for Satan as per 2 Cor.11:3 & Rev.12:9.

Snakes in LUKE 10:19 are symbolic of the forces of evil (like demons & evil spirits.) RICHARD SPECULATES: Could these *Reptilians* then be fashioned by the snakes, demons and evil spirits as a symbolic Biblical reference *to themselves,* and done so as part of a deception? {{*As odd as the following may appear,* a description of a Reptilian-like being was actually seen by Richard at age fourteen while in his backyard with his friend Jody; it was a sunny day, and the being stood about ten feet away; from what Richard remembers, it was "greenish scaly skin, with long sharp teeth, a short tail, one to two feet in length, long claws on the feet, three long claws on the hands with eyes he will never forget: They had a yellow background (iris) with pupils that were almond-shaped, which were black, and ran vertically across the yellow background." When questioned by me recently about this encounter, he also remembered that it must

59

THE CURS-ED NET

have stood about eight foot tall, *since it was higher than the clothes-line that it was standing by,* and Richard said that this line was approximately six foot high.}}

LET'S NOW TURN TO THE WORD *DRAGON*

This, of course, is another title for Satan (as per Rev.12:7) Allegedly it is a mythological monster, traditionally represented as a giant reptile, with lion's claws, long sharp teeth, a serpent's tail, wings, and scaly skin; it is also greenish in color, and I, *Richard,* am sure that the descriptions and color of the eyes pretty much matches what I saw when I had my Reptilian sighting. Using the same Bible as referenced before, Christ is speaking in LUKE 11:11-12:

"Which of your fathers, if your son asks for a fish will give him a snake instead? Or if he asks for an egg will give him a scorpion?" (Why were the **snake & scorpion** used? I believe they are also symbolic representations; here's how!)

Let's look at the word *scale* as it relates to the *fish & the snake.*

Scale is "a small plate-like dermal or epidermal structure; external coverings on a fish, reptile and certain mammals." Fish, reptiles & snakes have sharp teeth and fangs; they are also cold-blooded. Fish have tails, as do snakes and reptiles. Some colors of fish match the colors of snakes. In other words, there is a similarity between them, but what does a scorpion have to do with an egg? LET'S SEE!

VINE'S notes regarding LUKE 11:11-12, that the scorpion is an allusion to the egg, since it has the same shape of it *when at rest.* Is this a symbolic reference? I think it is!

Let's do a description list between the *scorpion* (evil forces—demons) to the *GRAY* "aliens" reported so often in the alien abduction phenomenon: The heads of *the Grays* are egg-shaped; the allusion here is that a scorpion at rest resembles an *egg-shape.* In concert with this, the structure of *the Grays'* eyes resembles the shape of almonds. To see how a scorpion is similar to a *Gray's* eye, we must first examine the word scorpion in Greek:

Here, (skorpios) is akin to (skorpizo) which means "to scatter." *Scatter* (diaspeiro) further means "to scatter abroad, as in ('dia') & ('spiro') to sow seed." *Seeds* are almond-shaped, and as indicated before, so are *the Grays'* eyes. Next, the eyes' *seeds* symbolically

60

THE CURS-ED NET

are black; the black eyes are symbolic. *Black* (as adjective) means "evil—wicked," and according to *Holman's Bible Dictionary,* black is "the abode of the dead." (There is also a reference to Job.3:5 & Jude13, with a further reference to *the Book of Enoch,*(68:18,) which was discussed in Chapter One concerning **The Bite of the Serpent** information.

Black (GK 'zophos') denotes the gloom of the region of the lost. In *Nelson's New & Illustrated Dictionary,* we look at the word *abyss* where it is described as a prison of disobedient spirits, as in the demons of the world of the dead.

So if then the color **black** symbolizes the 'abode of the dead,' and the prison of the disobedient spirits (demons) are by the same color black symbolized by the same 'world of the dead,' this would point to the possibility that the *Grays'* eyes symbolize evil. The color *black* also represents pestilence as in the scriptural books of *Daniel & Revelation.*

Now *pestilence* (as noun) means "pernicious evil influence or agent;" *pernicious* (as adj.) = a tendency to cause death (spiritual?) and serious injury, as well as causing great harm. The (archaic) meaning = evil—wicked.

So it seems that *snakes & scorpions* are symbolic for evil forces & demons. The symbolic similarities between snakes and the reptilians as to the facial descriptions of the reptilian images to dragons, serpents, the involvement of Satan & demons, as well as the appearance of phantoms, tells me that the snakes mentioned in *Luke* 10:19 & 11:11-12, symbolically, outwardly & spiritually **reflect the created images of the Reptilian race,** created & controlled by evil spirits. The symbolic similarities between *scorpions & Gray aliens* as to the detailed descriptions of each represent evil spiritual forces. The *Grays* are a created representation of its evil character & characters, (as demon & evil spirits.)

OH YEAII! In *Holman's Bible Dictionary,* the greenish-gray color of the **Grays** is also symbolic of death (especially spiritual death.) In conformity with this, the *Grays'* eyes must have an evil influence on us for hypnotic control, it seems to me. {{The reports that come in from the Ufological suggested data would tend to

61

confirm these observations, so that the symbolism suggested by Richard may not be far from the *reality* of the situation.}}

IN SUMMARY: The snakes represent the *Reptilians*, while the scorpions represent the *Grays*. The snakes are the **serpents of the highest rank**; the *Grays* are the scorpions, working under them as their underlings.

{{There you have it, folks, **THE HOSTS OF HEAVEN** — and what a sad and woeful lot they seem to be, causing untold misery in (what passes as) the "alien abduction phenomenon." I believe that Richard is doing a good service for humanity in exposing (from his point of view) what he sees as a *spiritual menace*. To ignore his findings and experiences may be disadvantageous to one's spiritual future health.

This same sinister scenario has been recently echoed in the novel by Michael Heiser called, ***THE FAÇADE, and although presented as fiction, captures some of the larger underlying truths that are being presented in this present non-fictional work.*** Dr. Karla Turner has also called our attention to the *Reptilian* menace and how they are negatively impacting on our reality; unfortunately her book, ***MASQUERADE OF ANGELS*** is not fiction, and was a clarion call back in the mid 1990s that something sinister was transpiring in the so-called UFO & ALIEN ABDUCTION phenomenon. Now, a good ten years later, Dr. Turner is no longer with us, but it may behoove some to pay ***more close attention*** to the findings and spiritual connections as are now being presented.}}

END NOTES:

Nelson's New and Illustrated Bible Dictionary
Publisher: Thomas Nelson, Inc. ©1995

Vine's Complete Expository Dictionary of Old and
New Testament Words:
Publisher: Thomas Nelson, Inc. ©1996
Used by permission of Thomas Nelson, Inc

CHAPTER SIX:

LIGHT DWELLINGS OF THE STELLAR ORDER

We will start with the book of **Ethiopian** Enoch, chapter seven, V7: "The whole number (of the Fallen 'alien' Angels) was two hundred who descended upon Ardis." (These unholy ones were figuratively known as 'stars' in *The Book of Enoch*, Jude 13, & Revelation [**The Apocalypse**.]) 200 Fallen Angels

Next we go to *The Book of the Secrets of Enoch* (**Slavonic** Enoch or II *ENOCH,*) chapter four, entitled, "Titles of the Angels Ruling the Stars." Stars, here, has two meanings: firstly, heavenly, then secondly, as angels. It reads as follows: "They brought before my face the elders and the rulers of the stellar orders, and showed me *two hundred* angels who rule the stars and their services to the heavens and fly with their wings and come round all those who sail."

Key words are as follows: 1) elders; 2) rulers; 3) stellar; 4) order; 5) wings; 6) round; 7) sail.

The word *elder* here in Greek (presbuteros) means "of rank, or of a position of responsibility." The next word, *rulers* in Greek (Archon) is "a ruler, chief, prince, and is translated as *rulers*". So ruler in Greek means "a ruler in the singular." Another Greek meaning of the word ruler is (kosmorator) which denotes "a ruler of this world." Now let's look at some of the titles of Satan:

1) The *prince* of this world (John 12:31)

2) The *prince* of the powers of the air, where air means sky, heavenly & stellar (Eph. 2:2)

3) The *ruler* of darkness (Eph. 6:12)

You see how these titles of Satan could reflect the meanings of "ruler" here? The next keyword is *stellar* which as (adj.) relates to stars, where the Latin (stella) = star. The next word to follow is *order* (a noun) meaning of an "established system of a social organization;" also, a foundation, seemingly a military one of the fallen angels and evil spirits.

Let's look at the word *star* in Greek. 'Star' is used also figuratively as angels described in the *Ethiopian Book of Enoch,* the book of Revelation (1:16, 2:1 & 3:1) and in Jude 13, as *wandering stars*. The book of Jude is a reference to Enoch. *Vines Expository Dictionary* describes these wandering stars as follows: They represent certain false teachers. Vines' analogy here is very interesting, considering the linkage to the UFO phenomenon. Read carefully and understand, as if the stars intended for light and guidance became the means of *deceit* by __irregula__r movements!

But it gets more interesting. Let's look at the word *wander* in the Greek; it means the word *deceit*! So if the word *star* is used figuratively for angel, then Jude 13 is stating that these certain false teachers are *deceitful angels*! **Now we have a stellar order of Satan at the top, and two hundred top ranking deceitful *stars*, fallen angels — next.**

It goes like this: the *elders* are the two hundred angels spoken of in chapter four of the *Book of the Secrets of Enoch,* and the ruler is none other than Satan, the *prince* of the power of the air. The word *power* here is used by metonymy as sometimes of persons and things (interchanged;) thus, the *angels* of Eph. 1:21 = *power*, which, in Greek is (*dunamis*). The word 'power' (Greek) is also (*kratos*) which, according to (RV BIBLE) = *strength*; see the word *dominion.*

This word *dominion* holds **very important meanings** and will show you that **aliens are NOT in control of the stellar regions, but rather evil forces of angels & demons are.** {{Of course, this heretofore has been the ***ongoing*** thesis of Richard in **the aforementioned chapters**, so the following adds yet another layer to this presentation. THE BOTTOM LINE: *The alien phenomenon is just a cover or smoke screen for the duplicitous dark sinister forces (from "their First Estate,") working behind the scenes.}}*

Follow closely! The Greek meanings will be listed in order to show how they reflect what this chapter of Enoch is stating; also, you can ascertain how the word *power* (as Satan's title,) plays a very important role here.

The word *dominion* in Greek (kratos) is "manifested power." (Kuriotes) denotes *lordship-power—dominion,* whether angelic or human, as per Eph. 1:21, Col. 1:16, 2 Peter 2:10, & Jude 8; in Ephesians & Colossians, it indicates a grade in the angelic order. (Kurieuo) in Greek means "to *rule over* or have dominion over;" lastly, we have (katakurieuo) which is Greek *to exercise or gain dominion over as* in "the power of demons over men" (Acts 19:16.)

These dark forces of angelic powers are evil spirits/demons under the control of Satan's rule of the stellar regions, the air, & the atmosphere. They exercise their rule/dominion over it, and **us** through crafty deceptions, and GUESS WHAT? **The UFO phenomenon** is *part of the show*!

The next key word is *wing* that is used here in chapter four of *The Book of the Secrets of Enoch* as a symbolic mode of transportation. The word *wing* in Greek (pterux) reflects symbolically in Revelation 12:14, as "the two wings of a great eagle," suggesting the definiteness of the action, where the wings indicate rapidity & protection. *Eagle* in Greek (actos) is connected with (aemi) which means "*to blow* as of the wind, on account of its wind-like flight." We know that the wind is invisible and it is often silent (stealthy) — **just as UFOs have been and will be.**

Two words, *rapidity* & *protection* reflect two characteristics of the wings: firstly, moving, acting or occurring with great speed, as in swift or instantly sudden; also, it is quick to act or react. We know these objects (UFOs) act or react with incredible speeds and in all directions, seemingly against the known laws of gravity. {{A good example of this would be the famous NASA STS-48 MISSION (1991) where physicist Dr. Jack Kasher clocked a UFO changing directions to avoid what appeared to be a missile being shot at it, and doing so at over 200,000 mph, according to the empirical evidence he presented as a physicist!!!}} It also seems that these wings have some sort of outer shell or protective covering. Remember, in *The Book of the Secrets of Enoch* (chapter five) we will talk about *houses* & enclosed structures — metaphorically.

I believe that if we looked at the word *wing* closer now, in the Greek we may uncover a few of their designs. The word *wing* in Greek (pterux) means *pinnacle* (pterugion) where "a pinnacle is a tail pointed formation such as a mountain peak, which resembles the shape of a TRIANGLE." {{Picture in your mind a peak, with steep sides tapered; below will be a reference to an actual illustration of how the above descriptions actually "translates" into a viable-looking group of UFOs!}}

A mountain peak (or mountains) in general has steep sides with a tapering projection to a pointed summit of a mountain. (This could depict a *triangle* **UFO!**) {{In Ufology, although I have heard about *triangular UFO* reports from police sources as early as the early 1970s, the popular notion thereof came into the public perception with the findings of UFO researchers in the mid-1980s, and an ever-increasing number of reports of these very large and silent craft drifting extremely slow over highways, so that many an automobile passenger gaped in utter wonder; some of these craft measured about two football fields in diameter or even larger, and the reports continue to this very day, from Belgium to Ohio & from St. Louis to Phoenix, Arizona, just to name a few of the more outstanding triangle cases on record with Air Forces and policemen. *Special note:* **Former governor of Arizona, Fife Symington, has recently announced on a 2007 LARRY KING SHOW, that he had actually witnessed the mile-long triangular-shaped UFO that had mysteriously situated itself over the city of Phoenix; as a former Air Force man, he assured Mr. King and the general public that it was *not military flares,* or for that matter, anything he was familiar with.}}**

We now look at the word *pinnacle* which in general means "a small *turret* &/or *spire.*" Let's take the meaning of this word *turret* in general: *domelike structure or enclosure.* A dome is a hemispherical roof. Do you know that in Latin (domus) means *house*? In Greek, (doma) means *house* also! So dome is reflective of the word *house*!

PICTURE IN YOUR MIND'S EYE A HEMISPHERICAL STRUCTURE. Of course these can be all different sizes and designs, but all are reflective of a *domelike look*! (Keep this in mind, for it will **sit atop** the next shape, after it is discussed.)

Now we take the word *spire* that is "a structure or formation that tapers to a point; a slender tapering, a gradual decrease in thickness, with an elongated object tapering at both ends." {{Although I cannot picture this in artistic form here, think of a hexagonal shape with the pointing at the east/west portions as so < > and spires -------- at both north/south portions, with tapering between each of the four cardinal directions; your mind's eye should picture a certain form of UFO, *especially when we position the dome on top of the northern spire!* So by putting the two drawing together, (the *dome* & the *hexagonal* shape with the pointed ends,) one should envision in one's mind a common UFO!

Dwellings of the Stellar Order & Outlines of their Wings:
These are three basic designs that show a variety of different shapes.
However, they do come in other shapes and sizes but still hold to
these three basic designs. Other UFOs incorporate these structured outlines.

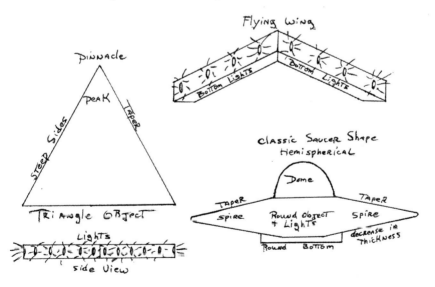

THE CURS-ED NET

I know that there are many different sizes and shapes of UFOs in Ufology, but as far as God's word (especially in *The Book of Enoch*, to me, Richard, this is no coincidence! The most seen and known shapes in Ufology are the traditional "saucer" or disc shapes, and more recently, the triangular-shaped objects (some of immense size.) {{For those familiar with the story of Bob Lazar, alleged physicist at Area 51, S-4, in Nevada, his depiction of the UFO he worked on and was "back-engineering" (the scout sport model) would look very much like the combination of the two descriptions given above by Richard as well as in the **graphic illustration** (dome on top of the hexagonal shape.)}}

There have also been reports of *Flying Wings*. {{To envision this, think of two rulers brought together at right angles, and each ruler has about three "portal windows" or lights ensconced equi-distantly within its surface; this may be reflective of this so-called FLYING WING and some have been seen to be as large as the trian-gles, usually dark, where the windows or lights appear as red in color, and sometimes amber.}}

So then these wings are possibly their mode of transportation, and by using *The Book of the Secrets of Enoch* by which these things were revealed by God through His prophet Enoch, three of the most common designs of the very same objects that have been seen by Man for a very long time become manifest! These are the most traditional types seen; of course, as I have said, there are all different kinds, but do we not have houses of all different shapes and sizes also?

The word *wings* is a symbol of their mode of transportation. Wings are not of one design, but many. It just so happens to be the basic designs of those objects we call UFOs. So what are the odds that any alien race (which we have no proof exists as they appear to be) would happen to have the very basic designs that God's word discloses through *The Book of Enoch*, and from specific verses of the Bible decoded? Is it coincidence that Satan and the fallen angels would have the same looking objects and agenda as a race of beings? I DON'T THINK SO!

The descriptions and characteristics of the whole phenomenon are too perfect through God's word to be anything other than what His word is reflective of, even to Christ's depiction of Luke 10:19,

THE CURS-ED NET

where we see the use of serpents & scorpions as symbols of evil demons, etc. The *Reptilians & Grays* are physical manifestations, sometimes as light images, (either in our minds or not,) and are shown symbolically as the serpents & scorpions noted above. These are **very dangerous** evil forces, i.e. fallen angels, with their accompanying evil spirits/demons. The scorpions and the serpents are as follows: the scorpions are the Grays (evil spirits, demons) while the serpents are the Reptilians (i.e. fallen angels.)

The last few key words of chapter four of *The Book of the Secrets of Enoch* start with round as in "to come round all those who sail." I believe the word *round* means the following: "to encompass, to envelop, to enclose on, & surround," yet it also has the idea of "to attack!"

Remember the first part of the chapter regarding **the Bite of the Serpent**, where, in Enoch 68:18, "the stroke of the spirit" & "the stroke which is given in midday" and the word in Greek means a blow; *blow* in Greek also means an unexpected attack! An assault! The word *round* in Greek (as per *Vine's*) is used in combinations with other words; round meant "shine and dwell" so that which comes ("round" all those who sail) is a light shining dwelling! {{A UFO?}}

The word *dwell* in Greek is (evoikeo) or "to dwell in; to inhabit." *Shine* in Greek is (lampo) which is "to shine as a torch;" also 'shine' (phaino) means "to cause to appear." In Greek we have (perilampo) that is "to shine around" & "to flash around" or "the lights on objects which flash on and off;" brilliant colors are characterized here. *Appear* in Greek is to become "evident" or "real!"

To *manifest* (emphanizo) can be used as a physical manifestation, such as images of creatures, whether by light, in the mind, or sometimes a being that could be felt, but not necessarily real as it appears to be. That would be the *Grays*, the *Reptilians*, or "humanoids" which I believe to be a specific breed of hybrid. Another very important aspect is the meaning in Greek of 'appear' (optomai) which is a reference to the person "creature" or thing seen and subjectively, as with reference to an inward impression or a spiritual experience, or mental occupation. The word *impression* represents "that which gives a false impression," from the word *deceit*, which, in the Greek

THE CURS-ED NET

is (apate). This impression is given as a deceitful appearance, statement, or as a deceiving influence.

REMEMBER that deceitful angels are the equivalent of wandering stars! Many times orbs of light are seen. We take the word appear and use the meaning (optomai) in Greek (to see;) from ops (the eye) where we get the English *optical*. We go to the word *orb* and in the *American Heritage College Dictionary*, one of the meanings happens to be "eye or eyeball." Did you also know that 'orb' in Latin (orbis) means "circle/disc/orbit" or "a disc shaped object"[?] So it seems we can connect the orbs to these dwellings of light! Oh yeah, *orbit* as a noun also means "a range of control or influence." So, during the *'alien'* abductions, the victims are physically attacked, mentally assaulted, and manipulated to do and remember whatever the abductors want their victims to remember.

We now end with the word *sail* that in Greek (diaperao) is "to cross over;" see 'pass.' *Pass* (parerchomai) from (para) means "to come or go;" also, the meaning (diodeuo) is to "travel along" and "to travel through." *Sail* as a noun means "to travel by means of a sailing vessel" So we have those today who come and go, traveling, whether by car, plane, ship, etc. Thousands of years ago the word 'sail' was a mode of transportation, as it is today. So these light dwellings (UFOs) come round all those who sail on water. Is this what has been happening in the **Bermuda Triangle**?

{{There is ample evidence from ship logs that some strange force (or "alien" space ships) have been witnessed to in this area, which some feel is a type of portal into another dimension; there are many documented books and film documentaries that have alluded to this sobering theory of some type of **'alien'** interference or kidnapping going on, which still cries out for a *final* explanation. Perhaps Richard's idea that the mysterious "powers of the air" (as referenced by St. Paul,) are **literally *diabolical***, that could account for the sudden disappearances that have been recorded, much like the *blow* of a light dwelling, whose venomous *bite* is both quick and deadly!

From what I can see, this theory is as good as any other, (perhaps better,) and we seem to have both *"Enoch"* & **"the Bible"** on *our side* of the argument, to boot! As I once alluded to in my own writ-

THE CURS-ED NET

ings: *the phenomenon seems an* **intimate** *one, and not merely the agenda of some curious space scientists from other galaxies, bent on improving their own situations* [as in some STAR TREK episode.] Whatever the harvesting going on, it again seems more sinister in nature, which, of course, is part of the overall dynamic of the warnings within **Holy Scripture.**}}

END NOTES:

Vine's Complete Expository Dictionary of Old and
New Testament Words:
Publisher: Thomas Nelson, Inc. ©1996
Used by permission of Thomas Nelson, Inc

CHAPTER SEVEN:

THE DOMICILES OF THE FALLEN ANGELS

(A Case for Abductions)

From The Book of the Secrets of Enoch, Chapter five:

> "And here I looked down and saw the treasure houses of the snow, and the angels who kept their terrible store houses, and the clouds whence they come out and into which they go."

Treasure is the first key word used here. Its Greek meaning (thesauods) is a noun denoting "a place of safe keeping." In Greek, *place* is referred to as "high place." The next key word is *house* where in Greek (oikia) is used metaphorically as "a heavenly abode or dwelling." *Dwellings* (as a noun) is "a place to live in," yet 'dwelling' in Greek (perioikeo) with (peri) "around" and (oikeo) means "to dwell around." The word *around* (adverb) means "to or among various places, here and there; also, to wander around."

Remember that *wander* in Greek means "deceitful." In Jude 13, it mentions the wandering stars — a reflection to the above dwellings, perhaps! These wandering stars move around various places, here & there. The Jude 13 of the Bible is a reference to *The Book of Enoch*. Wandering means also "deceitful" and the word *stars* is figuratively used in Enoch, Jude & Revelation as "angels." So we have heavenly dwellings moving (flying) around various places of

THE CURS-ED NET

(the world) by "deceitful" unholy angels, whose dwellings (houses) are used to keep something.

WHAT ARE THE TREASURES KEPT?

The next key word is *snow*, as in treasure houses of the snow. Obviously, this does **not** mean snow as itself, which might allude to its origin! Let's look at the evidence. The word snow in *The American Heritage College Dictionary* gives us two very interesting meanings here. The first is the origin. Snow is "solid precipitation in the form of crystals *originating* in the upper (atmosphere.)"

We look at the word *air* (noun) meaning "the atmosphere, the sky." The meaning of the sky here is very important. Sky is "the expanse of air over a given point on Earth, the *upper atmosphere* as seen by the Earth's surface, or the celestial regions, the 'heavens.'" Remember *house* metaphorically is used as "a heavenly abode." 'Snow' represents the dwelling place of origin, and also their habitat. Snow, as snow, originates from the upper atmosphere, **so as do the unholy dwellings of the deceitful angels**. "UFO" is just man's expression of something unknown 'flying', but these dwellings are **not** UFOs since we can now identify them as houses, the dwelling habitats of fallen angels, and we are identifying what these lights may be ~~ using scripture!

These UFOs, (objects seen in the sky) {{and also detected by radar both in the sky & underwater,}} were then the original flying sky dwellings of the fallen angels. Man coined the term "UFOs" but thousands of years before this, the unholy angels have been using their dwellings as a cover, pretending to be spaceships from another world, and having man worship them. Then, as now, they are deceiving us by using the UFO phenomenon (fashioned by them) to cover up their real agenda.

WHAT IS THE FALLEN ANGELS' AGENDA?

In my opinion, they are breeding hybrids for an evil purpose, but through deception have made us believe that an alien race is the one behind it all. The *Reptilians & Grays* are <u>all</u> part of the fallen angels' army, incorporating also the evil spirits & demons. These *houses* wander around where the word 'wander' also means "deceit!" We

THE CURS-ED NET

use the word *deceive* in general (Latin as decipere) which is "to ensnare;" *deceive* = de + capere which means "to seize!" The word *kidnap* in general means "to seize" also. To kidnap is to abduct! *Seize* in Greek (sullambano) means "to take or lay hold of" signifying to seize, as a prisoner.

The other meaning for 'snow' is symbolic. It is used in the Bible to describe several things. The most appropriate meaning stated here is from *Nelson's New Illustrated Bible Dictionary*, which uses the term 'brilliance.' *Brilliance* in general means "full of light-shining" & light is electromagnetic radiation. We now look at the word *shine*, & in the Greek (phaino) means "to cause to appear."

We have the word 'snow' meaning "house of the air, atmosphere;" also, these houses of snow are brilliant. They emit intense light, as in, light dwellings of the air. Let's now see if the word 'cause' — as in "cause to appear" sheds any light on the abduction phenomenon.

Cause in Greek *is (keterqazomai). It is "to work." Work* in Greek (katergaromai) has the meaning of "to achieve, effect by toil." *Toil* here means "to labor continuously," but let's look at the word *toil* in Greek. *Achieve* means to "accomplish their agenda", or "affect the power to produce an outcome," and also means "influence." Remember how these meanings rebound to the whole of the UFO phenomenon — how they adapt and reflect to it?

So *to cause influence over people* is "a power to sway or affect." It also means "to affect the nature of & development of" (as in breeding hybrids?) The meaning of *toil* in Greek that represents the abduction aspect is (basanizo) — "to put to the test;" then, "to examine by torture;" (cf. 'to vex or torment'.) To work to achieve an end where abductions become necessary as in (to test) in Hebrew (and as verb) means "to find out who is qualified for battle" (Judges 7:4,) but the word *battle* is not needed here, just the phrase "who is qualified." The **"chosen"** people are the **"donors"** who unwillingly, through torture, relinquish their needed tissue for the use of an evil end. {{Remember that *donors* were one of the three categories Richard designated for human beings as they are being used by the Fallen Angels & Co., the other two being *hosts & receivers*.}}

75

SEE FOR YOURSELF

The word *vex* (ochleo) in Greek means "to disturb, trouble" and is used in the passive voice as being troubled by evil spirits (Acts 5:16.) 'Trouble' is Greek (thlipsis) leads us to see *affliction* which, in Greek is (kakoucheo) & is from (kakos) which is "evil." *Affliction* is a condition of pain & suffering. (The abductees under hypnosis tell of much pain and suffering, but not only physically in time; they are very much mentally troubled.) {{**Thus, the information in the chapters of *The Bite of the Serpent* truly becomes a double-edged sword, metaphorically speaking, and the speaking with _forked_ tongue could not be better presented than with the image of a _serpent_, as part of Satan's lying entourage.}}**

The next key word is *terrible* as in *terrible storehouses*. The Greek for *terrible* leads us to see *fearful;* in Greek *fearful* (phobos) first had the meaning of *flight,* or that which may cause flight; also, fear, dread, terror. *Flight* in the following meaning is very appropriate here as a noun, which is a process of flying through the air by means of wings. It is broken down as follows: air/atmosphere/wings, which, as discussed earlier, is their mode of transportation, and depicting in drawings the appearance of UFOs — seen as flying wings, triangles, and the famous *saucer* shape. These objects represent terror, fear, dread, through evil character, such as fallen angels, evil spirits, & demons. *Terror* in Greek directs us to see the word *amazement*. This word in Greek explains the abduction process physically. A*mazement* in Greek is (ekstasis) quoting from *Vines Expository Dictionary* and is as follows:

"It is said of any displacement and especially with reference to the mind — of that alteration of the normal condition by which the person is thrown into a state of surprise or fear or both, or again in which a person is so transported out of his natural state that he falls into a trance." (Could this be connected to the *out-of-body* experiences reported by so many?)

Another Greek meaning is (thambos) for 'amaze' & "wonder," connecting it with a root to *render immovable!* (Abductees are put into a trance, then transported out of their natural surroundings, (out of body) and rendered immovable while abducted.)

THE CURS-ED NET

The next word is *store* (as in storehouses) that in Greek is (thesaurizo) & means to "lay up." *Lay up* as a general verb means "to stock up for future use." Remember, the first key word was *treasure* or to store up in a place of safekeeping. Houses here are their dwellings, so I believe that these so-called "**mother ships**" seen could very well be the storehouses. {{In Ufology, I am reminded of the haunting story of 200 men that went up a mountain in 1916 on Gallipoli Peninsula during a war engagement in Turkey, between the Dardanells & the Aegean Sea. I read the sworn affidavits of a witness to the scene that these 200 men went up the hill in a fog, but never came down the hill. Eight rather large "loaves of bread" (or elongated like clouds) were seen over the hill; one of the "loaves of bread" descended to this hill and then rejoined the other seven, and then the eight "loaves of bread' continued on their way. Charles Fort in the middle of his own book on strange happenings in our world (**THE BOOK OF THE DAMNED, as part of THE BOOKS OF CHARLES FORT,**) suggested that we (the human race were **property** but he never suggested *whose* property to the best of my recollection; maybe we now have a tentative answer to that question, by decoding the *Book of Enoch* and this activity via these fallen angels — perhaps!}}

STORE WHAT?

Let's see! We know firstly that we have the abduction; next comes the examination & the testing for donors & hosts. When found, the needed substance, tissues or sperm are chosen from specific people. They are for future use when needed, as in (for the possible implantation of the hosts.) This substance &/or tissue is held for mixture with a chosen male's sperm. The donors are implanted surgically with a tag, a monitoring device that tells the status of the tissue chosen, as well as the life signs and the ongoing availability for the use of said tissue. If the state of the substance or tissue needed is threatened by disease, death or removal, the devices *may very well be dissolved*. The implant also probably gives your location and is itself located at the exact spot of said tissue, so it is very possible that we have a *human physical logistical abducted donor agenda* occurring.

THE CURS-ED NET

Now as far as the **cattle mutilation** phenomenon is concerned, I believe it plays a very significant role here. After the fetus/embryo has been taken, it needs a place to incubate, to feed and to be nurtured. This is where the cattle parts come in — the parts taken with the *highest protein* for the feeding of the offspring. The blood of the cattle is the closest to human blood, so is needed for nourishment. {{I have seen evidence of obfuscation in this phenomenon from an ex-FBI agent as well as a so-called "Ufologist" (and ex-military man,) where both had strongly suggested that the **cattle mutilation phenomenon** is nothing more than "99% natural phenomenon at work!" Based on my own research, this is *a lot of hooey* where there are many anomalies that go *far beyond* natural *anything* which could explain this phenomenon. So again I can support the possible contention that what Richard is saying may have more truth to it than the *fanciful fiction of those who may have vested interests in not telling the **whole truth,*** and unfortunately, our government may be neck deep in being coerced to cooperate with these **fiends from Hell** — or else!!!}}

Let's go to the word *lay* as in *lay up*. *Lay* in Greek (epihallo) is to "lay upon" as of "seizing men;" also, *lay* (hupotithemi) has another Greek meaning, as in "to place under" (a trance.) (Thesaurizo) means to lay up, store up, akin to (thesaurus) which is a treasury or treasure house. *Stock* in general (as noun) is to supply or accumulate for future use.

The bottom line: *Stock* in Greek says to see the word *kind. Kind* in Greek is (genos) which is akin to (ginomai) or "to become" which denotes a family, as kindred & as offspring!

SUMMARY IDEAS OF THE AFOREMENTIONED

The treasure houses of the snow are dwellings that fly in the upper atmosphere, and over the world, in and out of the clouds. It is a dwelling for safekeeping, and a dwelling of light and brilliance. {{I suspect that they possibly have 'inter-dimensional' qualities just as had been demonstrated by certain UFOs, as in the famous 1952 sightings over WASHINGTON DC in the latter part of July.}}

Terrible storehouses are dwellings of terror and dread. These dwellings are used for abductions and breeding, for storing up, growing creatures, hybrids & offspring, which the fallen angels & demons choose to fashion. **Part of the human race is being used.** Specific people are chosen (as donors and hosts) while these dwellings are storehouses for hybrids, humanoid beings & *soulless creations* that are ruled by evil creatures and held for future use. {{That any government chooses not to speak to these sensitive issues is really not too surprising, given the *postures* of governments.}}

Treasure houses? YES! They contain substances and tissues needed for breeding, not to mention the storage places for cattle parts used for growth, food and nurturing. I believe that the giant sized dwellings (as **LIGHT DWELLINGS OF THE STELLAR ORDER**) are the *MOTHER SHIPS* and these are also *the storehouses!*

{{Final comment: Sometimes when we go through *etymology exercises* as that which Richard has put us through over the last four chapters of *The Bite of the Serpent,* it is important to **go beyond the words and phrases** so as to get to the essence of what is being presented; if Richard is truly being guided by the Holy Spirit, then it is **even more important** to see the overall effect being presented vs. just trying to connect the dots of the interrelationship of mere words and their kindred associations. There seems a *dark shadow within the forest* **scattered among the trees of Ufology,** *where sadly,* **these same Ufologists** *do not seem to see the forest for the tress, and, in effect, are throwing out the baby (of truth) with the bathwater.*

If the *two* aforementioned books of *Enoch* are indeed presenting us with a truth about Enoch's prophesying of the evil watchers, and what they are doing within their domiciles **to this very day** i.e., torturing victims to insure the success of their hybrid agenda — or worse — (not to dissimilar to what the malevolent Nazis did to the Jews on a more crude level during WW II with their fiendish excruciating experiments,) then it is important for anyone even mildly interested in these things, to actually read the **both books** of *Enoch,* and compare and weigh for themselves the connections being presented. This seems to be the challenge of what Richard is presenting, regardless of how "non-smoothly" or convoluted it may appear to be *at first glance!*}}

THE CURS-ED NET

END NOTES:

Nelson's New and Illustrated Bible Dictionary
Publisher: Thomas Nelson, Inc. ©1995

Vine's Complete Expository Dictionary of Old and
New Testament Words:
Publisher: Thomas Nelson, Inc. ©1996
Used by permission of Thomas Nelson, Inc.

CHAPTER EIGHT:

OF THE DEW THE OLIVE OIL AND VARIOUS FLOWERS

A reference from *The Book of the Secret of Enoch*, chapter six:

They showed me (Enoch) the treasure house of the dew, like oil of the olive and the appearance of its form, as of all the flowers of the earth; further many angels guarding the treasure houses of these **things and** *how they are made to shut and open.*

The first key word is *treasure*. In Greek (thesauros) denotes "a place of safe keeping." 'Treasure' in general (as noun) is "the accumulating of valuable things, highly valued possessions;" it also means "to store away." (Remember storehouses in chapter five of this same book; the place of safe-keeping is the 'house' which, in Greek (oikia) is a 'dwelling' — metaphorically of a heavenly abode.

In Greek, *heavenly* (ouranos) means the "aerial heavens" and aerial in general means "of or in the air," but also means "living in the air!" (Earlier, we established that these dwellings (objects) come from the upper atmosphere, the air, the sky & **not outer space!**) The inhabitants of these dwellings (fallen angels & evil spirits) appear to be storing valuable possessions of some sort.

(I can only believe that these valuables must be detained abductees, donors (abductees also), stored substances, &/or tissue,

THE CURS-ED NET

cattle parts, and blood among various other things, all to support a logistical line of needed nourishment to create a complete environment as some sort of facility to fashion hybrids & humanoids, while using incubators or glass containers, they themselves being filled with nourishment and growth materials.)

The first key word in this section is **dew.** 'Dew' in general is water droplets, but the verse indicates the phrase "dew like oil" so it could be construed as "water like oil." *Like* here means "similar characteristics to each other." What does water do that oil does also? Olive oil was used for cooking, and light lamps for lights & heat. Water, like oil, was used years ago to power grain wheels, & water wheels to power machinery. Today, by the use of dams and other devices, we extract the energy from water to make electricity. So water & oil **share the same thing, i.e.,** energy! The word *water* in Greek is (hudor) and this is where the English prefix *hydro* comes from. The word 'hydro' in general is "water, hydroelectric, hydrodynamic, hydrogen & hydropower."

Let's look at the word *hydroelectricity;* it is made by conversion of energy of running water. Could Enoch be telling us that water here could relate to some sort of energy used for these dwellings? We know that witnesses (of present day UFOs) have reported seeing objects going in and out of the water, and also moving at high speeds through the water. {{This is true in my own observations of the UFO field; specifically, a few years ago, there was a program on **UNSOLVED MYSTERIES** where, in Australia, a white spherical object was seen beaming down a white funnel-like white light into the lake, and extracting water from that lake. On another occasion, **THE HISTORY CHANNEL** had an interesting program (in the year of 2006) where the U.S. NAVY had tracked an unidentified object going faster than 150 knots at a depth of over 10,000 feet, which was admitted on the program – that **we *cannot do*!**}} Could these objects, then, be using the water (our waters) for this above purpose, as suggested by Richard? Let's explore the possibilities.}}

The words ***title power*** is a means of electricity generation achieved by capturing the energy contained in *moving water.* It is called "moving water masses." so when an object moves through the water at speed, it creates this moving water mass around itself.

THE CURS-ED NET

Two types of energy can be extracted: One is kinetic energy, created by the currents of the moving water mass around the object; the other form is potential energy. This is created by the difference in the height from the bottom of the object to the top of the object. This is called the *head*. The higher and wider the 'head,' the more energy can be extracted.

Kinetic energy is the work needed to accelerate a body (object) from rest to its current velocity. It gains this energy, its acceleration, when the body's speed changes (as in slower,) where the kinetic energy also drops. So, do these dwellings make hydroelectricity moving at speeds under the water, thereby creating the power to move at high speeds through the air and create kinetic energy? Potential energy may be obtained as a work against a specific force, such as gravity. What's very important here is that we must remember that these dwellings are inhabited by **supernatural beings,** such as fallen angels & evil spirits, who, by their supernatural power, have the ability to create all the mechanical devices needed to power their dwellings. The power probably is created from water, the likes of which we can only imagine!

How they most likely do this is in transcending the material order, changing the substances or metals beyond their natural structure. From what **God has already created,** these fallen angels had somehow fashioned the devices needed for their use, a use (or uses) that are at heart – **deceptive in nature**; for instance, at Roswell, a thin piece of metal crumpled returns back to its original state, or the changing of the molecular structure to act the way they wish by supernatural power. The same principle goes for aliens/alien bodies such as the ones that may have been "left" at the Roswell crash, which were *most likely* created hybrids, originally designed as humanoids. {{One may wish to speculate that it may have been a *Trojan horse* "innocently placed" **by dark & devious spirits** for the disposal of technologically *lustful* minds, such as would most likely have been the case with our blossoming military intelligence after WW II – *perhaps!*}}

I believe they can create (via implantation,) drawing from abductees (donors) that which is needed, plus possibly some tissue of their own make-up, which produces unnatural alien bodies,

THE CURS-ED NET

found **to be real!** Why not? They are flesh & blood living creatures, created by these fallen unholy angels. {{This solves the problem of the wrestling with those who are **not** of flesh & blood, as St. Paul describes in Ephesians 6:12, since the unholy mating of spirit and flesh *made possible* abhorrent flesh-earthbound creatures, and leading to the earth-bound evil spirits to boot, as was noted in *The Book of Enoch*!}} They must be real aliens, right? If you intend to deceive the world, and have the power to do so, you will do so! Seeing is believing, right?

BUT WAIT A MINUTE!

So then is Enoch showing us that these houses, dwellings (objects) have been and **are** extracting energy from water? Possibly! Below is a list of different types of energy. Some of these types have been reported cited by investigators at UFO and crop circle sites:

1) chemical energy
2) heat energy
3) electromagnetic energy, radiation, light
4) potential energy
5) mass energy
6) nuclear energy
7) kinetic energy

Let's say you travel under water at high speeds, with a "moving water mass" created around your vehicle. You now create from that energy hydroelectricity. At the same time, you also are creating potential energy from the *head* — the width & height of your vehicle. That power enables you to fly at great speeds through the air, which creates kinetic energy. In between, you create electromagnetic radiation (light) and heat. Add some outside light and colors, and what do you have?

The title of this essay is **OF THE DEW THE OIL & VARIOUS FLOWERS.** The *dew* is water. So what's the oil? To get olive oil, the olives are pressed, so oil appears as a form. Here oil is reflective of an appearance, a form that *is suggestive of flowers,* and the " appearance of its form" (as) of all the flowers of the Earth. 'As' here

THE CURS-ED NET

means when taken into consideration with a specific form, or as in some manner of. How does oil work with flowers?

The word *press* in general means "to compress or reshape, to press, flatten." In Greek, the word *appearance* (phantazo) is "to make visible." *Form* in Greek (morphe) is a "special characteristic *feature*" and (morphosis) is "an outline, image or (impress." 'Form' in Greek also is "pattern." The word *impress* in general is "a mark or pattern." A *pattern* is "an artistic or decorative design." The word *design* is "a graphic form," (perhaps the appearance of a graphic form?) *Graphics* (as noun) in general is "the making of drawings in accordance with the rules of mathematics."

Now the word '*flowers*' has more than one meaning that we need to use. To follow-up with the above meanings, the word used is 'flowers' (plural) in the verse. *Flowers* (as verb) is to "decorate with a floral 'pattern'" *Floral* is suggestive of a flower, and most all flowers are circular in outline, and have many patterns. So let's see what Enoch is trying to tell us here. We take the words *press* & *impress* patterns of 'artistic' designs to flatten graphics by the use of mathematics with the circular outline of flowers, and the flowers of different patterns, and what do we have? **CROP CIRCLES**!

Combine these crop circles with the presence of certain types of energies talked about earlier, such as heat, electromagnetic radiation, etc., and it sure sounds like what has been reported by crop circle investigators, doesn't it? {{For those readers not familiar with Richard's suggestions, patterns of crop circles worldwide, and possible theories as to their execution, please go to the below Internet link for a brief review:}}

http://www.crystalinks.com/croptheories.html

Let's now examine the other meanings of 'flowers,' as in "various flowers of the Earth." *Various* (adj. G.M.) is of "diverse kinds," "unlike," "more than one," "many-sided," and also an "individual or separate member of a group." (Many different designs are separate from or are the same as each other, with varying sizes, patterns, etc.) So we have (diverse kinds) of various flowers & (floral patterns) of the Earth & around the Earth.

THE CURS-ED NET

The other meaning of flowers is the Greek (huperakmos) from (huper) as "beyond" and (akme) as "the highest points of the Earth" with the word 'various' as different places.

So beyond the highest points of the Earth equals the atmosphere. The rest of the verse is cited as follows: "*how they are made to shut and open,*" but what shuts and opens?

The word *open* in Greek is a verb (anoigo). It means a "door or a gate" (dianoigo,) & "to open up" (dia) meaning "through" and as a noun (anoixis) — an "opening" (ope) or a "hole." So at various points, such as the highest points of the atmosphere, we have "portals, doors, openings" that they go *through.*

The word *shut* in Greek (apokleio) is "to shut fast" & (apo) "away from," as used in Luke 13:24 & 13:25 in the Bible. This reflects to and expresses the ***impossibility*** of entrance after the closing. In Luke 13:24-25 & Matthew 7:13-14, there is a reference about the small gate and narrow road which leads to Christ (as metaphor) while the large gate and wide road which does not (as in posing the good road to life vs. the evil roads to separation.) Those in Christ will be with Him after the flesh dies, since the spirit lives. Yet only in spirit form can we enter beyond to the other side; therefore, the meaning of the door shut, the impossibility of entrance after the closing where these *dwellings* go (through the doors, gates, portals) – we, in the flesh, cannot!

(Remember, they are fallen angels & evil spirits, not flesh. Their "beyond" the other side of the door is possibly **the abyss** or the realm of the lost, as in Jude 6; it talks about darkness for the fallen angels, and in Jude 13, a darkness reserved for the fallen ones. The word *blackness* in (*Vine's*) is the Greek (zophos) that is the gloom of the region of the lost. Could this be the beyond, or the other side of the gate? They have the ability to do this *at the present time*: **to come and go from our world to theirs.**

{{At the risk of complicating the phenomenon of the opening and closing of the gates or doors that Richard cited in the above analysis, suggestive of the portals of the *Fallen Ones*, allow me to cite an observation from the files of *FATIMA* of 1917, and what was witnessed there, according to the chief witness in this most amazing spiritual drama. It is a girl named Lucia, as reported in

THE CURS-ED NET

the book **HEAVENLY LIGHTS** by Dr. Joauim Fernandez & Fina D'Armada; after reading the citation, if you wish to read the whole review of this book (by Byron LeBeau,) just go to the below link on the Internet, but the point is to illustrate the anecdotal concept of entities leaving our dimension (possibly) via **portals or gates** "of a *vibrational* kind." WITNESS BELOW to a short citation from this essay:

> *Lucia indicated that as THE LADY left on one occasion (the June 13th one,) and Lucia said that THE LADY left and so did the object (cloud), then made this enigmatic remark: " There! Now it can't be seen. It has just now entered the sky and **the doors have closed.** (PIU) The authors give many examples of how UFOs use clouds to hide their identity; cf. pgs. 53-55.*

And later in the same essay, a different citation on another occasion:

> *The Being was then transported back to "the cloud" by the same way it came, appearing as if **"the doors had closed"** (as was referred to before in the words of Lucia.) Then "the cloud" streaked across the sky and superimposed itself in front of the Sun (and several witnesses saw a "ladder" next to the "Sun" (which may have been a cigar shaped second craft, according to the authors.)* http://theuniversalseduction.com/bookreviews/fatima-frank-facts-vs-illusive-fiction

I have had the sneaking suspicion that the **crop circle** phenomenon possibly revolves around the 'supernatural' as in activity of the *Fallen Angels*; obviously this cannot be proven, per se, but if Richard is connecting the etymological dots correctly, then it is a strong possibility that supernatural beings (not necessarily all evil) can drop into our third dimensional reality from their own "space" or "time" or "dimension" through their own "doors" or "gates" ~~ but more importantly, **with us none the wiser ostensibly!** This is what makes the subjects of **the cattle mutilations, the crop circles,**

THE CURS-ED NET

UFOs & alien abductions and, of course, the personages as represented by the Nephilim/Nophelim, such intriguing subjects when it comes to getting to the root of **"WHO DONE IT?"** *as in* **interfering with mankind?**

To carry this possible set of links **ONE STEP BEYOND** even the above, let us not forget that the UFO/*alien abduction* and anomalous phenomena also includes missing time of people, and even of planes (the latter of which sometimes includes strange green misty lights;) there was a program on "SIGHTINGS" a few years' ago, where an L-1011 was coming into a Florida airport, and mysteriously went off the radar scope for a full ten minutes, concerning the "reception committee" so much so that emergency fire engines, etc., were scrambled. Then, just as suddenly, the jet *reappeared* on the scope and landed safely. What made this case so bizarre (and to this day unanswerable,) was the fact that all the passengers had lost *ten minutes* off of their watches, as if they were in *another dimension* for those same ten minutes; also, the official jet clock had lost ten minutes! Did this jet *also* go through an inter-dimensional portal, gate or door?

Just maybe this *gate or door* does transport one to another dimension, where our time does **not** *interface in phase,* and once the door is shut, it is impossible to either go in or out...until...*the door reopens.* Some of us would call this the *spiritual* realm of existence, and death *triggers* that opening door; perhaps certain spiritual beings have the same power of opening and closing, and use it for their own designs that may include the gathering of things in their treasure houses, like cattle & people, <u>where</u> Enoch may have been warning us about this phenomenon, and prophesied accordingly a long time ago!

Perhaps not, and perhaps the above group of exercises may be nothing more than fanciful speculation based on misconstrued suggested data, but exploring these ideas in an open & non-prejudicial fashion, as Richard has attempted to do, may be a step in the right direction! Perhaps even Hamlet was right, echoing through the pen of one, William Shakespeare, or whoever was truly responsible for the lion's share of his writings when Hamlet said: ***There are more things in heaven and earth, Horatio, then have been dreamt***

THE CURS-ED NET

in your philosophy. Perhaps we should just go on to chapter nine and see if Richard can discover some of these "things" *not dreamt ~~ by showing and telling!*}}

END NOTES:

Vine's Complete Expository Dictionary of Old and
New Testament Words:
Publisher: Thomas Nelson, Inc. ©1996
Used by permission of Thomas Nelson, Inc.

CHAPTER NINE:

SHOW AND TELL

(GAME OF LIFE AND DEATH)

{{I believe Richard does an excellent job in *mapping out* this most important part of the *alien jigsaw puzzle!* If we understand the dynamics and certain reality of *familiar spirits* and how they are continuously bombarding their *receivers* to give out false and misleading information about the spiritual truth of our reality, then it goes a long way in putting the rest of the puzzle together, *a "puzzle" that is answered in* **THE BIBLE!**}}

INTRODUCTION TO **PART ONE**: This deals with many key words which come together explaining all of the ins and outs of the haunting phenomenon, and explains how demons (evil spirits) use and exploit mediums, i.e., how they lure them, teach them, & train them for their own benefit. The mediums become a service to these evil spirits in a way *so subtle* that they never know what danger their very spirits are in. They continue to live their lives, believing that they do indeed have this gift, but never realize that this power within is not theirs. They have, in essence, become deceived!

I try to explain exactly what has taken place in their lives and **I am trying to help them understand that they are being used.** It is an evil company beside them; however, they can overcome this evil and become saved through Jesus Christ.

THE CURS-ED NET

PART TWO will show the demons' attributes so you can see how they are more than capable of doing all of this deception.

PART ONE

We will start off with the word *demon* to see where this key word leads us. We will then take the information and see what it is describing. In (*Vine's*) the word 'demon' in Greek is (daimon.) In the New Testament, it denotes an evil spirit. Some would derive the word from a root *da* meaning "to distribute;" it also means "to know" and hence "a knowing one." The Greek (sunoida) is "to share the knowledge of or be privy to."

So we have evil spirits who possess knowledge & are called "the knowing ones." It seems they are also to share that knowledge — personally — but to whom?

The word *privy* is Greek (lathra) means "secretly & covertly" which itself is from the root (lath-) that indicates as being "unnoticed" & "unknown." It seems to me, that whoever receives this information is kept in the dark as to who is really giving them the information.

Continuing with the word 'privy,' another meaning in Greek is (pareisaktos) which is an adjective akin to (pareisago), & literally is "to bring in beside" i.e., secretly as from (para) "by the side." (Could this mean that the evil spirit becomes familiar to the spirit of the person receiving it?) At the end of the meaning of this, it says to see 'creep.'

The word *creep* in Greek (enduno, en, "in", duno) is "to enter" (pareisduno) & *to enter* is "by the side (para) 'beside' or 'in' which is to insinuate oneself into by stealth or to creep in stealthily." *Insinuate* here means "to introduce or insert (oneself) by subtle means." (Well it does sure sound like these evil spirits come into the people they choose to give this information to. It also seems that they come in as something "friendly," someone whom you would get used to because humans do not really have the powers without the one inside producing that power; yet — you feel you have received a ***special*** gift.) {{Is this just another ***Trojan horse*** from the dark side, similar to the possible "gift" given the military at Roswell back in 1947, as speculated previously?}}

92

THE CURS-ED NET

Let's look at this verse from the Bible, quoted here in (*Vine's*) dictionary for the meaning of 'demon:

"They (demons) disseminate errors among men and seek to seduce believers (1Tim 4:1). As seducing spirits, they deceive men into the supposition through mediums ("**_sensitives_**" today) and those who have familiar spirits (Lev. 20:6 & 27) that they can converse with deceased human beings ~~ hence the destructive deception of "spiritism," forbidden in scripture (Lev. 19:31, Deut. 18:11 & Isa. 8:19.)"

The next word is *know* which, in Greek is (oida) and is "a knowing one" from the same root as (eidom) — "to see" — which is a perfect tense with a present, signifying primarily "to have seen" or perceived, hence, "to know, to have known, knowledge of."

So I think that for these evil spirits to give certain information out, they would have to have seen (studied) that person or persons, or objects, locations, or structures, etc., to give one the knowledge one seeks; however, they **_set up_** the circumstances to what knowledge will be asked for.

Let's see if there is a way to find out how **the receivers** might go about getting this knowledge. We now take the words 'to see' from the root (eidom) in Greek and apply it to Hebrew. In Hebrew, the words *to see together*, a verb (ra'ah) is 'to see,' for "perceive," "observe," "get acquainted with," "gain understanding of" or (explaining every way someone could learn a good deal about something or someone.)

(Ra'ah) has several extended meanings: It can refer to perceiving or ascertaining something apart from seeing it with one's eyes (as in visions!) *Vision* in Greek (horasis) is "the sense of sight," where (horao) is "a spectacle sight," and *appearing* (optasia) is a form of (opsis) "the act of seeing," & from (optano) 'to see." The following will explain some basic ways the evil spirits go about gathering this information which they seek, and how through several means, disseminate that information which they wish the person to know, i.e., by means of visions, images, appearances, & conversing spirits (familiar spirits.)

The first word is *perceive* where several meanings are needed. In Greek (ginosko) is "to know by experience and observation,"

THE CURS-ED NET

and (theoreo) is "to be a spectator of." (It is basically the whole idea of how the evil spirits over time have gathered information on many people, places & things, which **they**, at the chosen time, and about the chosen subjects, choose to disseminate to those **chosen** people, (mediums) etc., when the time is right. They set up the time & place and how that information will be disseminated. They create the surroundings at the proper time for the event. They send you the information they know you will need by visions, appearances, or conversing with you. {{In order to fully comprehend how these *set-ups* are executed among humans for purposes of sexual *misuse, and done* by these same familiar spirits (that Richard is describing above,) please read Eve Lorgen's **THE LOVE BITE.** This spiritual "set up" uses the same modus operandi that you may be familiar with from the movie, **THE STING,** only the culprits in real life are of a nasty spiritual nature, but can interact with humanity from *behind the third dimensional scenes* as it were.}}

Next we look at the word *observation.* The noun in Greek is (parateresis) which means "attentive watching;" also, "to consider well" (tereo;) see 'keep.' *Keep* in Greek (tereo) denotes "to watch over." (So the evil ones watch over their servants attentively, those they consider well (as in *good servants!*)

The word *over* in Greek explains some familiar activity over their chosen ones. 'Over' means "to be to have" (proistemi) & in (Lit.) "to stand before," hence — "to lead," "to direct," "to attend to." This is translated 'rule'. They **rule** you! 'Rule' is "to lead." They are leading you __astray__, leading you to serve them & using you as an instrument. This becomes very detrimental to your spirit, for as long as you are serving them (the evil spirits) you **cannot and are** *not* **serving God**!

The next word here is *acquaint* which, in general, is a verb "to cause to come to know." (They cause the event that involves your receiving this special vision, etc., which, in turn, causes you to see things that lead you to believe that you have a special gift. **It's a set up, pure & simple** — {{just like in the aforementioned movie!}} Look at the word *acquaintance* (idos) in Greek: It reflects the notion of "one's own!" {{So who's the sucker?}}

THE CURS-ED NET

The word *gain* in Greek is a noun (porismos) which is "to denote, a providing," akin to (porizo,) to procure; it also means "of gain." (The evil spirits provide all the knowledge you need to know through an appearance, vision [mental] or conversing with your spirit!) This is a procurement process which is a means to their gain – **you**! These special efforts are to obtain or acquire a specific individual to be used for their agenda…**and you ghost hunters out there**: You are not seeking deceased people; rather you are calling out demons. You are literally playing with fire! Don't believe for one second that you cause things to happen at certain times, or take pictures of things you believe you have caught. *The demons* are calling all the shots! They allow things to happen the way they want. By your coopera- tion, **you are helping to destroy your very soul and spirit**!

Remember earlier it was mentioned that the demons disseminate errors among men. They scatter widely errors that are deceptive. In Greek *error* (plane) is a "wandering," a forsaking of the right path. In 2 Thess.2:11, it is "a working of error" & in (KJV) "a strong delu- sion;" see 'deceit.' In Jude 13, it is "a wandering, being led astray by wandering stars" (deceitful angels.) {{**In so few words, Jude** *said it all* **in his epistle!**}} The word *understand* in Greek is a verb (suniemi) that means primarily "to bring or set together," & (parati- themi) is "to place aside," (i.e., to bring your spirit and the evil spirit together — place beside.)

A noun related to the verb (ra'ah) *to see* is (Re m) which appears to mean "looking glass." (Mar'ah) means "visionary, an appearance or prophetic vision." *Visionary* is characterized and or given by apparitions which represent the "knowing ones" (demons.) Another meaning for visionary is "one who has visions, a seer or a medium." The means by which the visionary receives this knowledge is by an appearance (images,) visions (mental,) or conversing with familiar spirits. A vision in general is a mental image or even the *experience* of seeing, as if with the eyes of a supernatural being. The *chosen* people are shown these things as through the eyes of demons, {{i.e., *true receivers!*}}

The 'characterizations' of the evil spirits are the acting out of deceased people through images, sounds, speech, etc. They act out that which you are meant to see. They play the characters (*the ghosts*)

95

others see. **You are not speaking to dead people; you are speaking to evil spirits!** {{Does that scare 'little Bill'{?} — the phrase used by Clint Eastwood in the movie, **THE UNFORGIVEN,** since this was the derogatory expression he gave to the tin-horn sheriff, (Gene Hackman) who had no clue as to just how dangerous a gunslinger Clint Eastwood was, and of course, Gene's character **met with a terrible end !!!**}}

Looking glasses pluralized (mar'ch) refers to "an external appearance and can also connote 'sight' as a range of vision, or in the sense of a supernatural sight, 'image,' etc., or manifestation." The word *connote* implies the literal meaning here which is sight. So we have an external appearance, & supernaturally, a manifestation of something that employs sight.

We now look at the word 'appear' from appearance. *Appear* in general means "to become visible." In Latin (apparere): ad+parere is "to show." The meaning of show here as a pretense, is as "an outward show" in Greek; see 'observation.' The word 'show' in general also means "manifestation," as in the sense of a supernatural manifestation.

The word 'appear' in Greek (optomai) is "to see" as (ra'ah;) in Hebrew 'appear' from the Greek (ops) that means "eye" and in English "optical." 'Appear' as a verb is (phaino.) It signifies in the active voice "to shine." The word *apparition* in the meaning

(characterized by or given by apparitions,) is in Greek (phantasma.) The word 'apparition' is from (phaino,) to appear, so in Greek, apparition also means to appear or "to shine forth." An apparition is a phantasm or phantom; in Matt 14:26 & Mark 6:49 as "ghost." The meaning 'to see' & 'see' in Greek (blepo) is a verb that is "to have sight" so a supernatural appearance is an image of something which has sight.

We take the word *shine* in Greek (phaino) that denotes in the active voice "to give light" (photismos) or an illumination. *Light* in general is electromagnetic radiation, which could explain a good deal. In (Archaic,) 'light' means "eyesight" and one of the titles of Satan as "an angel of light" (2 Cor.11: 14-15.)

So we have a supernatural external appearance, a manifestation that is illuminated, and employs light that is electromagnetic radiation. We have the word 'appear' (ops) as the 'eye' that in English is optical. In (Archaic) light reflects eyesight. Apparition relates to a ghostly image, a form which then can be visible or invisible, and (either way) when it wants to, or when they choose it to be, so I have coined the word **"inavisible"** (devises, sort of speak that denotes a *dual* capacity.)

The aforementioned 'looking glasses' are a symbol for these "seeing" devises. Let's see if 'looking glasses,' the words themselves, can give any insight. The word *look* in general (as verb) is "to employ sight," especially in a given direction, and also means "to search." Now *search* in Greek means "to examine" (anakrisis) from (ana) which means "up or through." The device has the ability to search, can go upward, ascend, and go through things.

The word *glasses* in general means "to scan," as with an optical instrument. It is important to know that 'glass' in Greek (hualos) denotes "transparency."

Let's see if the word 'orb' plays a role here. Orbs are those illuminated transparent balls of light people have reported seeing at UFO encounters and "hauntings" (as in 'ghost hauntings.') The word *orb* (as noun) in general is "a sphere or spherical object." What also is important here is one of the meanings of 'orb' as an "eye or eyeball." Could this device then be representative of the orb being seen? Remember (ops) the eye and light in (Archaic) as eyesight. (Ops,) the eye in English is optical, so then these devices use some sort of supernatural set up. (I personally believe that these are being utilized — not only for sight as a roaming video camera — but also to record the real time study of their subjects, through vision & sound, as well as to send sound images outwardly, as through a "speaker." They can move about at will [both visibly & invisibly] projecting forms or images of things they want you to see, or project certain sounds [such as voices] here and there as the device moves.)

Remember the word 'glasses' = to scan and to search, and to employ sight. Well the word *eyeball* as in the meaning of the word 'orb' in general (as verb) means "to look over carefully," "to scrutinize," "to measure something or 'someone' by sight," "to examine," as to consider or choose through necessary qualifications (such as in a ***chosen*** person, abductee, donor & receiver?) Do the evil ones

THE CURS-ED NET

examine & measure us to consider certain people for future use? Are these evil spirits keeping eyes on us for future perspectives? {{It does seem that this may, indeed, be the case.}}

The word *scan* in general is "to examine or look over quickly." 'Scan' in Latin (scandere) is "to climb, the ability to ascend." Orbs are round, and eyes as eyeballs are round, i.e. spherical. So what have we uncovered so far?

1) a supernatural external appearance
2) has the ability of sight
3) shines, is illuminated and gives light
4) has electromagnetic radiation
5) is a manifestation
6) employs sight through optical means supernaturally
7) is suggestive of evil
8) is ghostly reflecting to an apparition; an image that can be visible or invisible
9) looks – searches – scans – explores — probes
10) in Latin, 'search' is (circare), meaning to go around, or the ability to move here & there
11) has the ability to climb, ascend
12) is transparent
13) can go through things
14) records both video & audio real time
15) projects images & sounds
(I call this device an Illuminating Roving Optical Transceiving Vehicle or I.R.O.T.V.)

TROUBLED HEARTS & SOULS

Now we leave the word **demon** and move to the word **scorpion.** In Greek (skorpios) means "to scatter;" see 'disperse.' The word *scorpion* is suggestive of the effects of scattering in the sowing of the spiritual seed. *An evil seed* in Greek (diaspeiro) is "to scatter abroad."

The demons 'disseminate' errors among men and seek to seduce believers (1 Tim 4:1) as seducing spirits. Earlier we looked at the word *disseminate* which in general (as verb) also means "to scatter widely," as in sowing seed & to spread abroad, to promulgate.

Promulgate (as verb) means "to make known." The meaning of scorpion in Greek & disseminate in general are similar, so if demons disseminate errors (1 Tim 4:1) and the word disseminate & scorpion have the <u>same</u> meaning, then scorpion is a possible symbol of demons. Let's go to Luke 10:19 within the (NIV BIBLE) "Life & Spirit Bible" with Christ speaking:

"I have given you authority to trample on snakes and scorpions and to overcome all the power of the enemy." (The Bible note on the bottom of the page for 10:19 states: Snakes & scorpions are terms representing the most dangerous forces of spiritual evil.) The word enemy above is representative of the title of Satan (Matt 13:39.) So you see, demons & scorpions are **one and the same** with scorpion being a symbol of demon. We also see that snakes & scorpions are associated with Satan, the enemy. {{*The scorpion injecting its poison into the whole Earth would therefore make an apt symbol within* **THE *CURS*-ED NET.**}}

We now look at the word *disperse*. The word in Greek (KJV) is "he hath dispersed abroad." 'Disperse' means "to scatter as 'one' who liberally disperses benefits," or (helpful aids) which are beneficially producing favorable results. In Latin (benfactum) < benefacere, is to "do a service!"

In order for evil spirits to make this work, they choose specified people after they "measure up" — so to speak, and make them believe they have received a special gift. All this is through a UFO encounter or vision, etc. Having these mediums now is to their benefit, a service that scatters information abroad to people seeking the mediums' help. They supernaturally receive their knowledge either through appearances (images) visions ('mental") or conversing with familiar spirits (evil spirits.) The mediums are not the only ones who believe they possess a power, but the people who seek them out also believe this falsehood.

'Disperse' in Greek from the root 'sharp' signifies "to cut asunder," akin to (skorpios) or a scorpion. *Asunder* is "to separate apart" or "to keep you away from anyone who is trying to tell you the truth," (and apart also from God.) They are sowing in you an evil seed. The word *cut* in Greek (katakopto,) in (Lit.) is "to cut down" as per Mark 5:5, referring to the demonic; also, (diaprio) signifies "to saw asunder,"

THE CURS-ED NET

hence, metaphorically "to be sawn through mentally, to be rent with vexation, to be cut to the heart." The word *rent* in Greek (diaspao) means "to tear asunder" & is translated "rent asunder." The word *tear* (sparasso) denotes "to tear, rend, convulse." *Convulse* (as verb) in general is "to shake violently," or "to affect with muscular convulsions!" [NOTE: As per Luke 9, even while the boy was coming, the demon threw him to the ground in a convulsion.]

This is being possessed, whether by conversing spirits talking to you at a séance, or a spirit possessing a person literally. The word *vex* from vexation in Greek (ochleo) means "to disturb." It is used in the passive voice as being troubled by evil spirits (Acts 5:16.)

'Vex' also means in Greek (basanizo) "to torment." *Torment* (kakoucheo) is "to treat evilly, evil entreated." *'Entreat* denotes "to use." They are using you (to use well or ill.) To use 'ill' is (kakos) as in bad, evil. To use 'well' *as in the mediums' case*, is in general (1) effectively (2) successfully (3) for benefit & gain (4) to put to good use, to exploit. (These are evil spirits using you for their means, not yours!)

Remember to be "cut to the heart" [?] In Greek, *heart'* spiritually speaking, by its usage in the New Testament, denotes the following: Evil affects the heart, and then affects

1) The seat of the physical life (Acts 14:17)
2) the seat of the moral nature & spiritual life, of grief (John 14:1; Rom. 9:2)
3) joy (John 16:22; Eph 5:19)
4) the desires (Matt 5:28; 2 Peter 2:14)
5) the affections (Luke 24:32; Acts 21:13)
6) the perceptions (John 12:40; Eph 4:18)
7) the thoughts (Matt 9:40; Hebrews 4:12)
8) the understanding (Matt 13:15; Rom. 1:21)
9) the reasoning powers (Mark 2:6; Luke 24:38)
10) the imagination (Luke 1:51)
11) the conscience (Acts 2:37; 1 John 3:20)
12) the intentions (Heb. 4:12; 1 Peter 4:1)
13) purpose (Acts 11:23; 2Cor. 9:7)
14) the will (Rom. 6:17; Col 3:14)
15) faith (Mark 11:23; Rom 10:10)

THE CURS-ED NET

All these human parts are affected when you keep evil spirits. Well we know where the word 'disperse' took us in Greek. Let's see where it takes us in the general meaning. As a verb, it is "to cause to vanish or disappear;" "to disseminate knowledge;" lastly, "to separate light into spectral rays." *Spectral* (as adj.) has general meaning "of or relating to a specter." A 'specter' is a ghostly apparition, a phantom, a haunting image. In Latin, it is 'appearance,' & a spectrum (as noun) means a distribution of electromagnetic energies.

A graphic or photographic representation of such a distribution: In Latin it is "an appearance." These electromagnetic energies create graphic 'images' & appearances (supernaturally,) as in "an outward appearance" as spoken of earlier; also there is a photographic (picture of these images) which is taken only by your camera. *Scatter* here, also has a meaning under (Phys.) of "separating and going in different directions." (How many times have people reported UFO objects coming apart, going in different directions, and then coming back together again?)

One more time we look at the word 'scattering' (which stems originally from the word **scorpion**) and as a noun, (phys.) represents " the dispersal of a beam of particles or of radiation into a range of directions as a result of physical interactions."

Interaction (as noun) in (Phys.) is "any of four fundamental ways in which bodies can influence each other, especially by supernatural means. They are the strong, weak, electromagnetic & gravitational forces." (If by supernatural powers they can make orbs float around, they can surely make UFOs fly about!)

Physics is "the interactions between matter & energy in fields such as acoustics, optics, mechanics, thermodynamics, cryogenics, and particle physics." Let's make a quick list of these things, and see which ones are involved with UFO encounters, hauntings & other phenomena:

1) electromagnetic energies — exhibiting electromagnetism
2) optics — involved in the use with orbs *as in the* Illuminated Roving Optical Transceiving Vehicles (or I.R.O.T.V. as mentioned earlier)
3) thermodynamics — heat & other forms of energy
4) cryogenics — relating to low temperatures (cold spots)

101

THE CURS-ED NET

5) acoustics — the total effect of sound, especially as produced in a small space (such as voices, noises?)

Added to the above are supernaturally imposed electronic voices at different frequencies and or other sounds, plus sound transmitted vibrations as through a speaker. Could these orbs (IROTV's) be roving speakers too? Well now you have much information gathered here. Read it over again carefully, and adapt it to your knowledge of all the above phenomena.

{{SPECIAL NOTE: Regarding the "voices" that Richard speaks of, it only happened to me **once** but it left an indelible impression on me, since I had experienced other "paranormal" activity, and naturally assumed that this was part of the larger picture; I had just finished my nap out in Ohio while staying at a friend's house temporarily. I know I was awake since I had heard some kids outside playing. I was lying on my left side, and all of a sudden, I distinctly heard a woman's voice whisper in my right ear the word "**ARBOR**" ~ but to this day, could not reconcile it with anything substantially, although I did later note that *Arbor Day* was the day of making my final decision about the illegal misapplication of the income tax by the IRS, since it was their "deadline" date (that particular year) to cooperate with them or not. I chose not to out of the conviction that *regardless how big the bully, if they are disrespecting the REAL law, then I must disrespect them*!

Anyway, since it was a woman's voice, I could only connect it to this "**ANASTASIA**" whom I had been led to believe was my former spirit lover. If Richard is correct in his surmise, it could have been part of a *real clever plot*" **by** the familiar spirits, *trying to lead me astray*! By carefully weighing Richard's words (as well as the admonitions from myriad books of the Bible, I do **now believe** that this particular "paranormal phenomenon" may well have been one of their (evil spirits') tricks, trying to take advantage of the vulnerability of its victim: **ME!** In closing this particular part, all I can say is: DO READ THIS ESSAY CAREFULLY! Be armed with *spiritual discernment* when it comes to the **myriad** seductions of the familiar spirits! This _**IS**_ spiritual warfare! Do not be a victim due to lack of discernment. Do not fall into **THE *CURS*-ED NET.**}}

PART TWO: CHARACTERISTICS OF FALLEN ANGELS

They are called the 'Devil's angels' (Matt 25:41; Rev. 12:9.)

They are called 'familiar spirits' (Deut. 18:11; Is. 8:10; 19:3.)

They are 'unclean spirits' (Matt 10:1; Rev. 16:134; Mark 1:27; 3:11; 5:13; Acts 5:16.)

They are 'evil spirits' (Luke 7:21; Acts 19:12,13.)

They are 'seducing spirits' (1 Tim. 4:1.)

They are 'wicked spirits (Luke 11:26.)

Modern man professes not to believe in demons, but they exist just the same. Satan has countless *hosts* of invisible demons to aid him in his dark designs against mankind. Do mediums really talk to the dead people or spirits? The Bible declares that the unsaved dead are in Hades, and _not_ roaming the Earth (Ps. 9:17; Luke 16:23; Rev 20:13.)

Fallen angels possess intelligence; they know Jesus (Luke 4:34.) They know of future damnation (Matt 8:29.) They know the saved from the unsaved (Acts 16:15; Rev. 9:4.) They experience emotion & fear (Luke 8:28; Is. 2:19.) They possess great strength (Dan. 10:13; Mark 5:24; Acts 19:16.) They disseminate false doctrine & information as noted in (1Thess: 2; 1 Tim. 4:1.)

They also (at times) commit the following afflictions on humans:

1) General affliction: (Matt 8:28; Mark 5:15; Luke 8:27-29.)
2) Insanity (Matt 8:28)
3) muteness (Matt 9:23)
4) immorality (Matt 9:33; Luke 4:36)
5) deafness (Mark 9:25)
6) epilepsy (Matt 17:15-18)
7) blindness (Matt 12:22)
8) suicide & mania (Mark 9:22)
9) personal injury (Mark 9:18)
10) physical defects (Luke 13:11)

They can also possess human beings: (Mark 1:25; Luke 4:35; Matt. 8:32; 9:33; 15:28; 17:18; 12:22; Luke 13:10-17.) {{Incidentally, if you wish to read a good essay on demon possession, please go to the Internet for LeBeau's review of Fr. Gabriele Amorth's book, and the title of the web page: "AN EXORCIST TELLS HIS STORY", located at

http://inspectorblebeau.pbwiki.com/ANEXORCISTTELLS HISSTORY It gives vivid descriptions of both serpent & scorpion demons.}}

In Galatians 5:19-21, Paul lists some evident works of the flesh, and mentions sorcery as one that would deny a man **entrance into the kingdom of heaven.** Condemned in verse 20, and from the Greek word (pharmakeia,) sorcery is the practice of magical or curious arts in whatever form the occult may take....

From the Topical Analysis of the Bible, by Walter Elwell:

Eph. 6 (NIV)—"For our struggle is not against flesh and blood, but against the rulers, the authorities, against the powers of this dark world and against the spiritual forces of evil in the heavenly realms."

("Demons" – Deceiving Spirits)

2 Cor.11: "For such men are false apostles, deceitful workmen, masquerading as apostles of Christ. And no wonder, for Satan himself masquerades as an angel of Light. It is not surprising then if his servants masquerade as servants of righteousness. Their end will be what their actions deserve.

1 Tim 4:1: "The spirit clearly says that in later times some will abandon the faith and follow deceitful spirits and things **taught** by demons.

James 2:19: "You believe that there is one God. Good! Even the demons believe that — and shudder."

Mark 3:11: "Whenever evil spirits saw him, they fell down before him and cried out, 'You are the son of God'".

Deut. 18:10-13: "Let no one be found among you who sacrifices his son or daughter in the fire, who practices divination or sorcery, interprets omens, engages in witchcraft, or casts spells, or is a medium or spiritist, *or who consults the dead.* Anyone who does these detestable practices, the Lord your God will drive out those nations before you. You must be blameless before the Lord your God."

Is. 8:19: "When men tell you to consult mediums and spiritists, who whisper and mutter, should not a people inquire of their God? Why consult the dead on behalf of the living? To the law and to the testimony? If they do not speak according to this word, they have no light of dawn."

1 Tim. 4:1: (earlier) where the word taught in Greek (didaktos) as an adjective, is primarily "what can be taught."

Where in **PART ONE** we saw that seers, mediums and spirit-ists can be taught that which they practice, and are made aware that they have a special gift. Then upon accepting that, they are shown through visions, conjuring spirits or appearances how to grow in this gift, i.e., the demon teaching them and molding them until they (the mediums,) **become that servant which is beneficial.**

{{Reflecting on the words and citations of Richard, I wonder **OUT LOUD** just how many unwitting mediums realize how they are being bamboozled *and so used*? The next time you have (what you think is) a paranormal experience, make sure you really have **a solid relationship with Christ.** If you are not fooling yourself, you should (by spiritual discernment) understand what is happening. If you cannot, seek advice, but do not just take it in *as if it were nothing more than* an unusual curiosity, since this is what those of the 'parallax view' are banking on, in my humble opinion! Remember, it is this same parallax view that leads one **away from God the Father** — a path — (upon reflection) I do not think anyone *who is God-fearing* would wish to travel.}}

END NOTES:

Vine's Complete Expository Dictionary of Old and New Testament Words:
Publisher: Thomas Nelson, Inc. ©1996
Used by permission of Thomas Nelson, Inc.

CHAPTER TEN:

THE ORIGINAL AGENDA OF THE SUPERNATURAL POWERS

[This chapter is based on *The Book of Ethiopian Enoch*, (ENOCH I) chapter 15, verse 8 & introduction to verse 9.]

The Origin of Evil Spirits (verse eight):

> *Now the giants, who have been born of spirits, and flesh, shall be called upon earth "evil spirits," and on earth shall be their habitation. Evil spirits shall proceed from their flesh, because they were created from above; from the holy Watchers was their foundation. Evil spirits shall they be upon earth, and the spirits of the wicked shall they be called. The habitation of the spirits of heaven shall be in heaven;* **but upon the earth** *shall be the habitation of terrestrial spirits, who are born on earth.*

In chapter seven it begins as the unholy angels (Watchers) who were holy angels in the beginning, but who left their heavenly home, and then became unholy angels. They said, "Come let us select for ourselves wives from the progeny of men, and let us beget children." (As recorded in this text, the *unholy* Watchers are considered to be about *two hundred*.) {{**This 200 # comes up again in the Book of the Secrets of Enoch (ENOCH II) and may be a clue as**

THE CURS-ED NET

to who those angels were in the Slavonic text.}} They then took wives each choosing for himself, whom they began to approach, and with whom they cohabitated, teaching them sorcery, incantations, and the dividing of roots and trees. In final, these are the races of giants brought forth.

The women bore to them (the unholy watchers) three races, beginning with the great giants. The giants brought forth (some say *slew*) which means "a large number." The nophelim brought forth ("slew") the Elioud, and they existed, increasing in power according to their greatness. {{Note: The alternate spellings of the general term *nephilim* had been briefly explained in the first chapter.}}

The unholy watchers became the fallen angels. The first two hundred were the *chief or higher angels*. Afterwards, many more followed. Several chief watchers began teaching men evil things. This below short list will show you how **evil (and its practices) began among mankind.**

Later you will see how the evil spirits (*these spirits of the giants*) who abide here on earth and who worked hand-in-hand with the fallen angels (their parents) have their own evil agenda for mankind. There are several key words, which through their meanings will define their actions. Within these meanings you will see the conformity among the key words and the descriptions of the supernatural phenomena which play out in this world, and which have been played out over the centuries.

We get to this list of the teachings from some of the chief unholy ones, who taught man evil practices that *continue to this day*, being controlled & spread throughout the population by *chosen* people, picked by these same evil ones. Their purpose, of course, is to deceive and control mankind, and use them for their own benefit and agenda. {{I wonder out loud if the picking of these people that Richard alludes to could not be done through so-called *secret societies*, that, in turn, owe their allegiance to the dark forces that they honor within these same dark societies! One example may be the *Skull & Bones* where, just recently, both presidential candidates hailed from, but neither wished to talk about their allegiances within same, and the major media did not seem *any too* curious about such allegiances.}}

THE TEACHINGS OF THE *UNHOLY*

1) The first chief unholy angel here is *Azazyel*, who taught men to make swords, knives, shields, breastplates, the fabrication of mirrors, and the workmanship of ornaments, as well as the use of paint, the beautifying of the eyebrows, the use of stones of every valuable and select kind, and all sorts of dyes, so that the world became altered. [NOTE: Impiety increased; fornication multiplied, and they transgressed & corrupted all their ways.]

2) Another chief angel, *Amazarak*, taught all the sorcerers and dividers of roots.

3) *Armers* taught the solution of sorcery, the method process of solving problems.

4) The chief angel *Barkayal* taught the observers of the stars, what is today called astrologers.

5) *Akibeel* taught signs (horror scopes.)

6) *Tamiel* taught astronomy.

7) *Asaradel* taught the motion of the moon.

As the giants died off, their spirits *became the evil spirits* (demons,) who enforce these teachings of their parents, or unholy watchers. {{This is probably the reason why a demon can be channeled through a **ouija board**, for instance. These spirits have agendas of their own. This agenda is connected to the supernatural phenomena that we see today, and has been around for many centuries. Incidentally, if one is looking for a connection between *ouija boards & UFOs,* there is an interesting anecdotal story told by Frank Salisbury in his 1974 book, **THE UTAH UFO DISPLAY. It goes like this:** The *ouija board* told some fourth graders that a UFO would appear above *Roosevelt Hospital (*in Roosevelt, Utah) at 8 PM, on the night of February 23, 1967. They were so excited that they told another fourth grader who informed her parents (*the Clyde McDonald family.)* At 8 PM the family indeed watched and saw a reddish orange ball about one third the size of the Moon *exactly where the 'ouija board' had predicted*! The author also mentioned that a man named Junior Hicks confirmed that five other people also saw the object in the same place about the same time. (If this is not a "clue" as to the root of UFOs, then I do not

THE CURS-ED NET

know what is, especially when you consider the warnings in *Enoch* as well as the Bible.) Incidentally, in the conclusion of the book, Dr. Salisbury could not help surmising that the various people he had interviewed throughout the book had somehow been *"conditioned,"* but wondered who or what possibly could have been doing this conditioning about viewing UFOs at exact times and in exact places! *Hopefully the answers may be found in this present work!*}}

The primary deceptive phenomenon is, of course, **the UFO phenomenon,** in which the following key words will reflect this agenda, with meanings that relate to this same phenomenon. As we move now to chapter 15, verse 9, this becomes evident. The spirits of the giants shall be *like* clouds, which shall "oppress, corrupt, fall, contend, and bruise upon the earth." This, then, is the evil agenda for the evil spirits among man. The meanings of these key words will define their workings. The three races of giants die, and their bodies rot away; their spirits become earthbound evil spirits (*demons.*) As they were conceived by the unholy watchers who had left their heavenly home, and they themselves became evil (as in the Fallen Angels,) how then are these evil spirits like clouds? What is their character?

Firstly, *cloud* in Greek (nephos) denotes "a cloudy shape, with less mass covering the heavens (sky.)" In Greek (nephele) or (nepheleim?) is a definitely shaped cloud, or masses of clouds possessing definite form. {{Again, cf. above "note" for the variant spellings of the root name of *nephilim,* and its variant alternative meanings as well.}}

1) Some clouds are shapeless (no likeness.) Evil spirits appear in ghostly forms that have no likeness such as *shadows.* Spirit shapeshifters do not want you to see what they truly look like, so appear as evil characters (images) unlike themselves.

2) Some clouds are of a definite form, i.e., evil spirits appearing specifically as a character needed for a deceptive purpose. These ghostly figures can be *Grays, Reptilians,* images of a man, woman or child, as in the '*hauntings*' phenomenon. Clouds are also water droplets (as Chapter Eight reflected upon.) Dew also reflect water droplets, so as clouds & dew, being **_both_** water droplets & giants, these clouds could represent the dwellings (UFOs) of the evil spirits! Could the text be telling us that the clouds (as dwellings) are inhabited by the giants (as evil spirits?)

THE CURS-ED NET

3) Clouds cover the sky as masses of clouds (evil spirits massed together as groups.) They are possibly roaming around the earth as clouds. They roam around the sky in their dwellings (UFOs) and may have been the same groups spotted in Mexico (in the early 1990s) or Washington DC (in the early 1950s.) {{Certainly the later reference was bizarre, since it seemed to smack of paranormal occurrences, like the "ships" (unknowns) or "clouds" could at first be detected on radar, and then, in a split second, would disappear, giving the observer the uncomfortable feeling that we were not dealing with "ordinary" ships, even if from *outer space*. See the 1956 movie, "UNIDENTIFIED FLYING OBJECTS" for visual details of this series of sightings in 1952.}}

4) A cloud obscures or (hides things.) Evil spirits are invisible; they are not readily seen or noticed. Many times they will hide their actions, perhaps by going (underwater.) They also deceive mankind by cleverly hiding from us the truths of God. They conceal their true agenda through these supernatural phenomena. They may appear in many forms, but never truly revealing themselves — **like excellent facades!**

5) Clouds are at times gloomy; they also have the meaning of being troubled (as in to make gloomy or to make troubled.) *Gloomy* (as an adj.) means to be "partially or totally dark." *Dark* in Greek as a noun is (skotia,) and is used here as "of a spiritual or moral darkness, emblematic of sin, as a condition of moral or spiritual depravity;" cf. Matt. 4:16; John 1:5; 8:12; 12:35; also 1 John 1:5; 2:8-9 & 11. Another meaning in Greek is (zophos) which denotes the "gloom of the nether world." (Skotoo) is "to darken" & metaphorically, of the mind or (deceiving in the mind) (Eph 4:18.)

To make *troubled* as in the Greek (thlipsis,) we see the words "affliction & tribulation." (Thlibo) has the meaning of "to afflict" & (skullo) is "to vex" as in tribulation & afflictions.

Now we take a look at the key words that define how the following meanings reflect to the supernatural phenomena that occurs today. We start with the word *oppress* which means to "keep down by severe and unjust use of force or authority" or a supernatural trance state to control us; another meaning is "to press against." *Press* (biazo) in the middle voice is "to force one's way into" (see

111

THE CURS-ED NET

enter.) *Enter* in Greek is (eiserchomai) which means "to come into" and (eisproeuomai) "to go into" and (pnabaino,) metaphorically, of "coming into the mind." Another meaning of 'oppress' is "to overwhelm," which also is to "surge over and submerge," & "to affect deeply in the mind or emotion."

The primary way I believe that the evil spirits or demons attack us is by coming into our minds, whether by a trance, or through the use of supernatural events that are **so real** we can only believe they exist by what they seem or appear to be, even though we are being deceived. {{If we do not have an anchor for a guide (such as *the Holy Bible & the Book of Enoch,)* it would be easy to see how one could be lost in this jungle of smoke & mirrors. I believe this is what has sadly happened to many people who follow the *'pied pipers'* of the New Age crowd.))

The word *surge* (as verb) is "to move freely back & forth or up & down in the air (UFOs?)" In physics, a *wave* also means "a graphic representation of the variation of a disturbance with time" (as in 'missing time'?) The word *submerge* is a verb which means "to place under water or to hide from view" & in Latin — (subvergere) where *sub* means "below or beneath (as in UFOs beneath the seas?)" In the *next* chapter on **Missing Time,** we mention about going beneath the 'sea' of the earth.

To affect the mind comes from the word 'overwhelm.' *Affect* in Greek (kakoo) is from (kakos) which means "evil" or "to make evil affected." *Evil* in Greek (kakos) is whatever is evil in "character." Evil in character is those deceptive supernatural forms, images, props, such as aliens: *Grays, Reptilians,* etc., or *ghosts,* and *UFOs.* {{If there are such things as "good" UFOs, I have not been convinced by the *scanty evidence presented.* In fact, in the story of Tobias in the Catholic rendition of the Bible, the angel **Raphael,** who was specifically helping the son of Tobias, did **not** ostensibly need any "conveyance" to make his way from Heaven to Earth, or so it appeared in the account within *The Book of Tobias. The good angel was sent to heal both Tobias, and his son by the same name.*}} They become evil characters playing a role in deception; also the word *base* is "evil in influence & effect." (Kakoo) is Greek for a

THE CURS-ED NET

verb that is "to ill treat or entreat evil." 'Base' is (agenes) which means "of low childbirth or negative family race" (as in hybrids?)

The word *influence* is used in every sort of deceptive event here, and will be reflected in its meanings:

1) A power affecting a person, or course of events.
2) A power to sway.
3) An effect or change by such power.
4) Produce effects by 'imperceptible' means.
5) Produce effects by intangible means.
6) To affect the nature, development or condition of; to modify (as in transcending the material order or changing materials to seem like they do not exist on this world.)

The word *effect'* used here is "to cause a specific outcome or a specific impression & phenomenon;" it also has the idea of "bringing into existence" as in (to create supernatural events.)

Let's look at the word *deceive* in Greek as in the noun (apate.) 'Deceit' is akin to (apatao) which is "to deceive" or (that which gives a false 'impression,') whether by appearance (false images) a statement (a declaration of something, a deception) or influence; also (phrenapatao) which is "to deceive in one's mind." (Remember the word *surge* also means to affect deeply in the mind or emotion.) 'Deceive' by appearance is also "to be evil in character, i.e., evil characters playing their evil roles to deceive us!" The word *appear* in Greek (phaino) is "to shine" or "to illuminate." (How many of these evil characters &/or props used in these supernatural deceptions emit light?) Another meaning of the word 'appear' is (phaneros,) "to manifest."

The word *apparition* in Greek reflects a meaning of appearing as follows: in Greek 'apparition' (phantasma) is the "phantom or phantasm from (phaino) which also means to appear." Another meaning of 'deceive' is by "fancies," which in Greek is (phrenapatao) where (phren) is "from the mind" & is "a sin against common sense."

The word *fancies* (as noun) is "the mental faculty through which visions, whims, and fantasies are summoned." (So by attacking your senses via supernatural power, you pretty much believe anything

THE CURS-ED NET

you see at the time because it looks real, yet, *as we know,* appearances can be deceiving.

During much of these events, one experiences the following as reflected in the meaning of the word *imperceptible* (as adjective) meaning "impossible or difficult to perceive by the mind or senses," & "so subtle, slight or gradual as to be barely perceptible;" the other word used as an "effect" (from the list above) is *intangible* which, as an adjective, "is incapable of being perceived by the senses, or unable to realize" (not able to comprehend.) The evil spirits can supernaturally put you under **with such subtlety** that one would never suspect what happened; also, they can deceive us through **such realistic venues (as in virtual reality,)** as to make us believe that they are true events.) {{Talk about your proverbial *animal being led by the ring in its nose!*}}

So the word 'oppress' explains a good deal in its meaning about the evil supernatural events which take place around us via UFOs, 'hauntings,' etc. {{**It seems obvious by now, that Richard is dramatizing this** *façade show* **that is set-up by the dark forces, whose tricks seem to seamlessly blend into the victims' sense of reality ~~ making the seductive process all the more** *tragic* **for the recipients; I would say that it is nothing less than** <u>**insidious**</u>**! Once we understand the true nature of this evil root, we can begin to take measures to protect ourselves;** *since it truly looks like a spiritual battle, spiritual armor will be absolutely necessary to protect one's self. Nothing less* <u>*will do!*</u>}}

The next key word is *corrupt* as in evil spirits look to corrupt mankind via "immorality, errors or alterations," to ruin morally, and to change the original form of (transcending the material order of substances or materials,) and also to evilly change a person spiritually: to do a service for them (alteration;) it also means altering the offspring of humans through implantation (hybrids!) *Corrupt* can mean "to contaminate" (your very soul & spirit by deceptions, making you stray away from all truths and believing in those things that the demons want you to believe in.)

Error in Greek is (plane) which is a "wandering" or "a forsaking of the right path" (2 Thess.2: 14.) *Form* in Greek (tupos) also is "a pattern in the way these evil events unravel themselves." They

THE CURS-ED NET

seem to have many of the same patterns connected to each of the different events and also in the patterns of the teaching evil things to us through these phenomena.

The next word on the evil spirits' agenda is *fall*, which in Greek (ptosis) is (metaphorically,) of the spiritual fall (Luke 2:34.) (Skandalon) = "a snare or trap," or "a means of doing wrong" (by believing in the 'trap' of deception by evil spirits through these supernatural phenomena) & is an occasion "to fall" (empipto) as in "to fall into" (a trap.)

'Fall' in general is a verb "to undergo capture, especially as in an attack," or "to give into temptation, to diminish, to pass into a particular state (trance) condition or situation." It also is "to occur at a specific time" (as in a personally appointed abductions?) It could mean "to occur at a specified place" (as at home or in your vehicle, etc.)

The next word in this report is *content*. In Latin this word (continere) means "to contain" (as in holding abductees, containing them while being examined, etc., at their (the demons') base of operations; it also means "to hold or contain in a trance." *Contain* in Latin (continere) = com + tenere, which is "to hold." (The evil spirits capture their victims and hold them hostage **under mind control**.) 'Contain' (as G.M.) also is "to have within." Here it might mean their *familiar* spirits within our spirit (those unfortunate enough to be subjected to this mind control.) When we accept that *false gift* or believe in a false deception to the point that we continuously spend an ***inordinate amount of time*** involved with these same evil spirits, {{we will actually find ourselves doing their work for them; Richard here is making a very important appeal for those so involved, so as to **break** this bondage (as in being wrapped securely within the *cursed net*) before it is too late, **since the stakes are very high indeed**! I personally believe that this is one of the key prophecies of ENOCII, since it involves *this very generation* as witnessed by the ongoing abduction phenomenon. We will also examine the curious remark by Jesus: ***As in the days of Noah, so shall it be with the return of the Son of Man***...where the days of Noah are not unlike what is going on right now.}}

THE CURS-ED NET

The key word *bruise* upon earth is a verb "to hurt," especially psychologically, (upon the earth to all mankind.) *To hurt* from the Greek (hubris) is "to harm" & also (kakoo,) "to do evil to anyone." *Psychological* (adj.) means "to influence or tend to influence the mind and emotions; also, by being associated with any of certain primary colors whose mixture may be subjective." The psychological primary colors are red, yellow, green, blue & the achromatic pair of black & white. (How many times have UFOs used flashing lights with these same color patterns? Could these same color patterns in certain sequence **subject people without their being the wiser?)**

Well, there it is — the *key words* for the agenda of the evil spirits; the meanings tell the story. Does this, or does this not explain that these supernatural phenomena are **not by aliens** but rather created & controlled by Fallen Angels & evil demonic spirits?

{{REMEMBER: the 15th chapter of ENOCH is _not_ about aliens, but concerns itself with these same fallen angels and their evil progeny, so it may not be coincidental that the examination of the words found within mean **exactly** as Richard interprets them to mean! Other theories about the origins of UFOs, etc., may be a clever trick (as part of the parallax view,) to steer us *away from the truth of the Bible!* The choice seems obvious, but there also is *no end to the skullduggery of these demons. It would not surprise me if* **so-called intellectual types** *try to sabotage the messages found within The Book of Enoch by* **doubting its "authenticity,"** **etc. My answer to this would be:** *READ THE BOOK, (especially as translated by Richard Laurence,) AND WEIGH IT FOR YOURSELVES AGAINST WHAT WE ARE FACING NOW IN OUR REALITY. DO NOT – ipso facto – TAKE THE WORD OF ANY GIVEN "SCHOLARLY SOURCE" AS* THE LAST WORD ON THE SUBJECT. *To do so would be an insult to your God-given right to know the truth in all the forms it has taken throughout the ages.*}}

CHAPTER ELEVEN:

MISSING TIME

This is a more in-depth summary of the abduction part of the UFO phenomenon. It concerns missing time among other important issues. We reflect back to *The Book of Enoch* (68:18) that was cited in the first chapter of this book. We look at the keyword, <u>***stroke***</u> and the particular meaning used here, which is to inflict a blow (a sudden unexpected attack.) It also has the meaning of penetrating or entering one's mind. This is presumably done by supernatural powers, i.e., the evil spirits and fallen angels working in conjunction with one another, and is *usually* executed during a UFO event of some sort.

I believe that there is a personally appointed arranged time and place for these events to transpire. It usually begins with an object seen in the night sky, with colored lights flashing in which these same lights are influencing the mind through primary colors. Then you stop to look and never realize that you have been put into a trance that was so subtle that you may have never perceived it. {{As an "abductee friend of mine" once said: ***The perfect abduction is not remembered.***}}

The word *blow* in Greek is (hupo) which means "under." It indicates repression or a trance state. We continue with the word 'stroke' from "enter one's mind." It also means to remove & separate. This sounds to me as when a person or persons are suddenly "tranced," where their consciousness could be separated and removed from their natural surroundings.

THE CURS-ED NET

Trance in Greek is (ekstasis) for which we also see the word 'amaze.' "It is a condition in which ordinary consciousness and the perception of natural circumstances are withheld, and the soul is susceptible (for the demons' evil agenda.)" A general meaning of the word 'trance' (as noun) is "a hypnotic, cataleptic, or ecstatic state, a detachment from one's physical surroundings; a semi-conscious state." (See 'transient.') 'Trance' (as a verb) is "to put into a trance; an entrance." To continue with this meaning, in Old French (transe) "to die," is "to be numb with fear;" the Latin is (transire) which is "to go across;" (also see transient.)

Let's look now at the word *amaze* that in Greek (as a noun) is (ekstasis,) and is literally "a standing out." The meaning of 'standing' here in Greek is (anistemi,) "to raise" & "for stand-in jeopardy." (See danger.) *Danger* is (enochos) in Greek, which means to be "held in" or "contained in" (en, 'in') & (echo,) "to have, hold."

(Once you are put into this evil supernatural trance, you are then held, contained in the demons' realm, for as ever as long as they need you.) As this is taking place, time goes by (***missing time***) and some of these people do notice this 'missing time' which they cannot account for, or someone reminded them of it later — especially if they had been missing for several hours. {{I know of a woman named Janet, who had this missing time, since she was almost two hours late for her medical appointment, but because she had no knowledge of what happened to her at the "time," she only was able to put the pieces together 33 years later after a qualified psychologist had regressed her to find "the missing time." Part of her remembrance under regressive hypnosis included being taken aboard a UFO, witnessing many things while she was so detained from her normal reality.}}

Most upsetting are the persons who themselves awaken in a different position or with their clothes on in a peculiar manner. {{I, speaking now as a "Ufologist," have actually met and interviewed people like this...such as the couple who were driving their car on one side of the highway, only to be driving in the opposite direction after the abduction to "God knows where!" Another incident involved a woman waking up in the morning to find her shirt inside out, which left this person perplexed — to say the least!}}

118

THE CURS-ED NET

Our minds & senses seem *not* to be able to perceive things like this it happening while they are happening. The person might feel that something "is not right" but doesn't know what to make of it. {{It certainly does not help living in a skeptical and insensitive society, where getting to the root of these upsetting developments can cost one his/her job, family disassociation — or worse!}} This is what drives many people to undergo hypnosis in today's world, to find out the root of their obsessions and "strange dreams." This, then, is how powerful the evil ones' trances can be and have been. The following will focus on what happens when you are in trance.'

We look at the word *amaze* in Greek & the summary of its meaning is as follows (from Vines Expository Dictionary.) It is said of any displacement — and especially with reference to the mind, of that alteration of the normal condition by which the person is thrown (cast) into a state of surprise, fear, or both, or again, in which a person is so transported out of his or her natural state, that he or she falls into a trance.

Another meaning of the word 'amaze' that is very important is the Greek (thambos) meaning "a wonder," or "an amazement" (such as a UFO sighting.) It has a root signifying as follows: "to render immovable" or "to make someone incapable of movement, to paralyze, or to be unable to move!"

The word *alteration* is "a condition of changing," (a change from your normal surroundings under a trance,) or "cast into a state of surprise as a sudden unexpected encounter, or an attack where one is captured suddenly without warning;" it also means "to cause wonder, astonishment or amazement (through the supernatural entrapment used by the evil spirits such as in a UFO encounter.)" A person so transported is "to carry from one place to another a 'condition' of being transported by (emotion) or (rapture.)

So either they {{the "demons, inc."}} can take your consciousness (if that is only needed,) or take your physical body by (rapture) and your consciousness (emotion) together! How many people through abduction or other events complained of not being able to move? {{I know of one VIP abductee who actually described her paralysis "process" started happening (at her toes) and in such a way that the only thing she could control before experiencing "lights out" before her 'Gray' intruder, was to be able to still move her eyes! The rest of this amazing tale was only remembered under hypnosis, and as I reported on in a previous chapter, this may only have been the tip of the iceberg concerning the layers of remembering under hypnosis, again, as per the research of Karla Turner and her famous *"Abductions in a Gingerbread House* story.}}

Transport in Latin is (transportare) as in trans + portare = "to carry." *Carry* in Greek is (diaphero) having the idea of "to carry through" (time?) while the meaning of (metatithemi) is "to place among" or "put in another place." When you're put into a trance, your body & mind (or just your mind in some cases) must be transported to another place & time among the evil ones (who are only presented today as hybrids, portrayed as *'Grays* or *Reptilians,* etc. In other words, your body (physically) and your mind (or just your mind) are carried among them to their place of operations, where that dwelling may very well be a UFO, and most likely under the water. {{These speculations were explored by Richard in chapter seven, and interestingly enough, in a major case in Ufology, reflected in a book by Budd Hopkins, the UFO that allegedly captured Linda Cortile out of her 12th story apartment near the Brooklyn Bridge, was actually seen by a female witness as going under that same bridge and diving into the East River, so here again, it tends to lend support to Richard's ideas in this area. [There were actually over twenty witnesses to this extraordinary event as noted in this book called, **WTNESSED.**] The real question for the inquiring mind is whether these *Grays* that abducted Linda were from some other planet or star system, or were they the 'hybrid residue' of fallen angels thrown down from their first estate thousands of years ago, as reported by ENOCH, and living perhaps much closer to our reality than the average person would expect or suspect?}}

We look at the word *entrance* (from 'trance' earlier.) In Greek, (eiserchomai) is "to come into." The evil ones come into your mind, control you, and abduct you through their supernatural power. The word *blow* in general comes into play here, as a verb contributing to the word 'transported' & its meaning is "to be in a state of motion." (This is a supernatural trance state that employs motion.) The word now is *transient* from trance in Greek (as adj.) whose (G.M.) is a "passing with time." *Past* in Greek (diaginomai) where (dia) means "through" is used in time to denote "an intervening elapse." The word *intervene* could possibly explain here about 'missing time' within the scope of the abduction phenomenon. 'Intervene' (as a verb in G.M.) is "to occur or come between two periods or points of time." In between these points of time must be the holding place, the containment habitat of the demons' evil workings, including examinations, implants, etc.

Does time literally stop at this juncture while you exist in some other state of reality [?] {{This is the $64,000 question; perhaps the victims are literally taken out of our reality, just as James LeFante (an abductee I had interviewed on public access TV back in the mid-1990s,) had suggested with his notion of "**time looping**," giving an example from his own life (witnessed by his friend Curtis,) where that seemed to be the only ostensible explanation as to why they were abducted at 4:30 PM, yet remember watching the same TV program that started "again" for them at 4 PM! Bizarre as that may seem, it begs the question as to where they were for that half hour period, and raises even more questions about the nature of our reality as we think we understand it.}}

The other meaning of 'intervene' is "to occur as an extraneous or unplanned circumstance" where the personally specified, chosen time in which the persons are involved in their collective event [UFO related?] are then, suddenly and unexpectedly attacked during this same "timeframe" (being subsequently supernaturally repressed.)

Time is an interval separating two points on the continuum, a duration of that time marked by events, conditions or phenomena, an appointed or fated moment (a personal event.) The interval is the amount of time between two specified instances, events or states (i.e., a trance state!) The events (usually a UFO encounter of some sort,) seem specifically arranged for a specific abduction. {{It doesn't seem to me, after having reviewed this enigmatic field for close to forty years, that there are *any* coincidences when it comes to who is being taken and why they are being taken; the dynamics of this phenomenon do not smack of simply inquisitive ET scientists from other galaxies gleaning knowledge for their planet or star system; rather, it seems — for the life of me — to be just the oppo-

THE CURS-ED NET

site: a sinister plan by very intelligent and crafty beings who are hell-bent on keeping to a *fiendish agenda*, an agenda that does not have our best interests at heart, as witnessed by the untold pain & agony attested to by countless abductees (from the little they can remember or retrieve from hypnosis.) AND WHAT ABOUT THE VERY MUCH THEY CANNOT REMEMBER? Should not this be of even greater concern for *anyone grappling for the meaning of these abductions?*}}

Remember *trance* in Latin = "to go over or across" where the word *across* in general here means "on or from the other side of." (Reality is your natural surroundings and should logically be the other side of.) Where then is the meaning "to cross through" as in from the other side (reality) and cross through time to your holding place (the destination) among the demons? The word *over* (G.M.) is "from one end or side to the other," or "from abduction reality to holding and then back to reality. *Time* in Greek is a "space" of time, and *space* (diastema) means "an interval." In Latin interval is (inter-vallum) = 'inter' + vallum as "rampart."

Now follow closely: *Inter* (as a verb in Latin) is 'in' + (terra) or (interrare) = 'earth' or "in earth." *Rampart* (the last of G.M.) is in Latin 'ante,' where 'ante' + the Latin 'parare' = "to prepare." *Prepare* (as a verb) is "to make ready beforehand for a specified purpose, as for an event," (as in a personal event set up by an abduction.)

(In earth) reflects earth (as noun, G.M.) which is the land surface of the world. *Earth* in Hebrew is (erets) or (earth as entire.) In *Holman's Bible Dictionary*, it is a created sphere or material realm, as in Gen 1:1 & 2 as the earth (erets.) Furthermore, 'erets' is what is beneath the earth or land, i.e., the underworld. (Earth) then is literally 'under' + 'world,' where *under* is a preposition with (G.M.) as being beneath the surface of.

Beneath in Greek (kato) signifies "down" or "downwards" (see bottom.) *Bottom* in Greek (a bussos) = bottomless from (intensive, & bussos,) which means "a depth." *Depth* in Greek (pelagos) is ("the sea!") Cf. Acts 27:5; the depth (of the sea) Matt 18:6.

The word 'bottom' is probably connected with a form of (plesso,) which is (to strike) and (plege) "a blow," suggestive of the tossing of the waves. Cf. (a strike – a blow) from *The Book of Enoch*, 68:18;

THE CURS-ED NET

also Jude 13, as in "wild waves" of evil teachers & evil spirits/ fallen angels.

So it might look like, when you are put into a trance and transported and "carried off" to a location, the destination may very well be below the surface of the earth (below the surface of the sea to be exact.) Is this where abductees are taken: far below the water?

{{Since the earth is approximately three quarters water, and since its very depths would be a very good "hiding" place to carry out physical examinations, etc., without much risk of being discovered, the above speculations by Richard does not seem at all far fetched, but may even be "*more* logical" than having these same abductees whisked off to a far away planet in a galaxy very *very* 'near'! This, then, becomes another reason for opting for the "demonic" explanation of the UFO & alien abduction phenomenon, as opposed to having some 'benevolent' [?] group(s) coming from afar, and *__intimately__* being involved with our species from the beginning until now. **[Remember the *ouija board/UFO incident* discussed previously from Dr. Salisbury's book?]** Holy Scripture seems to back-up the former, while, as far as the latter hypothesis, we only really have the "word" of the abductors as given to the abductees to communicate to the rest of humanity, and as we have learned bitterly from history, trust not the words of a potential adversary about their motives or intentions. A word to the wise is sufficient.}}

TO SEE A CONFIRMATION OF THE IDEAS OF RICHARD STOUT, WRITTEN BY A SCHOLAR (J. Timothy Unruh) ON THE UFO PHENOMENON IN RELATION TO BIBLICAL TEXTS (including *The Book of Enoch,*) GO TO THE INTERNET LINK:

http://inspectorblebeau.pbwiki.com/AUTHORCONFIRMSIDE AOFRICHARDSTOUTABOUTFALLENANGELS

FINAL NOTE: JUST REMEMBER, IN ALL OF THESE THINGS REGARDING FALLEN ANGELS, THE ENCOURAGING WORDS OF ST. PAUL:

"I am sure that neither death, nor life, nor angels, nor principalities, nor things present, nor things to come, nor powers, nor height, nor depth, nor any other creature will be able to

THE CURS-ED NET

separate us from the love of God, which is in Christ Jesus
our Lord."

(Romans 8:38-39 KJV)

END NOTES:

Vine's Complete Expository Dictionary of Old and
New Testament Words:
Publisher: Thomas Nelson, Inc. ©1996
Used by permission of Thomas Nelson, Inc.

CHAPTER TWELVE:

BREAKING the SCRIPTURAL CODE within PROPHECY

{{This chapter as well as the following five chapters, are dedicated to uncovering the demonic element of the alien abduction phenomenon as **potentially** encoded within scripture, reflected by the evidence presented in this treatise, based on the *key word notes* of co-author Richard Stout.

INTRODUCTION: Mr. Stout has seemingly pierced the veil of his initial explorations of *The Book of Enoch*, as reflected in "**THE BITE OF THE SERPENT**" *group* **of aforementioned chapters.** By diligently studying the scriptures, while being aided by scriptural dictionaries and concordances (as duly noted at the end of each pertinent chapter,) he has uncovered the potential actual *timeline* of **the curse of Canaan,** and how it is intimately involved within the heretofore enigma of the UFO and 'Alien' Abduction Phenomenon. Richard has found coded clues within the sacred scriptural texts of firstly, Zacharia, and then supported by Joel, Revelation (especially chapter nine,) with other supporting evidence from Isaiah & Deuteronomy, and minor references to other scripture.

- o This six-part *group of chapters* should truly help in our collective understanding of the UFO phenomenon, especially as it relates to **the spiritual reality as its underpinnings**, with the hope that it not only increases peoples' faith

THE CURS-ED NET

and *reliance* in God, but makes them acutely aware of the peril that lies lurking within this ostensible enigmatic UFO phenomenon and the accompanying demonic & deadly abduction phenomenon. To dismiss or simply ignore one's reliance upon the Father of All would be a big mistake *as the co-authors of this presentation see it.*

This *curse of Canaan* will be traced from just after THE GREAT FLOOD, and thanks to the prophet Zacharia, will be placed within a timeline that ends in our very time. Added to this is revealed the probable meaning of *the various types of locusts* of Revelation, chapter nine. How **THE TRIBULATION** will *end the curse* will also be explored within these six chapters.

THE SOURCES USED: This will involve the following:
1) NEW INTERNATIONAL VERSION (NIV)
2) VINE'S COMPLETE EXPOSITORY DICTIONARY (*Vine's.*) Any Greek word translated will always appear in parenthesis.
3) AMERICAN HERITAGE COLLEGE DICTIONARY (3RD EDITION) for all general meanings.
4) KING JAMES' VERSION (KJV)

LASTLY, *The Book of Enoch* will be referenced, usually through the aforementioned *group of chapters relating to **The Bite of the Serpent,*** to show how this beginning search into the connection between the so-called alien abduction phenomenon is actually, in effect, **the demonic abduction phenomenon,** but more importantly, how it is now being confirmed through specific canonical prophetic sources as well, *as per Richard's diligent research*!

And now I am delighted to present the full notes of Richard, with only minor corrections necessary. I will comment only where I feel it is necessary, to confirm some point or other, saving my own personal feelings for the end of this most important treatise, specifically as it relates to *reliance upon the Father of all & His blessed Son, Jesus.*}}

THE CURS-ED NET

KNOW THIS (NIV BIBLE)

[From Daniel 12:2: "*Multitudes who sleep in the dust of the earth will awake: some to everlasting life, others to shame and contempt.*"]

Those who still choose to believe that which is not of God's word and what is of false & deceiving nature (even when given the truth,) will awake to shame and everlasting contempt, but those who believe in God's word to be the truth and believe and accept His Son Jesus Christ as their beloved savior, will awake to **everlasting life**.

"But you, Daniel, close up and seal the words of the scroll until the time of the end. Many will go here and there to increase knowledge, will be spread throughout the world" (Dan 12:4.)

And Christ speaking:

"There is nothing concealed that will not be disclosed, or hidden that will not be made known" (Matt 10:6.) The truth will be known for those who accept it. {{Hopefully, what is being presented in this *very* treatise, is **part** of that very truth! I *pray* that this *is* the case.}}

THE FLYING SCROLL (An Introduction):

The Flying Scroll is connected to Joel 2, Revelation 9, and Enoch. Joel 2 & Rev. 9 mention a final judgment during the TRIBULATION, which will come down upon man and is **intimately** connected to what we know of as the UFO phenomenon.

Joel lists, in detail, the meanings of an **ongoing judgment** that is connected (I believe) to the curse as presented in Zacharia 5. *This curse* has been here for thousands of years, since after THE GREAT FLOOD of Noah's time. The curse explained in this chapter *is* explaining the ongoing supernatural, deceptive & evil project which is continually being orchestrated by the evil spirits & fallen angels, disguised as so-called "aliens" to distract us into believing that aliens do exist — *but they do not as explained in the Biblical commentary on the New Age literature!* As was cited above from Jesus' words, that there is nothing concealed that will not be made known, (and this **façade of benevolent or non-interfering aliens from elsewhere** is one of those things, I think.)

According to the most important four verses of Zacharia, we read the following:

127

THE CURS-ED NET

"I looked again, and there before me was a flying scroll. He asked me, 'What do you see?' I answered, 'I see a flying scroll, thirty feet long and fifteen feet wide.' And he said to me, 'This is **the curse** that is going out over the whole land; for according to what is said on one side every **thief** will be banished, and according to what it says on the other, every one who **swears falsely** will be banished. The Lord Almighty declares, 'I will send it out, and it will enter the house of the thief and the house of him who swears falsely by my name. It will remain in his house and destroy it, both its timbers and its stones." (5:1-4; NIV.)

The following is a breakdown that I believe, through KEY WORDS, is *exactly* what might be happening:

We will start with the word *fly* that, in general, is "to engage in flight or the act of flight; to move through the air." The word *flight* in general is "moving through the sky, atmosphere, or space; the ability to fly."

The word 'fly' in Greek is (petomai.) "To fly" has a root that is seen in (pteron) & (ptereix) as "a wing." The wings of the *locusts* (Rev. 9:9 & Joel 2:5,) both reflect similarities of "the wings" symbolically being in a mode of transportation. The word *wing* in Greek is (pteriex.) It symbolically, according to (KJV,) represents "two wings of a great eagle," which suggests the definiteness of the action, and the "wings" indicating rapidity & protection. Another meaning is (pterugion) which is a "pinnacle."

As far as we have established that this *scroll* indeed does fly, we must further understand this word *pinnacle.* You need to refer back to chapter six which explains the type of wings both sketched & described, only *this* scroll is what we call **cigar-shaped.** {{For those unfamiliar with Ufological lore, the "cigar-shaped" type craft have been reported often, and more regularly since the beginning of the 20th century; my father even saw one of these type craft way back in 1925, and he assured me it was *not* a blimp or zeppelin, and not too surprisingly, sent him on his life's long search to find the truth of this matter.}}

Moving forward, we look again at another meaning of the word *flight*, which, in Greek is (klino,) "to make to bend" & is translated "turned to flight." As we see in the word *turn*, it will express many important details that explain some of the 'wings' (or 'scroll') characteristics. (We are using the words "scroll & wing" symbolically for the characteristics of UFOs.)

Let's look at all of the meanings of the word 'turn' as it reflects in detail to UFOs:

1) To cause to move around an axis; cause to rotate or revolve.
2) Alter, and/or control the functioning of a mechanical device by the use of rotating.
3) To perform or accomplish a somersault, which is Latin (saltus, the past participle of saltre) for 'to leap' (Joel 2:5,) as in to leap over the mountaintops.
4) To change the position of. *Position* is here the arrangement of its body (UFO) parts; *posture*: "a changing arrangement of its body."
5) To reverse & re-sew the material of. *Reverse* is "transpose," while *sew* is "to make." The wings (UFO) make themselves transpose which is "to transfer the order of; to put into a different order."

So *turned to flight* possibly here means "transposing itself, changing its order, arrangements, or its body shape to another in flight." {{Just as the fallen angels have the ability to 'shape-shift,' (Enoch 19:2,) it also appears that so can their vehicles; on occasion, we get reports in the UFO literature of UFOs with the *most peculiar* shapes, i.e., definitely not "designed" with aerodynamic principles in mind.}}

To cement the statement further, we look at the word *turn* that, in Greek, is (anakampto, ana) or *back* (kampto) "to bend;" also, see the word 'return.' (Metastrepho) signifies in the passive voice "to be turned," or a change into something different. *Return* in Greek (anastrepho) is "to turn back;" also (anakampto) "to turn or bend back." (There have been many UFO reports of objects changing their shapes into something else from time to time. {{I once saw a video that had captured a UFO changing *literally* into the shape of a helicopter, so I believe that this is what Richard is alluding to, although we must be most suspicious of video-tape of anomalies

THE CURS-ED NET

being presented on TV for our amusement; I also suspect that the secret government may have developed a "stealth-type" of ability that they have *not exactly* shared with the people who pay taxes to this same government, adding another layer of intrigue to this already baffling enigma, so the layers of minions working in & through the dark forces may be, shall I say ~~ **LEGION! This shell game is best utilized under the general heading of** *compartmentalization,* **so that even if you wanted to put the pieces together to inform your "fellow man," the Military might, with their warnings and strict regulations in place, would, in most instances, thwart such endeavors.}}**

So now we have a vehicle, a wing type (scrou,) which can fly and have the ability to change its shape and back again. We must try to understand that this is only done by supernatural powers & I don't care how advanced the race could be. They would still be a "natural" entity and could never do most of the things found in the UFO phenomenon. THINK ABOUT IT:

1) Changing shapes of their craft
2) Changing their natural shapes — their very being
3) Being able to go through walls, where only a spirit mentioned in God's word which is invisible as the wind could do so and NOT a living organism, to the best of our knowledge.

Think about some of the things these so-called alien creatures supposedly do, and then you may ask yourself: is this possible, even for an advanced race, keeping in mind that they **are still flesh & blood!** ARE THEY ~~ or are they really spirits (evil spirits enclosed in a cloned or hybrid body to be able to co-exist with man in some way so they not only get their objective completed, but also accomplish all these things through a deceptive illusion of being aliens *to cover-up their true identity*! Could there be a better cloak of deception used? We accept them for what they seem to be, but are not, yet appearing to the whole world as they wish us to view them? {{It may be little wonder that *Satan will deceive the whole world*! Thinking on this point of Richard's, I think of St. Paul, who uses the apt expression of Satan cloaking himself as an **angel of light.** He compounds his insight by mentioning in Ephesians that we are

THE CURS-ED NET

NOT fighting against flesh & blood, but against the powers of darkness and wickedness from on high, which, when you think about it, resembles the crowd we seem to be confronting in the so-called 'alien abduction phenomenon.' Whoever believes in the truth as espoused in the New Testament (Covenant,) should also be able to follow Richard's ongoing dot connection with both the citations of Joel & Revelation, which the non-canonical *Enoch* seems to parallel and fill-in —~ and not just a little bit!}}

Let's now look at the word *scroll* in general, as 'a roll,' a rolled scroll of paper, an ancient book written on a roll of parchment or papyrus. The word *roll* in Greek is (apokulio) or (apokulizo) "to roll away." In English it means a cylinder (or perhaps a cigar-shaped flying object?) To 'roll' in general means "to travel around; to wander." (Check the **wandering stars** from chapter three.) 'Roll' means "to revolve on an axis or by repeatedly turning." The Latin is (rotula,) a diminutive of rota, "a wheel," (UFO?) as in to travel around, "over the whole land" (Zach 5:3.)

The word *away* which follows the words 'to roll' in Greek is the verb (airo.) Its meanings are to "seize lift up & to take away." It also implies a forcible removal. (Seize means to kidnap, and kidnap means to abduct;) the dictionary says to also see the word *bear* (as 9th meaning of *Vine's*.) In Greek the word seize (sullambano) literally means "to take together!" It signifies "to seize as a prisoner." (Refer to chapter seven where this was discussed.)

'Bear' is (airo) in Greek which means "to raise up, to lift, to take upon one's self and carry "what has been raised 'physically'" (as in the abductee?) It also means that it is "applied to the mind, to suspend, to keep in suspense." (*Suspend* means "to render temporarily ineffective or to paralyze!")

ONE POINT OF INTEREST: At the end of the meanings of the word 'bear,' it says to see the word 'begat' (apokeico) which means "to give birth, to bring forth" from (kuco) meaning "to be pregnant." The word *beget* also has a meaning in Greek of (ektroma) which denotes "an abortion, an untimely birth," from (ektitrosko) "to miscarry." So the word 'begat' has the implied meanings dealing with the abduction scenario of the possible implantation of a living organism, and then to extract that organism (the fetus) after the

THE CURS-ED NET

chosen amount of time. The word 'begat' has one more meaning here (anagennao) or (ana) which reflects the concept of "is again or from above," (as in UFOs? Aliens? I don't think so! It sounds rather like evil spirits and fallen angels, which seems more appropriate with the connotation being suggested.)

So far it seems we have a *flying scroll* (cylinder cigar-shaped object) that travels across the whole land. *Land* in Greek (ge) is "whole land;" see earth. *Earth* in Greek (ge) means "the earth as a whole" or "the world." So as it travels throughout the world, it seems to have the ability to change shapes in flight, and also seems by the "*curse*" to have an agenda, **including** abduction, implantation of the fetus, and the extraction of same, i.e., a forcible removal of the fertilized egg.

According to Zacharia, the *cylinder* "is thirty feet long and fifteen feet wide." (5:3; NIV) What do these dimensions mean? They apparently carry a coded message. Firstly, we look at the word *thirty symbolically* (other than just meaning the number.) It also carries a meaning that is very insightful. The meaning has "an indication of the **end of a story**." The word *story* here may not just represent the whole of a scripture from Genesis to Revelation, *but also* the beginning of the curse (of Canaan) to its conclusion. [The Canaan curse will be explained more in detail shortly.] The word *indication* in general means "serves as an indicator," but an indicator of what?

The number *fifteen* here is half of thirty. *Half* in Greek is (hemisus) and as a noun means " time." If we also look at the word *wide*, it also reflects "being at a certain distance from a desired goal or point." So the word *thirty* is an indicator of *fifteen* that is an exact point in time: "half-way from 'wide,' as a desired goal." (In my opinion, it would conclude in Revelation 9 as the judgment of the **locusts**, {{*as the "end of the story"*}} that will be addressed in a subsequent section.)

If Zacharia perhaps represents a type of **midpoint** in time for *this curse,* (discussed more fully below,) when did it begin and possibly when will it end? Zacharia was written about 470 — 520 B.C., so roughly 500 B.C. If we go ahead to our time, that would be approximately 2500 years. Now if you subtract the 2500 from 500 years before Christ, you will get approximately 3000 B.C. Why is

THE CURS-ED NET

this then *potentially* significant? 3000 B.C. arrives approximately at the period of the GREAT FLOOD. In Gen 9:25 (NIV,) Noah says, "Cursed be Canaan! The lowest of slaves will he be to his brothers." But why is this curse important? A curse was to begin with Canaan's bloodline. This was to happen after the GREAT FLOOD, when life began then to multiply. {{Before we go any further, I would like to interject two items from my own research: firstly, an item that deals with this number 15 plus the number 30. WITNESS another citation from scripture that deals with these very numbers: On the "15" & the "30" symbolism in the Old Testament, as per Craig Winn's observation and citation, below:

From CHAPTER TWO: *Enduring Love* http://yadayahweh. com/Yada_Yahweh_Going_Astray_Chesed.YHWH

['Gomer, however, was now owned by the temple priests of Baal. "So I bartered (karah - traded, exchanged money and bought) her for me for fifteen pieces of silver and fifteen bushels of barley. I said unto her, 'You shall live (yasab —dwell, endure, stay) with me many days (rab Yom — an exceedingly long time). You shall no longer be an unfaithful prostitute, and you shall have no other man; for I am indeed tying old and new together and expressing a relational agreement (gam) with regard to and concerning (el) you." (Hosea 3:2-3)]

According to historians, this **bartered** fee was the going rate at the time to **buy someone out of slavery** so as to offer them their freedom. It is a lovely picture of <u>our</u> salvation as we are "bought," literally redeemed, from the marketplace of sin. And it's interesting that the **thirty** cumulative units of silver and barley is equivalent to the thirty pieces of silver for which Judas betrayed Jesus.

Now I found this curious, since I just read about this after Richard had mentioned to me about the flying scroll & the measurements of **15 & 30**, and the possibility that this represented some parameter relating to the beginning, middle and end of the curse, that will be specifically shown to coincide (possibly) with our current problem of the demonic abduction phenomenon; I found it even *more curious* that these were the same numbers as in Hosea above, that represented "<u>*buying back*</u>" unfaithful servants, since they could not earn it themselves, in order to become "**uncursed**," if I can use that expression.

THE CURS-ED NET

To add to this mixed metaphor, the number **30** was itself a **cursed** number because it had to do with the amount of silver Judas got for betraying Jesus in the New Testament. So it seems that the numbers **15 & 30** show two sides of the coin of cursing **and** "uncursing," or it may *just be a coincidence.*

As far as the dating of THE GREAT FLOOD goes, I found confirmation about the approximate accuracy of the 3000 B.C. date. WITNESS:

As an interesting note, we know for certain that a flood of biblical proportions occurred five thousand years ago (around 3000 BCE) in the region where the men created in God's image (with a nesamah/conscience in addition to a nepesh/soul or consciousness) were said to have lived. Yahweh told us that Eden was at the headwaters of the Tigris and Euphrates Rivers, near the Black Sea, and that Adam's and Chavah's children ultimately formed the civilizations east and south of the Garden including: Babylon, Assyria, and Sumer. Archeologists have found cities 200 feet below the current shores of the Black Sea and a twelve foot thick layer of silt and mud was laid down all at once in Mesopotamia, precisely when the oldest Scriptural texts said the flood occurred

From link: http://inspectorblebeau.pbwiki.com/Conversations -with-YAHWEH-other-aspects

Craig Winn (who has penned on the Internet a comprehensive website called, *YADA YAHWEH.)* seems to be an accurate and excellent 'lay-scholar' when it comes to details surrounding the Old Testament, which he insists on calling a "Covenant," so Richard's timeline seems to be corroborated. Now let us return to Richard's treatise.}}

Before the GREAT FLOOD of Gen. 6:6 (NIV,) it states: "When man began to increase in number on the earth and daughters were born to them, the sons of God saw the daughters of men were beautiful and they married any of them they chose. The Nephilim were on earth in those days — and also afterwards — when the sons of God went to the daughters of men and had children by them."

The 'sons of God' in Job 1:6 & 2:1 was a phrase used for angelic or non-human beings. These were the Fallen Angels mentioned in the *Ethiopian* Book of Enoch, chapter 7. The Nephilim who were

THE CURS-ED NET

the offspring of this union is translated as **giants** in the KJV, and the New King James Version of the Bible. These *giants* **before** the Flood were the product of Fallen Angels and the daughters of men.

The **post** Flood giants were an intervention of the evil forces between men & women. We see the words mentioned earlier—"**and also afterward**"—meaning that they will return again. Their return began *during* the bloodline of Canaan. Canaan was the father of the Amorites, one of many tribes of offspring (Gen. 10:15-16.) The Amorites were a tribe of giants but the name also stood as an example of a class of giant, of which several different tribes existed. Other tribes included the Rephaim, and known as Emim (Deut. 2:11) and the Zamzummim (Deut. 2:20.) King Og of Bashan (Deut. 3:11) was the king of the Amorites and last of these giants. There was also the Anakim (Deut. 1:28, 2:10,11 & Josh. 14:12,15.)

The *curse* spoken of in Zacharia 5 is, I believe, the beginning of the birth of the tribes in Canaan's bloodline after the Flood. As was before the Flood, interaction from above (Fallen Angels) which created the Nephilim was also there after the Flood, but because God put an end to the ability of the Fallen Angels having direct human contact (intercourse,) these post-Flood giants had to be brought forth in another fashion.

The spirits of the Nephilim that became the earth-bound evil spirits came forth from the primary foundation of giants that existed before the Flood and by a judgment of God, killed each other off before the Flood. This proclivity, which then continued after the Flood, now, not only by the Fallen Angels (many who fathered the Nephilim before the Flood,) were thrown into *middle earth*, **the abyss,** by God as their judgment, but many other Fallen Angels remained, who together with earth-bound evil spirits, (the Nephilim,) have and used the method of human abduction as we know of it today, reflected in the UFO abduction phenomenon. It is through this method of abduction (**as *a fruit of* the curse**,) that seems to reflect how the post-Flood giants originated.

Instead of direct contact (intercourse) with the daughters of men, the method changed to the abduction of the people needed, employing supernatural power. They took (as they do today,) the needed DNA tissue through the donors used, the selected sperm

THE CURS-ED NET

donors, & impregnate the sperm with the evil mixture needed. More than likely it includes their own tissue types that were implanted into a woman's fetus. This then creates the hybrid organism they seek for their own nefarious uses. .

Times have changed since the Post Flood Giants. **They were the beginning of the whole abduction project.**

o **[This is what will be proved through the scriptures selected throughout these next six chapters.] As the project continued, so have the alterations of the (selected) organisms implanted in the human females. {{Remember that in Enoch 68:18, "somehow" Enoch was aware that this project would "diminish the embryo;" how did he know this, and what was he referring to? I have never seen any scriptural pundit address this issue *until now!*}}**

I believe that after the *Post flood Giants* were killed or died off, there was a temporary lull in the abductions, then, as we find out from Zacharia 5, where the Lord Almighty declares that He will send out *this scroll* (that I have perceived as a cigar-shaped object,) throughout the land. This then was the *mid-way point*! It was now *the curse* to begin again. (As I have intimated before, this curse <u>was</u> the UFO/abduction phenomenon that is both ongoing and exists to this present day!) In Zacharia 5 it states that certain groups of people will be inflicted with this curse, namely, the thieves & those who swear falsely (5:4.) {{I am sure that if this be true, these two categories alone may incorporate a huge number of people that have been amassed from the beginning of this curse (from the times of Canaan) until now; Richard will show that this curse will continue right up through the TRIBULATION, so don't expect the UFO/abduction phenomenon to end *any time soon!* I also believe that it is important to note that *we cannot be certain as to the whys or wherefores of any given abductee being* caught up in this *curs-ed* net, but some may be experiencing it in order to focus their attention on their true roots, or to think about why this is happening to them. To speculate any further would be, not only unwise *but downright foolish!*}}

THE CURS-ED NET

As will be mentioned in the forthcoming sections of the four *locusts'* types, as per the prophet Joel as well as in Revelation, this curse manifests and intensifies to a horrific state! It becomes a full-fledged invasion. Yet, as stated also in Joel, chapter 2, this curse has been an ongoing judgment, albeit escalating during the end-age period, {{i.e., most-likely, **in the present generation**, since the fig leaves seem to be ripening!}}

The Bible also mentions what is going to happen to those evil spirits and fallen angels who have carried out this curse from its inception. In the below link I had written that they are symbolic of the UFO, and the so-called "aliens" which have so deceived us over the centuries.

As per Isaiah 34:4 (NIV): "All the stars of the heavens will be dissolved and the sky rolled up like a scroll; all the starry hosts will fall like withered leaves from the vine, like shriveled figs from the fig tree." {{Of course Richard is citing a Biblical reference to the "wandering stars" (as angels) that Jude referred to in his epistle, which further had put the exclamation point on the accuracy of *The Book of Enoch* written so long ago!}}

The word **star** is symbolic of angels (Job 38:7,) as morning stars singing, as well as Revelation 8:10-11, & 9:1-2; it is also mentioned in *Enoch* where he actually equated angels with stars. "Heavens" is the sky-atmosphere. The word *dissolved* in Greek (katatuo) says to see the word 'destroy' (5th meaning) which reflects "to be taken down; to overthrow." The sky rolled-up is like a scroll "removed." The "starry hosts" are the evil spirits & fallen angels playing out the UFO **"façade show."** The word *fall* has as one of its meanings, "to be destroyed."

The word *whither* in general has an appropriate meaning here which is "to render incapable of action." So it seems the UFO phenomenon played out by evil spirits & fallen angels are to be ostensibly taken out of action & destroyed when our savior Jesus Christ returns at the close of the TRIBULATION period. {{This has often been referred to as the **Day of the Lord,** where there will be a total accountability for all who have had some allegiance with "SATAN, INC."}}

THE CURS-ED NET

So if 3000 B.C. seems to be the approximate time for *the beginning of the curse,* and this occurred 2500 years before 500 B.C., our present time (2500 years after 500 B.C.,) may portend that we indeed are in **THE LAST DAYS!** Just how close to the seven year TRIBULATION period, I don't know, but I feel it is very close indeed. {{The aforementioned Craig Winn, author of the website, *Yada Yahweh,* **had some very specific scriptural insight into the exact time of this period as being between 2026 & 2033 C.E. If you go to his Internet website cited below, you will read how Winn shows that the "indefinite period" has to do with the "catching up in the air" (i.e., THE RAPTURE, which will transpire sometime before the beginning of the TRIBULATION period. I caution the reader that there are several theories running about this dynamic, and it has always been my contention to *always be prepared since we know not the day nor the hour of our personal visitation.*}}**

Please review Winn's website for details: [From BOOK III of *Yada Yahweh,* SALVATION located at: CH. 6, also called "Salvation."] http://yadayahweh.com/Yada_Yahweh_Salvation_Yasha.YHWH

A SPECIAL NOTE: If you read the above-cited link, you will find that Mr. Winn feels that Jesus will return in November of 2033, so that the **Tribulation**, will in fact commence in November of 2026. It took Craig Winn (writing as a seeming non-denominational lay person,) about one thousand pages to explain the above dynamic comprehensively in his *Yada Yahweh* work; my only suggestion to the reader of our present work is to keep an open mind and examine Winn's work carefully, in order to surmise if he indeed has the timing of the prophecies specifically correct, since, after all, he uses the same type of approach as Richard, (i.e., the scriptures plus various concordances, etc., to arrive at his conclusions. As you will notice, 2026 is not that far down the pike!

BACK TO BREAKING THE SCRIPTURAL CODE

Now continuing with the word *thief,* in Greek (kleptes,) it literally & metaphorically means of 'false teachers' (John 10:8.) 'Teacher' in Greek (pseudodidaskalos,) alludes to a "false teacher" & occurs

THE CURS-ED NET

in the plural in 2 Peter 2:1. 'False' (pseudes) "of false witnesses" is reflected in ACTS 6:13 & "false apostles" in Rev. 2:2 (KJV.) It appears as "liars" in Rev. 21:8; also (pseudonumos) are those who are "under a false name" & are deceiving religions & (pseudos) "a falsehood."

The above is certainly one group of people who will be afflicted by this curse, the one which originated with Noah's curse on his grandson Canaan {{for the abhorrent act of Noah's son, Ham; one interpretation to explain the dynamics of this story was attempted by a Rev. Richard Gan, and you can read this fascinating account where the Rev. Gan uses Biblical references to put forward his argument at the web page located at:

http://inspectorblebeau.pbwiki.com/SATANS-SEED-Explored

The name of the web page is called, **Satan's Seed explored**, but I cannot endorse this interpretation, although it does seem to fit the facts of the accursed bloodline of Canaan, a bloodline that features the notorious Nimrod; I believe he was the grandson of Canaan, and not a very nice person.}}

Besides this group, there are those who swear falsely, with the meanings above connected to the word *swear*. We now look at the word 'swear' in Greek as (omnumi) which is used as "affirming or denying by an oath." The word *oath* (anathematizo) as per ACTS 23:21 (KJV,) reflects "having bound (themselves) with an oath;" see curse. The word *curse* here has a meaning of "describing this curse." In Greek we have (katathema) which denotes by metonymy, "an accused thing." (The object *cursed* being used for the 'curse' is "that which is the flying scroll" (or, shall we say **the cigar-shaped object**'?) {{It certainly is beginning to look that Richard may be ~~ in some respect ~~ cracking this scriptural code while unmasking the UFO menacing plague on humanity, but that's just me.}} If we look at the word *swear* in general, it also states, "to declare or affirm by invoking a deity or a person or thing." What group of people could this be? The word *affirm* is to declare firmly to be true.

Leaving the question aside for a second, we find that "to support the confirmation and to uphold" is that which you believe to be true, even if it is false. The word *invoke* is to "call on a higher power for assistance, support, inspiration," or to summon with incantations,

THE CURS-ED NET

i.e., conjure. (What higher power?) If you are not in God's word, and not heeding His warnings regarding evil uses and deceptions mentioned in the Biblical scriptures, then what are you calling upon and who then is answering you? God cannot go against His own nature, so if in scripture it warns you against the very same things you practice and share with others, who is accepting your call? Are they evil spirits, fallen angels, or perhaps Satan himself!

An *incantation* is the use of charms or spells, an utterance repeated without thought. To *conjure* is "to summon a supernatural force, to influence or affect by or as if by magic." It also has the idea of "calling or bringing to mind or evoking." To *evoke* is "to call to mind by naming, citing, or suggestion" (suggesting a form of hypnotism;) to *summon* is a "request to appear, to send for, and to call forth."

Look at the meaning of the word **medium**, (a person thought to have the power to communicate with the spirits of the dead or agents of another world or dimension.)

For all of those people who claim to have a special power from God, I urge you to refer back to chapter nine called Show & Tell since your true allegiance may depend on it. {{REMEMBER: being damned is simply being *separated* from God, which is bad enough, and if one chooses to be part of the '**Satanic Communion**,' well, it does not take a genius to figure out what God may think of this, especially since He made such a rather big point of this kind of conduct while giving the TEN COMMANDMENTS to His servant Moses; then there is the not-so-small matter of the **non-forgiveness of the fallen angels** for completely transgressing the laws set up by this very God, as outlined in The Book of Enoch.}}

I REPEAT A KEY SCRIPTURAL CITATION: "It will enter the house of the thief and the house of him who swears falsely by my name. It will remain in his house and destroy it, both its timbers and its stones" (Zach, 5:4; (NIV.) The word *house* in Greek is (oikos) which means "a dwelling." Literally, it seems that these evil agencies do go into your house and abduct you. Interestingly enough, 'house' also is "dwelling place of the soul" (within your body) as per 2Cor. 5:1. {{When Richard reminded me of this scripture, the demonic abduction phenomenon took on another *nuance* of reality!}} The evil within this curse will not only destroy your physical body but your spiritual body as well.

"ITS TIMBERS AND ITS STONES"

Timbers has the meaning in general here of a quality suited for above. It is a person "considered to have qualities suited for a particular activity." Those activities used and possessed by these people that are not done in a Godly spirit, the activities of which the Bible condemns, the activities for which the *thief* and those who *swear falsely* possess. IT IS THEY ON WHICH THE CURSE FALLS!

If we look at Gen. 9:25, we find that Canaan is cursed! This is fully discussed in

Zacharia 5, regarding **the flying scroll**. In the NIV Life & Spirit Bible, the Bible note for Gen. 9:25 states the following: "The curse indicated that the Canaanites (who were not black) would be oppressed and under the (control of other 'nations') to contrast Shem & Japheth's descendents (Noah's sons) other than Ham, who would be blessed by God. This prophecy of Noah was conditional for all concerned. Any descendants of Canaan who turned to God would also receive the blessings bestowed upon Shem & Japheth, but while any descendants of Shem & Japheth who departed from God would experience the "curse" bestowed on Canaan." {{BTW: Out of the house of Shem, the house of David would come to fruition, and from David's son (Nathan) would spring the savior through the virgin Mary; this is the reason that there were two lineages traced, one through Matthew (of Joseph,) and one through Luke (of Mary.) Is there any evidence of this *curse* historically? If you go to **my** web page called THE GIANTS OF THE MIDDLE EAST AND ELSEWHERE, you will see such evidence:

http://inspectorblebeau.pbwiki.com/GIANTS-IN-THE-MIDDLE-EAST-AND-ELSEWHERE

Here Steven Quayle documents ancient historical sources of "fierce giants" (the mighty men of renown in real history?) and indicative that some of the sons of Noah did not possibly make the right Godly choices, since giants crept up in their bloodlines (reflecting the curse,) and Quayle makes a point to mention that these giants were not the giants that suffer from "GIANTISM" with

THE CURS-ED NET

genetic defects, where they become weaker not stronger; no, instead these ancient giants who emigrated from the Middle East were the real McCoy, and what's worse, they continued on even into more recent history! His book, "Genesis 6 GIANTS" is very interesting *ostensible evidence* for the reality of *real giants*, large — mighty & for all we know — left over from the slaughter in the recorded scripture by Joshua & Co., after the FLOOD, and well documented in the Book of Numbers & the Book of Joshua, not to mention the Book of Jashar, which fills in some of the details not mentioned in the Book of Joshua (Joshua 10:13.)}}

Richard continues by making a point about the word *nations* that has another meaning that can be connected to the curse! The word 'nation' connects to that part of the curse that involves the abduction portion. It also means in Greek (genos,) a race; see kind. *Kind* in Greek (genos) is "an offspring" (which connects to the abduction part by being the final objective of the implantation, by and through these evil spirits.) (Allophulos) is "foreign" or "of another race." (In this case it would suggest evil spirits and fallen angels, who would deceive us into believing they were an alien race from **above**.) {{Again, if you were to read Michael Heiser's *THE FACADE*, all of this alien vs. demonic dynamic may start to fall neatly into place, having gone through Richard's exercises of scriptural code-breaking, using naught but God's inspired prophets of old, *__including Enoch__*! In short, the *facade* will fall like *scales from your eyes*.}}

So the word 'nations' as in the "control of other nations" could reflect that nation (or the race of false aliens) who possibly act as Satan's evil agencies that keep under control those people (abductees) that they choose. {{Many Ufologists do not wish to entertain its implied possibility because *the truth – unvarnished –* is not nicely *wrapped with bows* for easy consumption among the '*masses*,' or because your local church does not wish to "push the envelope" when it comes to this sensitive subject. Someone has to do the *dirty work* & call a spade a spade!}}

In Deut. 28:16,18 & 19, it mentions certain curses, among others, which would come upon Moses' people as consequences for turning away from God. I believe this is also true today, for all of us! The Bible note for 28:15 within the NIV Life & Spirit states the following:

THE CURS-ED NET

"Moses prophesied the consequences of turning away from God: chastisement, destruction, great sorrow, captivity & dispersion among the nations." {{As any Biblical student knows, this *diaspora* started around 70 C.E., and continues to this day, while the nation of Israel ostensibly was reborn in **1948**, which may, indeed, be a triggering of the last generation before the great TRIBULATION.}}

Several of these curses, I feel, impact upon the UFO phenomenon; for instance, in Deut. 28:16 (NIV) it says: "You will be cursed in the city and cursed in the country." (People are abducted in both, so, in other words, there is *no place to hide from these abductors*!) {{A curse is a mark, like the curse upon Cain, and it seems that abductees have been marked in some way, and I have read that many of these abductees will attest to this very dynamic, since when their abductors want them, they can even come through the walls for them, and the government simply looks the other way, or locks these poor unfortunates away in "mental institutions" for being — what they can only diagnose as <u>unbalanced psychologically</u> (crazy) for mentioning such "bizarre" topics. So when Deuteronomy says that it will cause both "great sorrow & captivity," it brings *new meaning* to the poor abductee sitting within a 'loony bin' with his or her fellow inmates!}}

Latin for the word *fruit* is (progenies < progignere) — "to beget." The word *beget* in Greek has a meaning of (anagennao) where 'ana' means "again, or from above." *Above* is "a connection with the angelic beings," like evil agencies who portray themselves as aliens; also (aktroma) denotes "an abortion; an untimely birth."

Another aspect of the ***abduction phenomenon*** revolves around cattle. Of course the word *calves* mean (cows & bulls.) Lo & behold the cattle are cursed in Deuteronomy as well. (MUTILATIONS?) In 28:18, it specifically includes the curses for not only the wombs of women, but also the production of livestock, (i.e., cattle.) IN VERSE 19: "You will be cursed when you go in & cursed when you go out." In other words, these abductions will & do happen indoors & outdoors, in the city or the country, and "all over the land" as is punctuated in Zacharia 5:3, as from the outside! And (5:4,) "the house" which, of course, is inside!

THE EXACT QUOTE FROM DEUT. 28:18 bears emphasizing:

THE CURS-ED NET

"The fruit of your womb will be cursed, and the crops of your land, and the calves of your herds and the lambs of your flocks." These things were introduced in ***The Bite of the Serpent*** (chapter one,) and may be worth a review.

The word *fruit* in general means "offspring" or "progeny." The word *progeny* is in general "one born or derived from another," (i.e., the evil spirits & fallen angels as "*alien*" beings;) also it denotes the "result of creative effort." The 'fruit' of exposing the agenda of these dark forces may surprise some, but it was alluded to in the Book of Joel, as well as Revelation. The next chapter will expose this agenda, and how it is continuing to this very day as part of the ongoing judgments.

END NOTES:

Vine's Complete Expository Dictionary of Old and
New Testament Words:
Publisher: Thomas Nelson, Inc. ©1996
Used by permission of Thomas Nelson, Inc.

CHAPTER THIRTEEN:

The Abduction Phenomenon within Joel & Revelation

{{In this chapter Richard explores how the prophet Joel (especially in his first two chapters,) actually seems to be expanding the story of the judgments as reflected in the Book of Revelation, chapter nine. It is also possibly *not too coincidental* that both authors saw (from different perspectives) exactly what Enoch had also seen & penned regarding his chapter 68, and how they were **directed by the Father God** to give warning to their people *and to us as well* as the children of the same Father of All. How all this may, in fact, tie-in with our current understanding of the "***demonic*** abduction phenomenon," I leave for your own inspection, after the data is supplied to you in these ongoing chapters of scriptural code-breaking, at least from Richard's stated position. Keep in mind that Jude referred to Enoch as a prophet, giving an example within *Jude's* epistle (vs. 14-15,) so for Enoch foreseeing what we frame as the **"alien abduction phenomenon"** in today's secular & *humanistic* world, *would have better been looked upon with spiritual eyes,* as is being done finally in this present treatise!}}

I, Richard, believe that Joel 2 & Rev. 9 are part of a **running story** regarding the coming of TRIBULATION judgment, with Joel itself containing the details, not only for this judgment, but also for an ongoing judgment taking place all over the world.

THE CURS-ED NET

This dynamic has been going on for thousands of years, & I will show why I believe this is so. Certain *key words & phrases* (that I have examined at my disposal,) match each book & chapter under consideration through these very key words and their meanings. We will see how all of these details will specifically explain much of what we presently have coined as the 'alien' abduction phenomenon & related phenomena such as *ghosts & spirits*.

What we will focus on in both *Joel & Revelation* is that both scriptural books contain **judgments**, as well as (who or what) may be executing these judgments, i.e., *those* taking the form of **locusts**. We shall start with several similarities in order to show how they are part of a continuing storyline of this same series of **ongoing judgments**.

FIRSTLY, *smoke* appears in Rev. 9:2 & "a day of cloud" in Joel 2:2. In Rev. 9:2, smoke from the abyss is mentioned, where, in Hebrew, the word 'smoke' is ('anan.') It means "cloud, fog, storm cloud," so both the cloud & the smoke meanings are *the same*!

Rev. 9 talks of locusts coming out of the smoke (clouds.) Locusts are evil spirits. In Enoch 15:9, it reads as follows: "The spirits of the giants shall be like (resemble) clouds," where the Greek word for *cloud* is (nephelas) and in Hebrew, 'smoke' is 'clouds' ('anan,) so in Rev. 9:2, locusts (as Evil Spirits) come out of the clouds where clouds are symbolic of the locusts' "wings" which symbolizes their mode of transportation. The clouds also are symbolic of the evil spirits who were once GIANTS {{as per the 15th chapter of *Ethiopian* Enoch.}} These clouds take the form of their transportation (UFOs?) (This was previously discussed in chapter six.)

SECONDLY, the sun & sky were darkened (Rev. 9:2.) In Joel 2:2, it says, "a day of darkness and gloom, a day of clouds and blackness," so in both scriptures they apparently color the atmosphere similarly.

THIRDLY, in Rev. 9:3, out of the smoke (clouds) are **locusts** (as we see as the symbol for **UFOs,**) that come down upon the earth. In Joel, an army of locusts is pictured in his first chapter.

FOURTHLY, in Rev. 9:4, the locusts are "told not to harm the grass or plants or trees." In Joel 2:3, it says "before them is like Eden but behind them a desert waste." It sounds like these verses

146

THE CURS-ED NET

do not agree, but follow closely. The word "desert" in Greek has the meaning of (eremos) as an adjective; it denotes with reference to persons, those who the locusts come down upon, as in "desolate," & "lay waste." Look at Joel 2:3 as ("a desert waste.") In yet another meaning (orphanos,) the English *orphans* signifies "bereft of parents or of a Father (God!)" (Eremosis) denotes desolation in the sense of "making desolate," <u>or </u>without God! The fire that devours in Joel 2:3 is symbolic of God's judgment of those who have rejected the **future** Christ. (Check Rev. 9:4: they were told "not to harm the grass of the earth or any plant or tree, but only those people who did not have the seal of God on their foreheads.") {{This sounds confusing, but the way I understand this is that *just as certain Hebrews rejected the words of Moses in the* **desert** *(and were judged harshly since Moses was a prophet of God,) so too will certain* **future** *generations who <u>refuse to heed</u> the words of Jesus (since they do not have "ears to hear,"* will be judged in a similar manner as those who will reject Jesus in the **future** (who represents in the flesh the one true Father's Son & messenger for God's true children.) In short, God's **true** children *always listen to* God's **true** prophets, of whom Jesus was the last to fulfill all righteousness.}}

FIFTHLY, in Rev. 9:7, "they (the locusts) looked like 'horses' prepared for 'battle'." In Joel 2:4: "they have the appearance of horses" (and in verse 5) "like a mighty army drawn up for 'battle'."

SIXTHLY, in Rev. 9:9, it states: "and the sound of their wings was like (resembled) the thundering of many horses and chariots rushing into battle." Joel 2:5 states "with the noise like that of 'chariots.' And like a mighty army (drawn) up for battle." Let's look at the word *drawn* as in the Greek (anabibazo,) a form of (anabino) meaning "to go up." (Anasao) means "up." (Exelko) is "out of." (In Rev. 9:3, it says, and "out of" the smoke locusts came;) also in Rev. 9:2, when he opened the abyss, smoke "rose." *Rose* is the past tense of 'rise,' and *rise* is "to go up," so Joel 2:5 & Rev. 9:2 & 3 are and mean the same.

AND LASTLY, in Rev. 9:11, they had a king over them (and angel of the abyss,) whose name in Hebrew is Abaddon and in Greek Apollyon. They both mean "destroyer" as in (the destroying locusts!) In Isaiah 34:4 it says, "All the stars of the heavens will

THE CURS-ED NET

be dissolved (where *stars* are symbolic for "angels," and *dissolved* means "to be taken out of action.") The fallen angels, who together with the evil spirits (who portray the UFO alien facade,) will be taken down; and the sky rolled up like a scroll, and all the "starry hosts will fall." (Refer back to chapter five for the details of this.)

The starry hosts are mirrored by the UFOs, (as well as the evil spirits & fallen angels within,) and at some point, toward the end of the TRIBULATION, will be destroyed.

In Rev. 9 & Joel 1 & 2, it mentions about locusts (demonic forces.) Symbolically we look at this word *locust* and compare the natural locust to the demonic locust in character & abilities. The word *locust* is also the name given to the **swarming phase** of the short-horned grasshopper. (This will be discussed in chapter fourteen.)

According to the Wik Encyclopedia of the Bible, in the Book of Revelation *locusts* with scorpion tails and human-like faces are to torment unbelievers for five months when the fifth trumpet sounds. One Old Testament book, *Joel*, is written in the context of a recent locust plague. {{This is one of the reasons we had chosen an *"alien looking scorpion"* for the cover of THE *CURS*-ED NET.}}

The below is a Bible note from (NIV) Life & Spirit Bible note on Joel 1:15:

"It can refer to a present-day judgment throughout the nations, and also to a final judgment during the Tribulation." (In other words, the locusts (demonic forces) are here now operating throughout the world and have been for thousands of years (starting perhaps some-times after the "curse of Canaan) as part of an **ongoing** judgment. Joel not only describes this in detail, but also explains what is to come during the Tribulation. This final judgment will manifest itself beyond the stage of operations taking place now throughout the world. Nations will be in anguish (Joel 2:6) as these locusts (demonic forces) will for five months set forth with a full earthly invasion as in relation to the ongoing UFO abduction phenomenon. {{This may indeed be in the not too distant future, if the dot connecting of this present work reflects the truth of these matters; the abduction phenomenon will only *gain in intensity*.}}

Continuing with the *Wik* Encyclopedia, the locusts are described in four different ways, i.e., as swarming, cutting, hopping, &

THE CURS-ED NET

destroying. Even though these locusts were identified in the Old Authorized Version as four different creatures, the (KJV) Bible is *also* known as the "authorized version," and the version preferred here. Modern translations <u>correctly</u> identify them as four kinds of *locusts*. (In this case, they are identified as certain *qualities* of locusts.) We look at the word *kind* and in Greek as (phusis) which denotes "the nature or power of a person or thing," (i.e., an individual or group's specific abilities.) The word *power* in Greek is (dunamis,) with the meaning of "ability or a power in action," (able to do something.) 'Power' also means "force," which itself has some interesting meanings.

Force Greek is (harpazo) which is "to carry off by force; to snatch away." *Snatch* has the meaning of "to grasp" or "seize" (suddenly;) "to kidnap," Now just look at the meaning of the word *abduct*. It suggests "carrying off by force or kidnapping." (So does this now reflect something of an agenda for which these *four kinds* (**qualities**) of locusts (demonic forces) work toward, where each has an ability that contributes to a specific end, and also through these other abilities we see, show how each group's contribution has its own detailed function?)

As it mentions in Rev. 9, these locusts also possess the deadliness of scorpion tails. So how would these demonic forces symbolically use this ability as compared to the natural use of a scorpion's tail?

We examine the sting of the scorpion that deposits the venom. In Re. 9:5 (NIV,) it states: "And the agony they suffered was like that of a sting of a scorpion when it strikes a man;" also, in Rev. 9:10: "They had tails and stings like scorpions, and in their tails they had power to torment people for five months."

The word *tail* symbolically means something that serves as a body part that delivers the sting (venom.) A meaning of the word 'tail' is "to connect by or as if by a tail," (where the key word is "connect.") {{The scorpion's tail *stinging the whole earth* on the cover of this book, we feel, is an apt depiction of what may indeed transpire with **THE BEAST** having power over mankind during the **TRIBULATION period, and these scorpions for "five months."**}}

THE CURS-ED NET

Let's look at the word *stinger* as "one that stings," especially (mentally,) and also "as a sharp blow;" (see Enoch 68:18.) The sting acts as a stimulus. The word *sting* means "a stimulus." A stimulus is an agent, an action, or condition that causes, elicits, or accelerates a physiological or psychological activity or response; in Latin it equals "**goad**." {{This word is *emphasized* since it will prove to be an important consideration in the *demonic* abduction phenomenon, subsequently detailed, especially in Kim Carlsberg's book.}}

If we now look at the word 'sting' again, it also means "a goad or spur." (A *spur* is a short spike that could reflect as the tail's stinger,) while the word 'goad' is a long pointed stick to prod animals, an agent meant for (prodding.) A prod is also used to stimulate. This prod or goad then, I believe, is *a wand* of some sort which is used to act against the "neural-transmission" of a person, used in a (electric capacity of some kind.) *Neural,* of course, is relating to the nervous system. {{I remember one abductee telling me (based on her hypnotic regression session,) that a type of "praying mantis" arm was holding such a stick, and actually "prodding her" after she had been taken into a type of "alien" craft (at least that's the way she described it,) and having "missing time" to boot; she was being prodded *especially* near her abdomen; she later confirmed that she was already then pregnant with her fourth child. This was the beginning of a sequential trip that led to her seeing a female child that she somehow thought she was connected to; besides this encounter she saw another small child that looked more "alien," and also had a tail.}} To finish this point, the nervous system consists of the brain, spinal cord, nerves, ganglia, & parts of the receptor organs that regulate the body's responses to (stimuli.)

How does the neural scorpion venom (sting) relate to a symbolic usage of the ability used by the locusts? Let us go back to the *Wik* reference: a scorpion's venom is neural toxic in nature. Neural toxins consist of a variety of small proteins as well as sodium & potassium cation (ions) that serve to interfere with the neural transmission in the victim. Scorpions use their venom to kill &/or to (paralyze) their prey. Incidentally, *paralysis* in Latin is "a loss or impairment of the ability to move a body part, as a result of damage to its nerve supply."

THE CURS-ED NET

We move on now to the word *torture* (Rev. 9:5,) which is "the affliction of the severe physical and mental torment." The word *torment* (Rev. 9:10,) is "to cause to undergo physical or mental torture." In Greek it is (basanismos,) akin to (basanizo) or (toil.) and is used for divine judgment; another meaning (akoucheo) is to "treat evilly" and "to be evil entreated" in the passive voice. (It is especially interesting that in Enoch 10:14, it records that the [evil spirits] shall *entreat you*.")

Entreat in Greek is (chraomai,) which denotes "to use well or ill." *Well* means "beneficial;" an example would be those people who unknowingly are being used by the evil spirits for their benefit. "To use ill" as an example would be *abductees* subjected to torment & torture, which in Latin has the meaning of "to twist."

The word *twist* adds several meanings here: in general it is "to alter the normal aspect of, & to alter or distort the mental, moral, or emotional character of; to coerce by physical force." If you *distort* something, you "twist it out of the proper or natural relation to its parts." It also means "to put to a wrong or improper (use,) as in *to entreat evilly;*" for example, to implant unnaturally something evil between a man & a woman through the man's sperm into the woman's fetus. To 'distort' also means a twisting of the mental part of it (Psychological,) & is the modification of unconscious impulses into (forms) acceptable by the conscious perception; in other words, modifying the impulses to the brain unconsciously to the form's (appearance) of what they (evil spirits) want you to remember by a conscious perception. This phenomenon includes reports by certain individuals that had indicated under hypnosis that they had allegedly been taken by beings from "elsewhere."

{{I would like to reflect (as we approach the end of this chapter,) by introducing some supporting data from a "documented abductee" *that may throw some light on* Richard's key words into what the evil spirits seem to be doing, but heretofore, have been passed off, *especially in the UFO literature,* as coming from some sort of possibly sinister ET ORIGIN, (or worse,) some "benevolent space brother/ sister who ultimately has our "best" interests at heart. I have found that *either scenario is* blatantly absurd, so the following will simply provide some *raw data* since the underlying dynamic is **not absurd**

THE CURS-ED NET

whatsoever, and moreover, that _most_ of the abductees are reporting honestly what they perceive to be true as far as can be ascertained through the investigation of said abductees by qualified observers over an extensive period of time. *In fact, this very treatise is trying to deal with the potential root of these abductees' real experiences, to put them in a proper framework that can be understood without prejudice; unfortunately, for some, a "spiritual understanding of the Bible" is absolutely necessary for the beginning of coming to grips with the bizarre aspects of THE UFO & ALIEN ABDUCTION phenomenon.*

One of the best books that pictorially (through a type of diary,) actually dramatized *"The Bite of the Serpent"* chapters discussed previously, and actually showing the evil functions of these malevolent spirits toward their victims under the abductors' controls, would be explained and illustrated in Kim Carlsberg's book, **BEYOND MY WILDEST DREAMS,** which is an alleged true accounting by Kim (who was a commercial artist and once worked for the TV show, *Baywatch*.)

In this book, Kim cites examples of what she had to undergo, parts of which are extracted via regressive hypnosis. The following is a brief list of some of her experiences, which _matches_ what Richard had just been outlining in his ongoing treatise; for instance, Kim is being captured and brought up to the ship in a light beam (25;) being given a "neural-transmission': *YOU ARE US* (82;) having a pre-mature fetus removed from her body by strange-looking entities. [NOTE: this fits nicely into the Enoch 68:18 motif of *"diminishing the embryo,"* where "the bite" occurs about the 8th week of pregnancy, or before Kim could even determine that she was pregnant; as per Kim, these same "aliens" suppressed her memory so she never even suspected she had been impregnated with (what we would now frame as) *the bite of the serpent!*] (94)

These scenes have been graphically depicted as well as commented on. On page 163, there is a picture of an "alien" with his *stinger or wand!* [NOTE: Kim refers to this type as the "Queen bee" (164;) another pictorial concerns an alien who has both a 'stinger' and candy cane in each of his odd-looking hands with *wandering stars* in the background, as a good extra touch, but most likely,

THE CURS-ED NET

unbeknownst to the illustrator of Kim's book (177.) Talk about a "sugar daddy" up to no good, but in actuality (if ___our___ treatise proves to be true,) this "sugar daddy" would be no less than an evil spirit masking itself in a costume as a GRAY or other form of ET!]

Lastly, (speaking of the devil,) there is a whole chapter dealing with "*shape-shifting*," which is a phenomenon actually reported within the *Ethiopian* Book of Enoch [chapter 19] as being a trait connected with **the Fallen Angels**; (this concept starts on page 243 of Kim's book in the edition cited under UFO references.)

One happy note: In the middle of the 1990s, I actually saw Kim on national TV talking about her ordeals, and commenting on the fact that she had *become more spiritually-minded*, and since then her abductions have completely diminished; she is seemingly not the only one where this ostensible spiritual "**quid pro quo**" is taking place, as occasionally recorded in the annals of Ufology, yet somehow many still cannot seem to make the connection between the intimate relationship of human beings with those who have fallen from their first estate, as recorded in the Epistle of Jude within the New Testament. How much more *connection of dots* needs to be presented for people to accept what appears almost obvious? *I am certain that there are other people like Richard (and Kim) who could attest to a "diminishing of the bite of the serpent" once they have realigned themselves with Jesus. After all, this IS one of the promises of the Bible, echoed from the prophet Jeremiah to St. Paul.*}}

Remember the **goad or wand** attacks the neural-transmitter that is a chemical substance such as acetyl choline, which transmits nerve impulses across a synapse. (They can interrupt the transmission to the brain, or from the brain to the body.) {{No wonder a person like Kim needs to recall these memories via regressive hypnosis, and remember that it was Karla Turner who had strongly suggested that there are more than one layer of obfuscation within the intrigue of the demonic abduction phenomenon, as she reported in her **ABDUCTION IN THE GINGER BREAD HOUSE** short essay, as cited in the INTERNET reference section.

Neural-psychology deals with the relationship between the nervous system & cerebral or mental functions. These mental func-

THE CURS-ED NET

tions deal with memory, perception, emotions, etc., that are found within the qualities of our soul & spirit.

Remember that torture & torment mean physical pain. The word 'pain' here also gives us some important meanings. The word *pain* in Greek is (panos,) which says to see the word 'labor;' another Greek word (odin) means a "birth pang." The word *labor* in Greek (kapos) is akin to (kopto,) which means to "strike, cut," (as in Enoch 68:18, echoing the strike of the embryo;) and the meaning of *cut* also identifies one of the kinds of locusts, i.e., the *cutting* locusts that will be the subject of chapter 15. 'Cut' in Greek (aphaireo) also is "to take away or remove" (as in taking a fetus out of a womb, perhaps, as well as during medical procedures, to cut or graft DNA tissue for future deposits into a male's sperm?)

We look at the word *strike* in Greek. It also says to see the words 'blow & smite.' *Smite* in Greek (patasso) metaphorically is "of judgment, and also of the infliction of the *disease by an angel*," but this meaning reflects back to the word 'goad.' (Rhapizo) is the Greek "to strike with a rod" (a wand.) As we review Enoch 68:18 again, it definitely refers to the abduction experience: the goad — the wand — the rod — the infliction of a trance, as well as the sting! 'Smite' also has the meaning of "wounding." {{*It seems to me that only a prophet of God could have known & written about these things thousands of years ago,(as in ENOCH,) and we have only "caught up" with the beginnings of this knowledge within the last thirty years or so, without even fully realizing what was truly going on.* **This process is still ongoing. AMAZING! When Richard drew my attention to this same 68:18 verse, it** *literally* **threw me for a loop!**

Richard, in showing (**"through the HOLY SPIRIT"** *as he keeps reminding me,)* layer after layer of connecting key word "dots," seems to leave the lingering impression, at least to me, that **all of these aforementioned prophets,** including, not only Enoch, but Joel, the author of Revelation, Zacharia, and even Isaiah, are, in fact, "*tuning into* the unfolding of the abduction scenario" as we can plainly see it operating right up to this present day as part of the *ongoing judgments* being rendered until the time of *the coming* TRIBULATION; if it is true, would not God forewarn us about these judgments, giving ample "proof" through his sacred prophetic scribes

THE CURS-ED NET

of the inherent danger lurking and skulking about in our midst, while the governments, media and churches say little or nothing of import about this percolating crisis among the populations of the world? It certainly appears to be the case, which includes as many spin stories as any "good" politician could muster up when faced with the awful prospect of *telling the truth, the whole truth, and nothing but....}}*

Blow in Greek (hupopneo) has the meaning of "under" indicating repression, (as in a trance?) *Wound* in Greek (plege) is "a blow, a stroke," *echoing the words of Enoch again;* lastly, (epitithemi) which has the Greek idea of "to lay on."

Lay in Greek (tithemi) is to "put, place or set." (Perhaps it is to place the evil seed into the fetus?) (Epihallo) is "to lay upon, as of seizing; to imprison." 'Lay' is (hupotithemi,) "to place under" (a trance.)

The last very important meaning here is (thesaurizo,) which is to "lay up," "store up," and is akin to (thesaurus,) "a treasury, a storehouse!" The next four chapters will dismantle the *UFO & ALIEN ABDUCTION PHENOMENON,* by an understanding of the different functions of **locusts,** *as Richard understands the scriptures in relation to the aforementioned mystery.*

END NOTES:

Vine's Complete Expository Dictionary of Old and
New Testament Words:
Publisher: Thomas Nelson, Inc. ©1996
Used by permission of Thomas Nelson, Inc.

CHAPTER FOURTEEN:

The Swarming Locusts

{{This is a very intriguing chapter, the end of which will discuss the dynamics of both the ''soul & spirit'' as it possibly related to the demonic abduction phenomenon; it is very technical, so I will be adding an actual anecdotal story from the life of Ted Rice that may help throw some light on this sensitive subject that seems rarely addressed in the field of Ufology. Maybe after reviewing Ted's story in light of Richard's treatise, you may be able to draw certain conclusions about just what is going on in Ufology. This "swarm" Richard is examining revolves around the possible symbolic meaning in both the 9th chapter of Revelation, as well as its corresponding symbolic language as stated through the prophet Joel in the first two chapters of his own book. It all culminates in a potentially better understanding of the demonic realm, and how it should possibly be viewed in our own present reality.}}

In *Joel* 2 (NIV,) it says, "Like dawn spreading across the mountains a large and mighty army comes." The word *like* means "resembling in appearance &/or form." *Dawn* in Greek as a verb is (augazo,) and it has the meaning of "to shine." Let's see what other meanings here in Greek will be helpful. (Phaino) is "to cause to appear," and denotes in the active voice, "to give light or shine," (so like the dawn spreading across the mountains, so is this swarm that shines & gives off light.)

THE CURS-ED NET

There's a word here in Greek (lampo) that is "to shine as a torch," (which I believe to be symbolic of verse three, the *fire* (meaning judgment) being executed as the army moves forth. 'Fire' is used symbolically as divine judgment upon those who rejected Christ (Matt. 3:11.)

Concerning the judgments of God at the close of the present age include 2Thess. 1:8, & Rev. 18:8, that is being reflected in the second chapter of Joel & the ninth chapter of Revelation. Let's see if we can establish what kind of a swarm is "as the dawn." We know that the swarm gives off light and is executing judgment, yet there are more details of what the swarm refers to, and what the judgment may be. [NOTE: Joel is not only mentioning a divine judgment here, during the TRIBULATION period, but also includes the details that are enclosed as referenced to an *ongoing* judgment taking place now and which has been going on for a few thousand years; also, from the 'NIV Life & Spirit Bible,' we note in 1:15, *the Day of the Lord.* It can refer to the present-day judgment throughout the nations, and also refers to the final judgment, which contains these **locusts** as "evil agencies" during the TRIBULATION period, both as ongoing judgment and Tribulation judgment. They contain basically the same details, only the Tribulation judgment is going to be manifested *to the maximum,* & cover the nations of the world.

In verse six of the Bible note it mentions that toward the end, which at this point is the same as in Joel, it refers primarily to God's present judgment through it, as a reminder of that coming TRIBULATION judgment. Continuing on, we will see the uncovering of what this "dawn" represents, and what the judgments may contain.

We start with the Greek word *shine* as (perilampo) while 'flashing around' or 'shining round about' is (perinstrpto,) & 'cause to appear' is (phaino.) *Around* is as follows in general: "in a circle or with a circular motion, or on all sides from all directions." NOTE: as an adjective, it also means being in "existence." As in the above, it has the meaning "to appear."

So far we have the *dawn,* which is symbolic of an appearance of an army, and appearing by light or shining. This light seems to be shining around & flashing around something. It also appears as

THE CURS-ED NET

a type of circular object and possibly rotating while the lights are flashing in a circular motion.

The word *appearance* in general also means an "outward aspect." It is interesting to note that the word 'aspect' would have a meaning of "something that 'appears' from a specific vantage point." Like the dawn, it appears in the sky.

Aspect has another interesting connotation; the word 'mien' in general "is an appearance or bearing" (exerting pressure, force or influence on; to overwhelm, to effect,) especially as it reveals an inner state of mind, a form of alteration through influence by appearance. The word *dawn* in Greek is "to shine" and shine further means "to emit light." As we look at the word 'light' in reference to the meaning above, in Greek (phos) is akin to (phao,) "to give light" (from its root 'pha' & 'phan,' expressing "light as seen by the eye." Metaphorically, it has the idea of "reaching the mind," (i.e., trance-like effect.)

Light is also electro-magnetic radiation, an illumination derived from a source of light. The word *illuminate* has a very interesting meaning, and that is "to adorn with brilliant colors." (Let's see if colors used through light could have a trance-like effect.) *Color* is "the characteristic of light by which the individual is made aware of an object, objects or light sources described in terms of dominant wavelength; to give a distinctive character to, and to exert influence on, affect." (So now we have the 'dawn' as symbolic of something which shines, emits light, flashes light, suddenly appears, and emits different kinds of colored lights flashing round-about, and it seems to have an influential *trance-like* effect used as some sort of an attraction mode.

WHO AM I?

To get closer yet to the meaning of all this, we continue with the word 'color.' It also has the meaning of an "outward appearance." The word 'shine' (as noted earlier) means to emit light, and light has the meaning of being an addictive primary color; yet *light* is "to illuminate," meaning also "to decorate with lights" (as in different patterns!) It also is "to expose to or reveal by radiation." (So now we are being shown the intricate & illuminating meaning of what

THE CURS-ED NET

seems to be detailing the "dawn" of what is representing the actual appearance of what people and & nations will see.)

WHAT AM I?

FOLLOW CLOSELY NOW: We continue with the primary colors acting as a type of influence. Primary colors are of three different groups: addictive, psychological, or light primaries. *Psychological* primaries are red, yellow, green & blue, as well as the achromatic pair of black & white, so these objects will have basic colors of red, yellow, green, blue, and white lights called *physiological*. From the group of primary colors, I believe, also reflect to colors that influence or tend to influence the mind or emotions, or the mixing of primaries becoming subjective. Changing colors would have a subjective effect on a person, depending on how they were presented. *Subjective* means "to take place within a person's mind; it also has the sense of being particular to a given person," ('personal.')

'Psychological' is another meaning, existing only within the experiencer's mind (a person having a **UFO sighting**, for instance,) so we add to these objects the most basic colors of red, green, yellow & blue, which, if used in a particular flashing pattern, becomes (by the lights) *an influence* as a result of this. They are meant to attract, to bait, to hold our interest, and to, at times, put us into a trance state, such as *those people who are chosen for* abduction! These objects contain all the detailed information, explaining the exact overall form and appearance of *WHO AM I/WHAT AM I? Simply stated: UFOs!*

BUT WHO'S INSIDE?

The word *dawn* also symbolizes *the swarming locusts*! Looking at this word, we find 1) it moves in large numbers; 2) it gathers in large numbers; 3) it overruns as the 'swarm' in Joel 2:2. And what does this army do? *Overrun* is "to seize locations that usually are occupied." This is alluded to in Joel 2:9: "They climb into houses; like thieves they enter through the windows." The word *house* here is "all the different types of dwellings we live in today." (I believe that these are the occupied locations that are mentioned in the meaning, "to overrun."

THE CURS-ED NET

Now is Joel 2:7, we have: "They charge like warriors, they scale walls like soldiers" (as in a military operation.) It means they have and are experienced in this type of tactical nature. (I must remind you that *this* they have supernatural abilities.) In Rev. 9 of 'NIV BIBLE Note (9:3) it states, "These locusts represent an increased number of demons and demonic activity released on the earth during the Tribulation. They have the power of scorpions." This means that they have a supernatural ability to render a person paralyzed with the same effect that a scorpion would have, only including a quite different usage. [Thus, to answer the question, WHO IS IN THESE UFOs? – our response would be, *DAMNED DEMONS THAT STING, THAT'S WHO*!

WARFARE TACTICS

If we examine the key word *scale* as in verse seven, it has the idea of "to climb up and around." When we look for the word in *VINE'S,* it shows the words "climb up," which says to see the word 'arise.' In Greek as (diegeiro) it means "through, intensive." The word *intensive* relates to "the method used," (as in how the wall was 'scaled' or "how they could have 'climbed' into the houses.") It seems by the meaning above, that the locusts, (evil spirits) *could have* done this by going **right through the walls** and then be in the houses, which would be, in effect, a form of military supernatural *stealth* tactic!

AFTER BREACHING THE WALLS

Look at the word *arise* in Greek as (egeiro,) which has a meaning of "causing to appear" (or in the passive) "appearing." So then after they go through the walls, they have the ability to appear {{just like one would expect of a spirit! In the aforementioned book as outlined by Kim Carlsberg in a previous chapter, interestingly enough on page 125 we have a picture of four "aliens," two of whom are in the process of *going through a wall*, while two are already in the bedroom of their victim; the scene also has a 'blue light' coming through the ceiling, which may be the *modus operandi* of abducting human beings in this instance. These beings (or in our view, demons,) also seem to have the ability to change the molecular structure of

THE CURS-ED NET

the wall for this "exit way" of the human, which will be explained subsequently via another abductee's experience which I had noted some time ago.}}

The word *cause* here in Greek is a verb (peien) and it is "to do" as in to accomplish. The meaning of the word *appear'* in Greek is (phaino) & in the active voice signifies "to shine;" in the passive voice, "to be brought forth into the light." When these evil spirits (as locusts) move through the walls, they are *in spirit* form. When they appear, coming forth into the light, they appear to be in physical form, but could still be a ghostly figure {{*as one might phrase in phase transition, or words to that effect.}}* In any case, they do appear to us as we can see them as they show themselves to be. How many UFO reports of aliens are & have been seen in a person's house, (usually the bedroom) [?] The abductees remember seeing them in their rooms. {{Two other books that may throw some more light on the high strangeness of the abductee encounters with these elusive beings can be found in David Jacobs' book, *SECRET LIFE*, as well as Eve Lorgen's book, which emphasizes spiritual warfare, called *THE LOVE BITE.}}*

We move to the word 'shine' which is "to cause to appear." If we look at the word *apparition* in Greek, it is "phantasma" from (phaino;) it also reflects a sense of "to appear," and is translated as "apparition" (Matt. 14:26, & Mark 6:49, from the (KJV) & means "spirit." So I believe, without a doubt, that these locusts, are in fact – SPIRITS, and ghostly evil spirits who deceive man by appearing as alien facades, & taking the form of *GRAYS or otherwise*! {{This is the ongoing theme of this treatise, where the envelope is continually being pushed to show the reality of this important *deception being perpetrated upon the minds of mankind!}}*

REMEMBER — as a spirit they can *go through walls!* I believe that their objective, as stated in Joel, (using the *tool* of key words,) translates into the conclusion that *can only spell the word*

A-B-D-U-C-T-I-O-N-S-!

These *swarming* locusts are the first of four kinds, and their first operation (military style) is to enter into houses! The verse "like thieves" shows the manner of approach. {{Richard believes

THE CURS-ED NET

they come through windows, and this may be, but I will recount an anecdotal story where they do, in fact, come right through the walls, and they can leave with their victim(s) also through the same wall. According to a woman named Mary, they accomplish this by making the wall separate in a circular fashion so that the human being would have no trouble going *through the wall*, if they decide to take the person bodily. Whether these spirits climb through the windows or go through the walls, they are spirits, so neither would pose a problem; even in **The Bite of the Serpent** material, discussed previously, we had posed that they have the ability to transcend the material order.}}

If we look at the word *enter* in Greek, we have (suneiserchomai.) This means "to enter together," yet not into the house, but enter the window when leaving the house. We look at another meaning of 'enter' as when they are going into the house. The word (pareiserchomai) means "to come in besides," where 'beside' means to be at the side of or next to, or very close to, (as of being in the same room as you, and practically right next to you,) appearing within the location of the abductee. There is yet another meaning, from the word (pareiserchomai,) that confirms the military tactic of stealth and the meaning is "to enter secretly by stealth," and to "come in privily." *Privily* in Greek is (lathra) meaning "secretly, covertly," from the root 'lath,' indicating "unnoticed or unknown." {{This would certainly support coming in as spirits through solid objects without even being seen, as previously cited via the Carlsberg book, and the anecdotal story by an abductee named Mary, remembering that back in the 1990s, neither Kim nor Mary thought that these things were anything other than *aliens* from *elsewhere*, where **the Pleiades or Orion** were prime candidates being bandied about in Ufology. WE KNOW BETTER NOW, at least according to these expanded chapters regarding *The Bite of the Serpent.* When we get to the chapter regarding **THE CURS-ED NET,** the Pleiadian & Orion connections will be dealt with in their *proper context   as part of the cursed net!*}}

We've looked at the word 'besides' in general, but if we also look at the words and meanings of "beside one's self" in Greek, it may explain a part of their agenda, by putting a person beside

THE CURS-ED NET

themselves via supernatural means. In Greek *beside one's self* is (existemi) primarily, and literally it is "to put out of position, to displace," hence, "to amaze." To *displace* is "to move from a position, to force to leave." How do they 'prep' you for abduction? The key word to follow now is 'amaze.' The word *amaze* in Greek is (ekstasis) and literally means "a standing out."

In **Vine's** we find the following: It is said of any displacement, and especially with reference to the mind of that alteration of that normal condition by which a person is thrown into a state of surprise or fear, or both, or again, in which a person is so transported out of his natural state, that he falls into a trance (as in a supernatural trance.) Then another very important meaning which follows the reaction of the trance is (thambos,) as "amazement" which is connected to the root of "render immobile" (as in 'paralyze'!) It is also associated with terror. All of these meanings are literally described in the abduction *process.*'

A very interesting follow-up here in *Vine's* is the meaning of the word *trance that* in Greek is (ekstasis.) It states a "condition in which ordinary consciousness and the perception of natural circumstances were withheld and the soul was susceptible."

We have covered a good deal of territory so far about "entering," "trances," "abduction agendas," as well as the supernatural ability there to accomplish this, but I feel we must look at the further meanings of the word **swarm**! These meanings hold very important information for an overall view of this type of invasion; for instance, it also is "to climb something in this manner." This is in relation to Joel 2:7-9 (as in a deeper detailed agenda?) And how is the word 'grip' involved here? *Grip* in general means "a tight hold of" & a "manner of holding." The word *manner* means "a method of" as we have seen. One method was the "trance." If we look closer at the word 'manner,' in the Greek (ethos,) it is primarily "a haunt." (Remember the word 'appear,' especially after coming in through the walls.) *Haunt* means either "to visit or appear to in the form of a ghost or other supernatural being," or it can have the meaning of "visiting often." How many abductees have been interviewed stating that they have been abducted more than once?

Another very important meaning of the word 'grip' is to have an "intellectual hold of." *Intellect* is that part which has the ability to reason (as in a normal mental state.) In Latin we have (intellectus) meaning "perception" as a passive participle of (intellegere) meaning "to perceive." So does this trance target your mental state? *Mental* is "mind." *Perception* is "the process, act, or faculty of perceiving." The neurological processes are that which interpretations are effected. *Perceive* in Latin is (percipere): per-, per + capere, having the meaning of "to seize" as well as "detain, abduct."

The word *abduct* in Latin is (abducere,) for "away." We look at this word *away* in the Greek as the verb (airo) "to seize, to lift up," & "take away." It is translated as "away with," implying a forcible removal for the purpose of putting to death. In this specific case of a spiritual judgment, it could mean "spiritual death." At the end of the meaning, it directs us to look at the word ('bear' #9.)

We have seen that the physical body is taken, but what of the spirit?

It is important to note that (*bear* #9) in Greek is (airo) like above. It signifies "to raise up," to lift physically, and also can be applied to the mind; it further means to "suspend" or "to render temporarily ineffective," i.e., to hold in suspense (paralyzed?).

Here is where it gets interesting.

We look at the word *suspense* in Greek. It is "to hold in." (Of course it means also "to hold someone in suspense over something," but what could it possibly mean here?) A Greek meaning *hold* (teresis) is a "watching, guarding," hence "imprisonment" & "to watch." (In Enoch the Fallen Angels are also called **Watchers**.) Another meaning (epilambano) is "to lay hold of, to take hold of." (But what is being imprisoned here? Remember when we mentioned a possibility of spiritual death? We will examine just what the locusts are holding.) Firstly, however, when we look at the word 'suspense' (hold up,) it mentions to see the word (*about* #6,) a verb as follows in Greek (psuchen) (airo) & 'Literally' "to raise the breath, or *to lift the soul*." It signifies "to hold in suspense" (as in lay hold of, to take hold of, imprison.)

165

THE CURS-ED NET

Does this sound like an 'alien' abduction, not only of your physical body, but **of your own soul & spirit as well**? Parts *of each* could also be taken and held in suspense, but for what reason? {{There is an actual anecdotal story in Ufology that covers this very dynamic, which I will present after Richard finishes examining this complex & intriguing subject.}}

In order to try to come to any sort of understanding here, we must break down the qualities of the soul & spirit. A quick analysis of this follows: Could they, the evil spirits, be taking parts of the soul and parts of the spirit *to eliminate* certain qualities during the abduction or examination, possibly to render our bodies empty of certain emotions or qualities, that if, if they were present, would be a hindrance to these evil spirits in some way? Of course we would "forget" all of this by the aforementioned procedures they seemingly have in place, causing amnesia. {{This may not be too far-fetched a concept; in Ufology we have the alleged *true* story of a hybrid girl (Raechel) from the book, *RAECHEL'S EYES*, where Raechel knew she was different looking from her "fellow-man," so she wore big dark glasses and large baggy clothes to conceal her 'hybrid' qualities; the sad and tragic part about this story, told by her biological mother, was that Raechel was "tainted" by the alien (evil spirit) DNA. Anyway, Raechel was apparently having human qualities being "bred out of her" and one of those qualities was that of *compassion*. Whoever her guardians were (and I surmised by end of book that they were evil spirits of some sort, who did not take too kindly to her having this quality,) so before the story is ended, Raechel is **terminated!** To me this sounds like an agenda of the dark forces, whether you wish to call them evil spirits or fallen angels, or whatever, and after I relate the story of Ted Rice's eye-witness account, the reader may wish to reappraise certain aspects of Ufology that may, indeed, have a dark spiritual root at the base of it.}}

In Greek (pneuma) primarily denotes "the wind," (akin to pnco) "to breathe, blow" & "breath;" in regard to *the spiri*t, it is "like the wind ~~ invisible, immaterial & powerful." The New Testament's use of the word may be analyzed approximately as follows:

THE CURS-ED NET

1) "The wind" John 3:8
2) "The breath" 2Thess. 2:8; Rev. 11:11, 13:15; Job 12:10.
3) "The immaterial invisible part of man," Luke 8:55; Acts 7:59.
4) "The disembodied man" 2Cor. 5:3-4; Luke 24:37-39; Heb. 12:23.
5) The resurrection body, 1Cor. 15:45; 1 Tim. 3:16; 1 Peter 3:18.
6) The sentient element in man, that by which he perceives, reflects, feels, desires, Matt. 5:3; Mark 2:8. Luke 1:47.
7) Purpose, aim, 2Cor. 12:18; Philemon 1:27; Eph. 4:23.

NOTE: The following information to end this chapter is from *Vine's*:

In Greek (psuche) is the "breath, the breath of life," then "*the soul,*" in its various meanings. The New Testament's use may be analyzed approximately as follows:

1) "The natural life of the body," Matt. 2:20; Luke 12:22; Acts 20:10.
2) "The immaterial, invisible part of man," Matt. 10:28; Acts 2:27.
3) "The disembodied man," 2Cor. 5:3-4; Rev. 6:9.
4) "The seat of personality," Luke 9:24; (explained as one's "own self;) Luke 9:25; Heb. 6:19, 10:39.
5) "The seat of the sentient element in man, that by which he perceives, reflects, feels, desires," Matt. 11:29; Luke 1:46; Acts 14:2.
6) "The seat of will & purpose," Matt. 22:37; Acts 4:32; Eph. 6:6.
7) "The seat of appetite," Rev. 18:14; Ps 107:9; Isaiah 5:14.
8) "Desire," Isaiah 29:8.
9) "Character," Luke 1:17; Rom. 1:4.
10) "Moral questions & activities. bad, as of bondage, as of a slave," Rom 8:15; Isaiah 61:3; '*phantasma*' *is* rendered as "spirit," Matt 14:26 & Mark 6:49 (KJV) see apparition.

THE DISTINCTION BETWEEN THE SOUL & SPIRIT IS AS FOLLOWS:

That which the soul possesses which the spirit does not:

1) The natural life of the body.
2) The seat of personality (one's own self.)
3) The seat of will
4) The seat of appetite.

That which the spirit possesses which the soul does not:

1) The wind
2) To blow
3) Powerful
4) Resurrecting body {{as I understand this, and hence, this IS the spirit that was given to Adam (as the first man) by God in Genesis 2:7, so it would have the potential to resurrect *as a spiritual being that will be "changed" as per St. Paul.*}}

The qualities *shared by* both the soul & spirit:

1) The immaterial invisible part of man
2) The disembodied man
3) The sentient element in man, and that by which he perceives, reflects, feels, desires.
4) Purpose.

They would _leave_ **part** of both the soul and the spirit where each contains their own separate qualities. The spirit part is to keep the body alive, and the remaining part of the soul with the spirit left in the body would allow that person's eyes and brain to still function to a certain extent, but yet keep the body as ineffective & immobile throughout the examination as is *humanly* possible.

[REMINDER]: Directly from *Vine's:*

THE CURS-ED NET

The language of Heb. 4:12 suggests *the extreme difficulty* of distinguishing between the soul and the spirit, which are alike in their nature and their activities. Generally speaking the spirit is the **higher**, the soul the lower element. The spirit may be recognized as the "life principle" bestowed on man by God, whereas the soul is the resulting life constituted in the individual, leaving the body as the material organism *animated* by soul & spirit. Body & soul are the constituents of the man, according to Matt 6:25, 10:28; Luke 12:20; Acts 20:10; **body & spirit** according to Luke 8:55; 1Cor 5:3 & 7:34; Jas. 2:26; Matt 26:28; the emotions are associated with *soul*, in John 13:21, (emotions) associated with the *spirit*: cf. Ps. 42:11 & Kings 21:5. The emotions are shared by both soul and spirit.

Richard's hypothesis:

If you eliminate the emotions and the sentient element in man, which is the way we perceive, reflect, feel & desire during the abduction examinations, I believe you then reduce the victim to an ineffective willing body able to be used and probed at will. Let's say that it is by this method **and** by the use of the "goad" (rod; trance) that form the elements of the *anesthesiology*. Look at the word *anesthetic* which causes the loss of sensation, with or without the loss of consciousness.

In the Greek, the word (anaisthetos) or an + (aisthetos) = "perceptible." This is what is (**eliminated**) with the soul/spirit, where both share these same qualities, such as *emotions*: an intense mental state, a strong feeling; that part of the consciousness which involves feeling & sensibility.

The *sentient* element is "eliminated," which is having a sense of perception, where the consciousness of a given person is taken out. In Latin we have "to feel." You lose the experience of sensation which is a perception associated with a *stimulation* of the sense organ or with a specific body condition. The stimulus could be the contact with the **goad**, the rod that puts you into a trance, which could also mean that specific body condition is being left for examination on the table with **parts** of your soul and spirit taken out. You would never even know what happened to you, unless you were hypnotized to remember.

THE CURS-ED NET

{{I remember viewing the movie, **COMMUNION**, where it depicted Whitley Strieber being confronted by malevolent-looking small bluish beings, and one of them was holding a *goad* that he applied to Whitley's head; we also have Dr. David Lewis, reporting on the same person via Strieber's book, *"COMMUNION"*, quoted Texe Marrs, in his own book, "MYSTERY MARK OF THE NEW AGE," where apparently a woman named 'ISHTAR' touched the head of Strieber with a "magic wand," so that images began to swirl about in his mind; these entities were described as "demonic." [Source: *"UFO: END-TIME DELUSION,"* p.164.] This, then, seems to add another level of credibility that the things Richard is referring to revolve around the dark side of Ufology, where the roots seem to point to demonic entities — *and not ET's* from else-where, stopping off on Earth just to pick up a few samples/people for experiments.}}

The aliens (evil spirits) just minimize what is relative to keeping you alive and able to function enough through the examination. Your mind cannot perceive what is happening, but yet still func-tions enough that when the parts of your soul and spirit are *reunited*, under a skill like regressive hypnosis, you *do remember things*! {{Because of what may lie in store for the abductee, especially if he or she does not have a solid foundation *in faith,* it may become a shattering experience, especially if Karla Turner is correct about finding the truth of the abduction experience but *only after* the first level of remembering which may be acting as a "screen memory;" it could also be a natural defense mechanism of *our very psyches* to cushion the blow of some traumatic experience.}}

The stages of intense probing &/or extraction of DNA &/or tissues (the initial operating part of it,) are almost all the time missing, usually by a supernatural process of an anesthetic. {{Richard may be alluding to the fact that the military of various governments may have a vested interest in monitoring "legitimate" abductees, and will abduct these same people to glean information about the alien/demonic threat; cf. the book, *LOST WAS THE KEY*, by Leah Haley, for her documentation on this particular dynamic operating and also complicating the abduction phenomenon.}}

THE CURS-ED NET

Under hypnosis you will only remember so much, i.e., what you were allowed to remember. {{James LeFante, I believe, fits into this category, since he became a type of *PR MAN* for his captors, trying to put a *positive spin* on the agenda being perpetrated upon his friends and himself, as I witnessed in a mid-1990s "SIGHTINGS" series of episodes on commercial TV. Some of the things that he & his friends had to undergo (via alien experimentation,) seemed down-right immoral, and certainly not Biblically oriented...*which led me to suspect, even back then that the ET phenomenon was seeming more like the demonic agenda. Now I am sure of it ~~ some twelve years or so later.*}}

{{Before ending this section, I wish to dramatize what happened (or what was observed by Ted Rice, and reported by Karla Turner, in her *must read* book, *MASQUERADE OF ANGELS.* It may serve as a good example of the complications that are involved with the abduction phenomenon, but were not totally appreciated back in 1994 when Karla had penned the book; of course the information you have read in this chapter is — in effect — *'breaking relative new ground'* in our understanding of the demonic abduction phenomenon, but in any event, I think this example may help us in our endeavor to secure *a potential* truth as to what is *really* going on within the phenomenon:

CAVEAT: {{I do not believe the following is *completely* true, per se, (remembering that Richard solves this problem because of the use of the "partial soul/spirit," but it is instructive to see *that if it is a form of disinformation*, just how effective these demonic forces can be in lying to us; of course, if false, it probably would have to do with the orchestrations of the *dark demons* rather than what Ted Rice witnessed in a possible *altered* condition. This is yet another reason to *rely on THE HOLY BIBLE* when it comes to the strange & unusual.}}

An excerpt from Ted Rice's story, cited within page 243 of Karla's book:

Ted was recalling what he saw with his *cloned body* as related to hypno-therapist, Barbara Bartholic.

THE CURS-ED NET

"When the cloned body was placed on the table, it was completely inert. The woman (the alien) placed the black box with my soul on the new body, and then they did something that activated the body, because I saw it twitch and jerk, and then the chest started expanding as it breathed. That's when I found myself in the new body.

"Remember that they **didn't** remove my soul from my original body **until** I drank the green liquid and apparently died," Ted went on. "Looking at both procedures, I think I understand now that the soul is apparently locked into the body by an energy field, the aura that forms once the body is breathing. They can't take the soul out without killing the body, and it isn't locked into the body until breath is drawn."

{{Needless to say, this is a controversial monologue from Ted back in the 1994 book, and I merely offer it as just another piece that *has been offered* about the alien abduction phenomenon that Richard & I prefer calling the demonic abduction phenomenon. (The **bold words** within the above quote were emphasized by the co-author of this work.)

Since we may very well be dealing with demons to begin with, who knows where the truth ends and *the spin of lies* begin when it comes to what abductees are *reporting to us* about their experiences. I hope that maybe this example will get some thinking about what we are offered in the Ufological literature, and how it may veer (ever so slightly) from what scripture tells us — especially when it comes to the dynamics of both soul and spirit. I can see a danger in accepting what may be a half-truth to sign-off to concepts like abortion, with the notion that it is not really killing a human being, but we must ask ourselves: *Is this anecdotal story the whole truth or just a clever part* thereof!}}

THE CURS-ED NET

END NOTES:

Vine's Complete Expository Dictionary of Old and
New Testament Words:
Publisher: Thomas Nelson, Inc. ©1996
Used by permission of Thomas Nelson, Inc

CHAPTER FIFTEEN:

THE CUTTING LOCUSTS

{{This short chapter is meant to show the symbolism that may have been employed by the Biblical prophet (as seen by Richard,) to execute one of the functions (or qualities) of one of the types of **locusts**, i.e., the *cutting* processes involved in the ongoing demonic abduction phenomenon (as part of the aforementioned **curse**.)}}

The word *cut* in Greek is first (kopto) "to cut by a blow," as for example, branches; also see the words (lament, bewail.) The word *blow* in general means "a sudden stroke." Enoch 68:18 mentions the **stroke of the embryo,** {{which would otherwise seem a very curious phrase, except in the light of the ***demonic abduction phenomenon.***}} The word 'blow' also in Greek is (rhapisma) meaning "a blow with a rod." 'Blow' repeats the meaning of (hipopneo) — (hupo) "under" here (indicating repression.) [The rod or goad puts the abducted person in a trance, *as discussed previously*.]

Let's look at the word *branches*. In the Greek (klados) from (klao) means "to break," as in a young tender shoot "broken off" for grafting. *Break* in Greek as a noun (parabasis) means a "transgression," "to go across." We will see that the following act involving grafting here is a **transgression against God's law** toward humanity. *Transgress* (parabates) is "one who oversteps a prescribed limit." Transgression implies the violation of God's law {{as was done by the Fallen Angels, and documented by Enoch in *The Book of Enoch*.}} (So these evil spirits who abduct people and follow out their evil agenda with these same people victimized and known today as 'alien abductees' are transgressing the law of God as regard to man.)

Now the word *graft* in general means 1) to unite by insertion; 2) to join; 3) to transplant or implant surgically. The word *implant* has several meanings here that represent this detailing of the abduction phenomenon sequence. In general, 'implant' means a) to insert or embed an object or a device surgically; b) to insert a tissue within the body; c) (Embryo) is to become attached to and embedded in the uterine lining used in reference to a fertilized egg. (See Enoch 68:18 that is **coding to us** this very process.)

In the Greek (apokopto) is to "cut off, or cut away," 'Literally' of the members of the body. (Could this **s-p-e-l-l** cattle mutilations as in the bodies of cattle being mutilated to provide nourishment for the hybrid demons?) Yet another meaning of the word 'cut' is to follow with the general meaning of "reaping or harvesting" (as by the abduction of people so as to use them as a harvest, where the word *harvest* has a meaning of "to receive the benefits from an action," (where the abductions **ARE** the action!)

The word *reap* means "to obtain by an 'effort' which is an earnest attempt to accomplish something." The word *effort* in Old French is esfort < esforeier, "to force;" (check chapter twelve for the word *force*, which in Greek means to "carry off" by force, and to "snatch away," "seize," & to "kidnap" (as in an abduction?) The evil spirits gather the abductees DNA/tissue, etc., to complete their evil agenda, which I believe to be (as fruit thereof) forms of hybridization. {{Remember the example of *Raechel* in "RAECHEL'S EYES" where poor Raechel was terminated by her evil captors (the evil spirits and their possible military minions) simply because the quality of COMPASSION was not "weeded out" of her; if this is a true story (which it is presented as in the Ufological literature,) it should be of **grave** concern to anyone trying to figure out the end game in the agenda of these same evil captors; Richard may well be fingering the true agenda of these captors, i.e., *the evil spirits* who are themselves operating as part of the overall Fallen Angel agenda!}}

Now in finalizing the idea of the word 'cut,' we look at the meaning of "to separate from a main body." (This could relate to

THE CURS-ED NET

a cattle mutilation or to an abductee's examination where DNA/ tissue, etc., is taken; it could also involve {{and usually does, according to the "track record" of the abduction literature,}} the fetus being taken.

If we review the word *branches*, (to break a young tender shoot for grafting,) a *shoot* means "a young growth arising from a germinating seed." (I know we are mainly addressing plants here, but **look between the lines** and you may be able to see the larger picture.) The word *germinate* means "to begin to grow," but also "to come into existence."

We can now look at the word *gut* in relation to *cut* as to the details involved, and we come to a meaning of "to extract essential or major parts of" — (which when applied to what we just penned, could very well reflect the cattle mutilations & the abduction examinations.)

{{A reflection on this chapter: If we can understand & appreciate what had been addressed in the beginning chapters regarding *the Bite of the Serpent,* about the rather **explicit** reference to the evil spirits' attempt at transgressing God's law ~ by interfering as in *the serpent biting the embryo & diminishing it,* with both the changing & development of its fruit, (the hybrids,) the most likely intent of Enoch 68:18, as per our previous treatise presentation, then it should provide a venue for having absolutely no trouble connecting this most recent "dot" while integrating it into the ongoing process that is percolating before our very eyes, and hence, *__the function of the cutting locusts__*!

The implication that this process will be accelerated during the Tribulation period (since the various locusts are the agents mentioned during this horrendous time,) should help the reader to fill-in the symbolism being decoded — as Richard has attempted to do with his "key word" approach in understanding the potential scriptural code that we really do need to understand in these potentially "end time" dynamics.

CHAPTER SIXTEEN:

THE HOPPING LOCUSTS

{{This chapter will show very clearly (via **key words**) how these *hopping locusts* represent, in fact, the **UFO** advance of the **LOCUST INVASION**, as part of the ongoing judgments of God, culminating during the TRIBUALTION period.}}

Let's put these meanings into perspective as compared to *UFOs*. The *hopping locusts* have wings that symbolically represent their mode of transportation. The wings are *not* naturally attached to the locusts here, since they are evil spirits & Fallen Angels from the Abyss (Rev. 9.) {{Since the *evil spirits* are earthbound spirits of the aforementioned *giants* of Enoch (chapter 15,) it may reflect that there are *different levels* of THE ABYSS, and that this *abyss* may run very deep into our own Earth. One may imagine the dramatic scene from J.R.R. Tolkien's **LORD OF THE RINGS,** where he may have *metaphorically* depicted the **evil that lurked in the Middle Earth, and perhaps thrust down there from their "second estate;"** I mention this as a possibility since Tolkien may have been aware of Richard Laurence's translation of Enoch, having gone to the same university as the Hebrew scholar Dr. Laurence, although they were separated by many years. Being a Roman Catholic in good standing, Tolkien may have been reluctant to broach such a sensitive topic in real life, but it would not have been immune from his "fiction," (*in the form of metaphor of which he was fond,*)

THE CURS-ED NET

especially if *The Book of Enoch* captured his imagination from a scriptural point of view.}}

We begin with the word *hop* which in general means "to move with bounding, skips or leaps, {{perhaps as the UFOs that Kenneth Arnold had spotted in June of 1947,}} to move quickly or to move over. {{In the UFO literature, some UFOs have been tracked on radar going well in access of 8.000 mph in our own atmosphere, and also tracked by Naval sonar as going far in access of what any submarine could achieve right up to the present day.}}

Another meaning relative here is "to stimulate with or as if with a narcotic." The word *stimulate* was discussed earlier in chapter twelve with the word **stinger**. The effects of certain narcotics that are alluded to here are those which alter, induces sleep, &/or cause narcosis. *Narcosis* is a condition of unconsciousness in Greek (narcosis,) as "a numbing." *Numb* here relates to the UFO abduction phenomenon as having the meaning "deprived of the power to feel or move normally, emotionally unresponsive." The meaning above relates to "paralysis" — a loss or impairment of the ability to move, usually of damage to the nerve supply (where the "goad" reacts.) 'Numb' in Middle English is 'nome,' variant of nomin, past participle of nimen, (to seize or abduct.)

Other meanings of 'hop' are as follows: the word *bpind* means "forward &/or upward." *Skip* is "to pass from point to point, to pass over." *Leap* is to "bound upward from the ground, to move quickly or abruptly from one position to another or one place to another, to act impulsively; also an abrupt or precipitous passage, shift or transition."

Let's put these meanings into perspective compared to a UFO. Its characteristics:

1) bound, moving forward & upward;
2) skip, passing from a point to another point (a localized position) and to pass over (above) or to another specified place or location;
3) leap, move upward from the ground quickly or to move abruptly from one position to another;
4) to act *impulsively* (having the power & force to impel or 'incite' forcefully.

THE CURS-ED NET

Incite here has a meaning in Latin "to stimulate" (as a UFO could or would do with its supernatural movements & flashing colored lights,) while *impel* has a meaning of "to urge to action through moral pressure," (or, in other words,) to force, entreat by moral force – as in evil behavior.

(There's that word ***entreat*** again; cf. chapter twelve under torment & torture.) Then there is the word *impulsively,* which in (physics) means "to act within a brief time, interval, a space between two points." (Could that mean *here* and through a portal to *there*?) Interval can also mean time. The word *abrupt* means "sudden, touching on one subject or position after another with sudden transition."

Precipitous, as indicated earlier, is being extremely rapid, (as in to move very fast from one point to another; steep.) The word *passage* is the "act or process of passing from one place to another," or "the process of elapsing," especially (a passage of time.) The word *elapse* is "to slip by." *Slip* is to move quietly, to move stealthily, to pass "imperceptibly." (Cases of UFOs passing imperceptibly means that which is "impossible or difficult to perceive by the mind or senses," or, (in other words, supernaturally beyond anything we know of.) {{One like myself, as a forty year observer of the UFO phenomenon, has only to point out the famous WASHINGTON D.C. sighting regarding July of 1952, which was cited very well in a 1956 documentary movie called, "UNIDENTIFIED FLYING OBJECTS," where these elusive UFOs sighted and picked up on radar over the sensitive area of our Federal capitol, when chased, __simply disappeared __(possibly into hyperspace,) and when the jets that were chasing them went back to base, **the unknowns suddenly _reappeared_**!' It doesn't take much thought to realize that these UFOs had "spatial" abilities (as in ***dimensional shifts***) that were far beyond what we could have done in 1952 — or for that matter — today!}}

Two words are of interest here: the word *shift* means "to alter (position or place or time)" plus the word *transit* from the earlier citing of the word "transitions." 'Transit' in Latin is transitus , past participle of transire, "to go across;" see the word 'transient.'

Translent means "passing with time;" in Latin, transient, tran siens, transeunt — as past participle of transire, is "to go over." Check in the beginning of this chapter for the word "hop" as in

181

THE CURS-ED NET

hopping locusts: it has a meaning of "to move over," showing that in their name **hopping**, it holds an ability to "pass with time."

So the title, *Hopping Locusts* involves many details of how their wings (mode of transportation) operated and how it all relates to the abilities and characteristics of today's UFOs within the abduction phenomenon. From the movements to even the ability to elapsed time, they **all** involve supernatural powers. {{To a Biblically knowledgeable person, these abilities would have come as no surprise since St. Paul had mentioned who are enemies were & are: spiritual wicked dark forces from ON HIGH! (Eph. 6:12) — so these enumerating insightful details from Richard should come as no real surprise *either*.}}

CHAPTER SEVENTEEN:

The Destroying Locusts

{{These *destroying locusts* are the final piece of the spiritual puzzle (the ongoing invasion) and not surprisingly, it will be demonstrated by Richard (as usual using **key words**) just how intimately the UFO figures into this mix — (and what will become a caldron during the Tribulation.) It will be a mix that has been distorted, making it hard for our eyes to truly see, but with the proper understanding of the Biblical codes ensconced within the prophetic writings of the canonical Bible which will be cited below, I believe the **unsealing** of the Book of Daniel (chapter 12) is slowly but surely being made manifest in what looks very much like the last generation before *the day of the Lord*! Witness:}}

There are several meanings that relate to the information provided in chapter sixteen, so we will start with the word *destroy*, which in Greek (kathaireo) means "to cast down, pull down by force." Another meaning (luo) is "to loose, sever, break." (CF. 1 John 3:8, regarding the works of the Devil.)

We look at the meaning of *cast down* as applied here, which reveals the phrase "to cast, throw or put." 'Down' has the meaning of "in or into an inactive or inoperative state," (to paralyze?) It further means to "lower into a condition of subjection." *Subjective* is "the taking place within a person's mind, being personal & particular to a given person; existing only in the mind." This makes a good deal of sense when one considers that in chapter twelve the

THE CURS-ED NET

evil spirits (considered as *the Grays,*) put one into a "trance" by a goad (rod) which connects in between the nervous system and the brain. To 'cast down' is to put into a condition of subjection (trance.) Remember that it is also "by force" (as mentioned above.)

There's a meaning of (apoleia) where the Greek indicates *loss of well being,* where 'well being' is a state of being "healthy." Through abductions, our bodies are not made whole anymore. They are not as healthy as they once were. Physically they have been tampered with; also mentally, many of these people who have witnessed sightings or have been involved in whichever way with UFOs, have had their lives changed (albeit with subtlety,) but changed *for the worse!*' - {{and may I say, as in *"the bite of the Demon serpent"* that this change occurs!}}

Destroy in Greek also is (apollumi) — "to perish." This meaning includes being unhealthy (spiritually.) The meaning of *perish* (diaph-theiro) is "to corrupt." THERE IS MUCH EVIL TIED IN WITH UFOs. If you do decide to involve yourself within this realm, *do not do it out of mere curiosity* since it may very well become a *bait* for the beginnings of unnatural (**paranormal**) occurrences in your life, or your life may change in some way — usually not for the better. {{My own forty year investigation of this subject did, in fact, lead eventually to having **paranormal experiences** of one kind or another over the last 14 years, so what Richard is cautioning may be wise council indeed; of course, if one prays for spiritual discern-ment while encountering these wiles, it may help one's faith, but one should proceed with all caution. A word to the wise. I invite anyone to visit my poem, *"RELIANCE"* for my reflection on this very sensitive subject, where I started to understand the *serpent's subtle ways.* Go to the Internet web page located at http://inspec-torblebeau.pbwiki.com/RELIANCE}}

Most times we simply get so obsessed, we have to make it part of our lives. (*Satan is acutely aware of this lure, bait & hook.* Now, at that point, we have been "snuckered" — charmed — seduced & {{may I say, *captured within the curs-ed net*! Is there a way out? YES! Simply put your *reliance on the loving Father* (Yahweh, the proper name of God,) and His Son *Jesus*, whom we call Jesus today. Remember the words in 1 John 4:4: "greater is he who is within

THE CURS-ED NET

you than he who is in the world." This focus, combined with much prayer & piety should get you through the storm that is yet to come. Yes, Richard & I share the same sentiments when it comes to this *reliance,* since after all, it is what Jesus had asked us to do.}}

BACK TO THE TREATISE:

To *corrupt* (kapeleuo) is to be a "retailer, to peddle, to huck-sterize." To *huckster* in general is to be one who "uses aggressive, showy, and sometimes devious methods to promote or sell a product." (In this case, Satan and his evil agencies are continuously deceiving us in every way they can to *sell* their products — {{the fruit of which is spiritual DEATH!}} The UFO phenomenon is simply one of those hooks as bait that is alluring, since it looks *merely* strange and "alien," but is cleverly disguised to hide themselves and their evil agenda for which you may be an unwitting dupe for! {{Now if you read or re-read Michael Heiser's *THE FACADE*, you may then enjoy a deeper appreciation for the set-up or *sting* being perpetrated upon you daily, in the tantalizing paranormal news as presented on cable TV and through the contactee literature of Ufology. It is ALL meant to steer you away from the foundation truths within the Holy Bible, but it is done in such a curious and seductive "parallax" manner, we do not necessarily recognize it for what it truly is, like being caught in a *rip tide* with the end result that you will be swept out to sea, and not *rest in peace*!}}

Speaking of which, we now look at the word *corrupt* which in Greek means "to destroy by the means of corrupting, and so bringing us into a worse state of affairs." Simply put, we are deceived fully through the supernatural abilities as utilized by the evil entities. If we look at the word 'destroy,' in general it has several meanings to add to the character & qualities of these *locusts*, the very symbol used as evil spirits:

1) to seduce
2) to render useless or ineffective and in Latin it means "to pile up."

Pile has a meaning of accumulating, which is to "gather" and 'gather' has the meaning of "to harvest" ~~ as in (having to do with abductions & cattle mutilations.) It also contains the idea of "amassing," (as in the coming time of unprecedented abductions all over the world!) {{This, of course, is what has been symbolized (through **key words**) and reflected in Revelation 9:5, with the troubling indication that for **_five full months_** there will be unrelenting torture (via the abductions as per the present interpretation) of these various types of locusts, acting (with permission) in all sorts of fashions upon a non-repenting mankind, left behind to face the "music." IT IS NOT A PRETTY PICTURE, and thank God that many will be spared by being **_caught up_** before these things start to happen, as per the writings of St. Paul; of course, it is during this time that others will gain their salvation by finally making the right choice, regardless of consequence, i.e., put through the CRUCIBLE, **_and dying rather than turn one's back or deny Jesus Christ._**}}

THE CHEESE NOW "BECOMES MORE BINDING"

Gather alternately means to "forage." 'Forage' has a meaning of "to wander in search of" (like **wandering stars**?) It also means "fodder." *Fodder* is used as a way to describe the abduction scenario involving humans, and cattle has a meaning of "a consumable, often inferior item or resource that is in demand and usually abundant in supply."

Lastly, *destroy* means "to subdue" which also means "to quiet or bring under control by physical force or persuasion" (trance;) furthermore, it offers the idea of "bringing under cultivation." In Latin (subdere) = subdue meaning "to subject" or "to cultivate" as of addressing the abduction phenomenon. Here, as far as the fetus is concerned, we have both to prepare & to promote the growth of a biological culture. *Biological* relates to, or affects living organisms *Culture* means the breeding of animals or other life, to produce & to grow stock. They are affecting life by growing & producing stock, such as "with hybrids," (possibly injecting man's sperm with not only abductees' DNA or tissue, but also their own DNA via the hybrid agenda. The name **destroying locusts** certainly explains a good many details. Incidentally, this hybrid DNA dynamic will be addressed in more detail in the next three chapters, and may offer a clue about those **Giants of Old** who died, but whose evil spirits remained **Earthbound, and searching for a place to inhabit**!

Some reflections by co-author LeBeau: {{There you have it, folks, six chapters addressing the evil spirits & Fallen Angels' massive, long-term, ongoing judgments (allowed by God) but presented to humanity in a stealthy fashion within the cloaking facade of the UFO & alien abduction phenomenon, where only an apparent few seem to be comprehensively aware of the data in Ufology and how it can be linked to Biblical prophecy in **the way** you have seen presented in this treatise as well as the groundwork that was fashioned via the first group of chapters relating to **the Bite of the Serpent.**

IS THAT ALL THERE IS?

Happily, the answer is "NO!" Richard & I (Byron LeBeau,) decided to add "THE THIRD WAVE" that is being presented in the last three chapters, centering our attention around (what we frame as) THE *CURS*-ED NET, which will entail the actual origins of those who have **left** their FIRST ESTATE as per the writings of Jude. Further comments will be addressed regarding **the Lord of the Stings** (SATAN) as well as those **Grays with their goading rods** who are prodding their poor unfortunate victims in their diabolical "end-game agenda" to control all of this world under the auspices of THE PRINCE OF THIS WORLD. A look at **astrology** and how it fits into this **curs-ed net** will also be addressed.

CHAPTER EIGHTEEN:

The *Curs*-ed Net

(Exposing the HOOK)

{{This chapter starts the *third* layer of the three-part thesis which is trying to put this phenomenon **of the Fallen Angels & earthbound demons** into proper perspective as a reflection of the storyline of **The Book of Enoch,** a book that is a *type of comprehensive prelude* to our understanding of what **Sacred Canonical Scripture** had indicated *ever so* cryptically, especially as it relates to a more comprehensive understanding of Genesis 6:4.

By putting certain key verses together (such as Enoch 68:18) as well as using key chapters within certain prophetical scripture (such as in Joel, Zacharia, Isaiah & Revelation,) it became clear (at least to Richard,) that the *wandering stars* that St. Jude referenced in his **canonical** epistle (Jude 13) were *none other than* the Fallen Angels that seduced men, who were responsible for the bitter fruit of the *Giants of Old*, whose very spirits became subsequently *bound to the Earth as unclean spirits*. This is the long & short of the story that is ***imperative to understand*** if we are to make any real sense out of what we see today: *UFOs seemingly flying about without too many people in "**officialdom**" taking serious notice of; the national MEDIA which only parrots the **official line;** confusing and vague stances by certain churches who (for various reasons) do not connect the **clear dots** of 'The Book of Enoch **with** the canonical

THE CURS-ED NET

texts of the Old & New Testament (except for the **Ethiopian church as a rare exception.**) Is it any wonder that the average 'Joe' on the street is both baffled and ignorant about the underlying truth of all of this? This is the reason we have called this chapter **THE *CURS-ED* NET, echoing the very title of this book.** It is our purpose to untangle and expose this net for what it truly is: *the ultimate deception of Satan and the dark forces from* **ON HIGH,** *who firmly desire to ensnare us in the same net that they themselves were cast into or freely joined as part of the evil Watchers who did not stay steadfast in their appointed tasks*!

So what is this NET that is accursed? St. Jude also talked about these fallen ones as losing their **First Estate**, and being thrown down (Jude 6.) We feel that they were not only cast into this *curs-ed* net, but they also (out of anger and jealousy toward the children of men,) were thereafter enticing men to be caught up in the same net as they; therefore, when we see that the sacred scripture **condemning** either honoring or serving the sun or the moon or the stars (Deuteronomy 4:19,) know that it is condemning the homage man pays to ASTOLOGY, (which, according to 1 Enoch 8,) was taught to men by these *same* fallen ones who had already been judged, awaiting final condemnation. We also see this same condemnation in the Book of Jeremiah, where it states the following:

"The children gather wood, their fathers light the fire, and the women knead dough to make cakes for the *queen of heaven*, (which was the fertility goddess, *ISHTAR*, and the cakes were made in the shape of stars to honor *this same Ishtar* who was identified with the planet Venus,) while libations are poured out to strange gods in order to hurt me. Is it I whom they hurt, says the Lord; is it not rather themselves to their own confusion? See now, says the Lord God, my anger and my wrath will pour out upon this place, upon man and beast, upon the trees and the field and the fruits of the earth; it will burn without being quenched" (7:18-20.)

It is clear to both Richard & myself that *from the above citation,* as well as the one from Deuteronomy, that anyone who gives homage to the wandering stars as fallen angels, will **sorely distress** the very living God who made all the stars and the planets and the moons to begin with! The Bible is warning such foolish people

THE CURS-ED NET

that by so aligning themselves (i.e., hitching their wagons to *the demonic* stars,) *each one who does such a despicable thing* is – in effect - being trapped (like glue) in the fallen angels' *CURS*-ED NET! The NET itself can be symbolically seen as in the air (where the **powers of evil** are) as well as in the ocean of near space, represented by the sun, the moon and various constellations, all of which contain symbolism that would identify these same signs as part of the demonic realm — which somehow needs to be adored & honored, *due perhaps to the pride and hubris of such pompous & arrogant 'angelic' fools who had formerly been adorned in such glory ~~ especially Lucifer*!

This chapter is meant to prove this very point. This will be done, firstly, by citing the key constellations mentioned in the Bible, which itself begs the question: Why are only certain constellations mentioned? [According to H.A. Rey in regard to his book, *THE STARS,* there are 88 constellations in the entire sky *that can be viewed from Earth*, where only about two dozen of which can be seen at any given time, and the Zodiac only represents twelve of these constellations,] *yet* in The Bible, Orion, which is not in the Zodiac, is specifically mentioned, while the Pleiades, which is only a *part* of the constellation of Taurus, the Bull, are both mentioned in Job (see below.)

It is our feeling that THE *CURS*-ED NET incorporates the entire **Second Estate** of the fallen ones (and their fashioned minions,) and each portion thereof has its own specific function within the **Satanic 'Corporation.'** This will be discussed as we focus on the key elements of Richard's notes regarding the parameters of the *NET*work.

Once we understand what is really behind this *façade of lights*, and remember that Enoch himself referred to the fallen angels as wandering stars (1 Enoch 43:1,) it will be much easier to comprehend how **Astrology** may be a *lure* by the fishermen with the net to trap man into thinking that they are man's gods, and therefore should be honored and adored, which is exactly the opposite of what God wants of us to do, as enumerated many times in the Bible, especially in the book of Jeremiah.

THE CURS-ED NET

After we view the Biblical references, and Richard's analysis of same, I will give some examples from the Ufological literature that **_not so coincidentally_** mention these same constellations! Such coincidences stretch credulity, especially when the first two parts of our thesis clearly show that the *façade show of wandering stars* is responsible for the UFO & DEMONIC ABDUCTION PHENOMENON, so, per force, the fallen angels and demons (which will be shown to be the *Reptilians & Grays,*) are the same culprits that have been harassing mankind for at least the last five thousand years or so, perhaps longer.}}

BIBLICAL REFERENCES TO WANDERING STARS IN THE FORM OF CONSTELLATIONS OR PARTS THEREOF

For the record, *constellation* is defined as "any of the various configuration of stars to which names have been given" (such as CANCER [*the Crab*]) and in *astrology*, the "grouping of relative positions of the stars as supposed influencing events, especially at a person's birth."

1) "He (God) is the maker of the Bear and Orion, the Pleiades, and the constellations of the south." (Job 9:9. NIV)
2) "Can you bind the beautiful Pleiades? Can you loose the cords of Orion?" (Job 38:31.)
3) "or lead out the Bear with its cubs?" (Job 38:31.)
4) "He who made the Pleiades and Orion." (Amos 5:8.)
5) "Can you bring forth the constellations in their seasons?" (Job 38:32.)

{{So why are these constellations (or parts thereof) specifically mentioned in Job & Amos? Below Richard explores some key words to see if we can unravel this mystery:}}

God is the maker (demiourgos) of The Bear, Orion & the Pleiades. {{NOTE: The Great Bear (URSA MAJOR) includes a familiar sight in the night sky called *the Big Dipper*.}} The southern constellations belong to the boundary territory of which the Bear & Orion also belong; *south* also in Greek means "region" which was made by God. {{If you think of these symbolic places (even as states or vibrations of being) designed for temporary dwellings as part of the fallen angels' *Second Estate* until final judgment and destination are

192

pronounced, then you may have a more clear idea of the dynamics that is ~ perhaps ~ being presented here. Remember, these are basically spiritual beings we are dealing with, even though it seems they have the capacity for having a physical component, which may rightfully confuse some until *other* dynamics are understood; this will be addressed in this third leg of the treatise.}}

The *binding* referred to, describes the binding of prisoners (abductees?) with cords (trances?) {{I get the impression that this may be a double metaphor since I mentioned in the introduction that the fallen angels are both prisoners within the second estate net, and also are trying to lure **their own prisoners** (the abductees;) Job is being asked rhetorically if he could so bind such a powerful force or stop what they are doing? It seems that only God has the power to bind and control the activities of the prisoners, so why would anyone wish to cooperate with the fallen angels or demons under such restraint? Is this a **code** to Job to have some respect for the power of God and what only He can control, since Job himself is only part of the *potter's clay [?]*}}

Richard notes that the Pleiades are *beautiful*, and that in Greek, (horaios) describes that which is seasonable, from (hora) — *a season*, which is "a suitable time or recurrent period." (Richard sees this, [from an abduction point of view,] as being set to certain recurrent times or seasons.) {{Of course, in Ufological literature, many abductees talk about being *"taken"* sometime between 3 and 4 AM, so there may be a legitimate connection here.}} *Season* from Latin (satio, sation) means "sowing," and (satus) as past participle of (serere) as "to plant;" {{Implanting seed within the womb of the female human may remind the reader of 1 Enoch 68:18, so again the imagery is consistent with the abduction phenomenon.}}

Orion & the Pleiades have been mentioned as the home of the **Grays**, and because the *Reptilian* are also seen with the Grays from time to time, possibly their home also. {{I, myself, have a video documentary that bears out the connection between the Grays & Reptilians, as reported on by Linda Moulton Howe regarding the Ron & Paula Watson story, where both Ron & Paula witnessed a cow being abducted by Grays and levitated into a UFO; they also saw a large green Reptilian standing nearby, with large yellow eyes

THE CURS-ED NET

& vertical pupils; later Paula recounts (under regressive hypnosis) that the Grays were extracting something from her uterus area, while a Reptilian looked on. As far as from where the abductors say to an abductee or "contactee" like Billy Meier *they hail from,* we can take that information with a grain of salt, since, if they are either fallen angels or demons, their very lies will look like the truth to their victims, and since Satan is the father of lies, what they say proves nothing! For an interesting look at what Meier's contact "Semjase" had *instilled in him as her "wisdom,"* please consult Jim Marrs' book entitled, **ALIEN AGENDA,** as part of *his* chapter seven called *'The Pleiadian Connection,' pages 299-313;* the **New Age** literature has spawned many fuzzy stories dealing with what seems to be Fallen Angels, of which Semjase may very well be one of. Richard Thompson had noted in another UFO related book how the very name is reminiscent of one of the Fallen Angels that **Enoch himself had mentioned,** which was addressed previously in an earlier chapter.}}

Richard also came to the conclusion that if Orion & the Pleiades are the "cubs" and the Bear is the mother, then it is quite possible, symbolically and perhaps literally, that the Grays & the Reptilians were produced by their mother (the Fallen Angels) and they are *therefore* the hybrids and the workers! The Pleiades belong to TAURUS — (*the Bull)* as part of the Zodiac, but the Bear & Orion are mentioned here to also represent two other constellations which belong to the boundary territory, i.e., the second estate which Jude referred to as the abode of the Fallen Angels; therefore, as part of that estate (*NETwork,)* the demonic hybrid beings from Orion and the Pleiades would seem to work together for that end. {{If you look at a star map, the Pleiades are a cluster of stars on one of the horns of *the Bull,* which, to me, would symbolically reflect part of an **advancing attack group**, since a horn can be used as a weapon of attack, just as was mentioned in the beginning chapters regarding *the bite of the serpent* with the blows given, as in the aforementioned 1 ENOCH 68:18. Does this dynamic not only make sense, but connect some dots in our understanding of the relationship among the "ufonauts," astrology and the *curs*-ed plan of the Fallen Angels & demons? I believe it does!}}

194

THE CURS-ED NET

The *cords of Orion* in general are the force that binds and restrains. ("The abductee," i.e., the female victim, is the one diseased [diminished] by being implanted with the malignant cancerous organism.) As mentioned before, how can mankind stop this type of activity? Can mankind free the abductee from their prison? NO! *only Jesus Christ, the true Son of God, can do this*! {{I have heard of certain female abductees who have developed a relationship with Jesus, and have become more spiritually-minded, and their abductions have lessoned or disappeared, similar to the testimony of Richard Stout in chapter four, where he *broke through his own cursed net*. If we are correct in our surmise that the abduction phenomenon is, in fact, connected to the Fallen Angels and their demon minions, then it would not be surprising to see this *spiritual quid pro quo* as a literal dynamic, a dynamic which is being attested to by other people as well, in varying degrees. Ann Druffel wrote a very interesting essay called, *'Techniques for Resisting Alien Abductions,'* that reflected the success of spiritual warfare against these nefarious "aliens;" I am including the details about this essay in the "UFO & OTHER BOOK & ARTICLE REFERENCES," and I heartily recommend your reading this 1993 piece.}}

When Richard focused in on "the Bear," he found that in general, it is an omnivorous animal. The word *vorous* is "eating, feeding on" and in Latin, it is "to swallow or devour," but what does it feed on? *Feed* in Greek (bosko) is used by a herdsman from (boo) "to nourish," where the special function being to provide food: the root is (bo) found in (boter) – "a herdsman" and/or herd and (botane) "fodder, pasture." (So herdsman is symbolic of those whose job it is to mutilate the "herd" cattle.) *Fodder* in general is "raw material, (food) as for a creation;" also "a consumable, often inferior item or resource."

Pasture in Greek (nome) "is a feeding." In Greek, *feed* also is (trepho) and is "to make to grow, to bring up, nourish" (hybrids?) Let's look at the word *cattle*, which, in Greek is (thremma) from (trepho) that means "to nourish, nurture, feed." (So cattle is that which is fed on earlier from 'Bear.')

The meaning of 'cattle' in Greek (ktenos) means "cattle as property;" see beast #3. This in Greek is (ktenos) *property* with the connected verb (ktaomai) that is "to possess." It signifies in scripture animals for slaughter. *Slaughter* has a meaning of "a butcher;" also the word 'slaughter' in Hebrew (zaban) is "slaughter for eating." *Buthcher* in Old French is (bouchier < bouc, boc,) signifying a "he-goat" and probably of Celtic origin. (If we connect these dots: 'He-goats' are **evil spirits** working with the herdsman who have the job of mutilating cattle for food.)

WHAT IS SIGNIFICANT ABOUT THE BEAR'S CUBS?

{{The below may be technically difficult to follow, but it revolves around the notion of the cubs having a deficiency (that parallels the hybrid scenario in the demonic abduction phenomenon,) If there is this same association in scripture, and if the Bear's cubs are, in fact, *Orion & the Pleiades* who function as the *hybrids*, then it would give more credence to Richard's analysis that follows.}}

The bottom line in this analysis is this: if the cubs are represented as hybrids, created by the Fallen Angels, and they need an essential (but bio-chemical) element to sustain themselves, it may answer the puzzling phenomenon behind the cattle mutilations, where certain parts of the cattle (such as eyes, jaw parts, tongue, blood, rectum & sex organs, etc., are excised from the cattle *expertly* and without proper explanation heretofore, and according to Richard, are used to feed the hybrid workers who may be deficient in certain chemicals in their bodies, and they need the cattle parts to sustain themselves. If indeed the hybrid bodies are given life and movement by the evil spirits within the body, (which they cannot afford to rot completely,) so they must be maintained physically, and if not possessed by this same evil spirit, would not have life movement. {{This seems to revolve around DNA mixing and cloning, and therefore, *how evil spirit and flesh may conjoin,* which, of course, would reflect yet another transgression from the law of God.}}

As to the Biblical phrase mentioned above, Can you bring forth the constellations in their seasons? Richard has the following observation, again, using his *key word* approach to understanding these phrases from scripture:

Bring in general is to "lead or force, persuade or induce." *Forth* in general (obsolete) is "away from a specified place" (or time.) 'Forth' in Greek (exo) means "outside of their habitat, territory."

Constellations (astron) is "an arbitrary formation of stars" & in Latin (stella) which means "star;" it is also symbolic of "Fallen Angels." In their *seasons* represent "a specified period of time – a recurrent period. " (Is this a specified time period that comes up periodically where the human abductions take place?)

Repeating the reference to Job 38:31: Remember the beautiful Pleiades[?] where *beautiful* in Greek means "seasons" (horaios) as mentioned before. It is also used "as the outward appearance of whitened sepulchers in contrast to the corruption within — (within the constellations, of which the Bear, Orion & the Pleiades are at the forefront.) *Whitened sepulchers* mean "evil people," or in this case (evil creatures such as *Grays & Reptilians*) as part of the Fallen Angels within. {{One may recall that Jesus referred to the Scribes & Pharisees in the New Testament in the same way, since, although looking fine and 'beautiful' on the outside (**like the *Pleiades*,**) within are full of dead men's bones and all corruption! Perhaps when the author of the *Job* scripture used the **coded** word 'beautiful' for the Pleiades, he meant exactly what Richard had surmised! I remember vividly illustrating the example of Semjase (allegedly from the Pleiades,) giving spurious information to Billy Meier, as observed by Richard Thompson in his book, *ALIEN IDENTITIES*, and mentioned preciously, *emphasized again with the Jim Marrs' reference to the same.* Perhaps Richard is not overstating the case, as we try to connect the **astrological** dots between Biblical references and Ufological folk stories.}}

THE LIVING BEAST: HOW DOES IT FUNCTION?

{{It is our contention that there was no coincidence that The Holy Bible mentions certain constellations in Job and elsewhere, and that there is a very good reason that these areas are **bound** since these are the *temporary* holding pens for angels who have transgressed the laws of God, and must suffer the consequences of their actions. *The Book of Enoch* has laid out very specifically this scenario, so when we try to connect the dots of Ufology & Astrology

THE CURS-ED NET

with the Biblical story, it slowly begins to make a certain sense, provided one can agree that there is a loving powerful God whose children include both angels & men, and that all had been or are being tested to see exactly where His children stand when it comes to doing the will of the Father. *The Living Beast* did not fair too well, so both he & his companions have been thrust into this **curs-ed net** and now wish to do battle with men, so as to claim mankind for his body and soul property; even the aforementioned J.R.R. Tolkien pictured in his writings the *Elves* as God's first children, who were to administer to men (**Watchers over**) so in his "fiction," the *Orcs* (as the fallen elves) might take on a new dimension of meaning; cf. *THE SILMARILLION*, for details. Go to the Internet link for a summary of this most fascinating book @ http://www.indepthinfo. com/tolkien/sil.shtml

To repeat a previous speculation on my part, I became enamored with the idea that both Tolkien as well as the first translator of the *Ethiopian* Book of Enoch, (Hebrew scholar, Richard Laurence,) hailed from the same English university, Oxford, (and not too many years apart,) so it would not be surprising to me, despite the fact that Tolkien was a good Roman Catholic, that he would have been aware of this scholarly translation, and – perhaps - incorporated some of Enoch's prophecies and knowledge of the Fallen Angels into his own "fiction" where he could get his metaphorical ideas into public consciousness without incurring the wrath of his church. After all, MAN was described as a secondary creation by God, just as *Iluvatar* was depicted creating both the Elves & MAN within the framework of Tolkien's masterpiece, popularized in "THE LORD OF THE RINGS" trilogy, which was published before *The Silmarillion*, which only came out after Tolkien died, and published by his son.}}

Richard uses Job 9:9, to draw the portrait thusly:

"God is the maker of the Bear and Orion, the Pleiades and the constellation of the South." *South* in Greek is (notos) meaning "a region." *Region* in Greek is (chora) and has the sense of "a space lying between two limits;" for regions beyond, see 'part.' *Part* in Greek is (meros) which means "a portion." 'Limit,' – for limit, see define.' *Define* (horizo) is in English 'horizon,' and in Greek primarily "to

THE CURS-ED NET

mark out the boundaries of a place, to appoint." *Appoint* in general is "to arrange, to prescribe."

Horizon in Greek means "a limiting (circle,) a boundary." It signifies territory. Boundary in general is "a border." The Pleiades is located in the constellation TAURUS, in the northern hemisphere. ORION is a constellation located in the celestial equator near GEMINI & TAURUS. ZETA RETICULUM consists of Zeta Reticuli 1 & Zeta Reticuli 2, and is a constellation in the *southern* hemisphere. Latin for Reticulum is (of rete,) or **net**. 'Reticulum' in general is a netlike formation. {{'Net' is the English constellation name of the Latin Reticulum according to the aforementioned *THE STARS* astrological reference book.}}

'Net' in Greek is (diktuon.) A general term for a 'net' (from an old verb diko) is "to cast". The Greek (diskos) is *disk* in English or a circular object (the UFO.) 'Net' in general is something that entraps you — a snare. In general, it is "to fish for or to catch" and *catch* means "to capture or seize, and also a stroke, as in to strike" (and also as in abduction.) *Zeta* is the sixth letter of the Greek alphabet & is of Phoenician origin. (The **giants** also settled in Phoenicia.)

Now *six* in Greek is "hex" and likewise in English. *Hex* in general is "a curse." The German (Hexe) is "a witch," which is "to bewitch." *Bewitch* in general here is "to captivate completely, entrance." *Captivate* is "to attract by charm – beauty or excellence," and (archaic) means "to capture" as in a Latin prisoner. *Entrance* is "to enter, a means or point in which to enter."

The word *hemisphere* means "a half of sphere" (circle), and if we refer back to the word 'horizon,' it means "a limiting circle or half of sphere; hemisphere is a limited circle or boundary."

{{At this point, Richard introduces the name *Diana* — the virgin goddess of hunting, childbirth, and is associated with the moon; if you recall, the name ***Ishtar*** came up as a footnote of the Jeremiah quote in the beginning of this chapter, and she and Diana are one and the same – as a *queen of heaven*. This "lovely" lady plays a rather large role in astrological circles, and was the center of the Whitley Strieber nightmare if you recall the Texe Marrs citation mentioned previously.}} According to Richard, 'hunting' = "abductions," 'childbirth' = "hybrids, implantations," and the moon represents the

THE CURS-ED NET

crescent's two horns, which refer to the northern and southern hemispheres of the **Zodiac.** {{This *Zodiac* will be discussed in full later in this chapter.}}

One of the meanings of the word *moon* in general is "a crescent-shaped" where a crescent is a limited circle. *Hunting* involves the use of the net, where 'childbirth' — the catch, is the product of the prey which has been abducted and implanted. The Moon refers to the limiting circles (or the boundaries of *the Zodiac*.) *Moon* also has a meaning (selene) from (selas) which is "brightness." The Hebrew words are (yareach,) "wandering" & (lebanah) "white." Richard sums it up thusly: bright-white-wandering disks are UFOs, while remembering 'net' in Greek is (diskos) for disk! {{Certainly these connecting dots are not just coincidence, are they?}}

Now *the Zodiac* is divided into twelve equal parts called signs. *Sign* in Greek (semeion) is "an indication, a token of that which distinguishes a person or thing;" also, a sign may be a warning or admonition by Satan through his special agents (as in 2Thess. 2:19) of tokens "portending future" events (serving as an omen & by indicating by prediction of horoscopes!)

Token = (endeixis) which reflects a "pointing out," and (endeigma) which indicates a token (sign) as acknowledged by those referred to. (Endeixis) points more especially to the inherent veracity of the token (sign.)

Veracity is "the adherence to the truth — a conformity to the truth or fact;" in Latin it means "true." *Indication* is "a sign" where 'indicate' is "to show the way or direction of; to point out." In Latin it is (indicater.)

Thus, *the Zodiac* is an indicator, an index, a dial of twelve signs which (represent the actions and character of a living creature or beast & is symbolic in their meanings through these signs of those who inhabit the constellations.) *Show* in Greek (logos) means "a reputation" — (but what type of a reputation do these signs expose?) A *reputation* is "a specific characteristic or trait." Let's look now at each individual sign in *the Zodiac* to find out.

DIAGNOSING THE ZODIAC SIGNS

{{Richard & I both agreed that *the Zodiac* had to be a large part of **THE *CURS*-ED NET** for the simple reason that not a few people seemed to be influenced by astrology — of which the Zodiac is the chief segue into…so…there must be a causal connection between it and the Fallen Angels, since it is these very beings who were the instruments of giving "knowledge of the stars, signs, and astrology" to man; refer to 1 Enoch 8:5-7 for details. This also seems to answer the question of how mankind became so knowledgeable about these matters, since it would have taken man quite a long time to figure out things like the "precession of the equinox." If you go to the Internet web page, http://inspectorblebeau.pbwiki.com/COSMOLOGY-THE-BIBLE-AND-WORLD-MYTHS you will get some idea from my book review of Paul Laviolette's book (*EARTH UNDER FIRE*,) just how complicated this subject really is, and how hard it would have been for man to gain knowledge of his galaxy without some form of help — which Enoch is suggesting man did receive!

Another Internet web page actually discusses some of the ideas we are addressing in this chapter; go to http://inspectorblebeau. pbwiki.com/CONSTELLATIONS-and-ZODIAC-FACADES-for-SATAN In this report, based on a book written by Texe Marrs, (the same man that "fingered" Whitley Strieber's connection to *queen of heaven Ishtar*,) addresses the *lures* of the **New Age** thinking, embossed within **the Zodiac**, especially in "THE GREAT BEAR," "VIRGO" and the Mother Goddess, THE SUN GOD (**Ba'al**,) as well as other pagan & Satanic symbols ensconced within this same zodiac. This is a very revealing book review of just what is wrong with *New Age thinking*!}}

Richard starts this section of the chapter off by reminding us that if we truly want a relationship with the Father & Jesus, His Son, we **cannot** rely on these false & deceiving signs in any way, shape or form. He punctuates this point by quoting 2 Kings 22:19 NIV (or 4 Kings in the Catholic Bible):

"Because your heart was responsive and you humbled your-self before the Lord when you heard what I have spoken against this place and its people, that they would become accursed and laid

THE CURS-ED NET

waste, and because you tore your robes and wept in my presence, I have heard you, declares the Lord."

(This place, *Temple,* was full of idols to Baal & evil worship of Satan, just like today can refer to those things around us which are **not of God** and that which God teaches us in the Bible to refrain from.) {{Today, our *Godless* TV may, in fact, be the *new temple* of loose moral seduction & degradation. Be careful! Be selective! Understand that the *New Age* temples are probably in almost every home, *crouching* like lion-snares — patiently waiting to pour out its poison upon its unsuspecting victims. Does that make all TV programming bad? Of course not...but by being spiritually discerning, especially with young children in the domicile, you will not have reneged on your responsibility to be good parents, both for their sakes as well as your own.}}

In a Bible note from the NIV LIFE & SPIRIT BIBLE: Regarding the above quote, Josiah pleased God because he humbled himself before the Lord. Humbling one's self before God is a primary condition for becoming renewed and receiving God's grace. It involves

1) Believing in God's judgments toward us are right and just, in accordance with what we deserve.
2) Knowing that we, without His grace, are captive to sin and evil, and that we are dependent on Him for all good (Pr 3:7, Romans 12:3, & 1Cor. 1:4.
3) Having a contrite heart before God because of our spiritually poor condition (Ps 51:17; Lev. 26:40-41; Num. 12:3.)
4) Fearing God's word with deep sincerity.

We also see in 2 Kings 23:5 NIV, the following:

"He did away with the pagan priests appointed by the kings of Judah to burn incense on the high places of the towns of Judah and on those around Jerusalem — those who burned incense to Baal, to the Sun and the Moon, to the constellations " (as **Zodiac** signs.)

{{Although I mentioned this Biblical verse in the beginning, it may be instructive to quote it in full at this juncture, **confirming** the Bible's extreme caution to us about honoring and adoring these false signs:

THE CURS-ED NET

"And when you look up to the heavens and behold the Sun or the Moon or **any** star among the heavenly hosts, do not be led astray into adoring them and serving them" (Deut. 4:19.) WHAT COULD BE *CLEARER* THAN THIS – if you believe The Bible as being true! I might add here that this is the reason for doing this book: We must have no doubt that there is a seductive influencing evil being perpetrated upon man to worship false gods (even unwittingly) but tragically causing a major offense against the ALMIGHTY FATHER! This *curs*-ed net is cursed in more ways than one. BEWARE! Incidentally, I found a clue within this above-cited verse in scripture that I will be commenting on *at the end of the book* that may very well be germane to this entire thesis of Richard's.

We have mentioned in more than one place the importance of 1 *Enoch*, chapter eight. Now Richard addresses this key chapter in full, as part of being aware of the pitfalls of astrology, and how the fallen ones were chiefly responsible for the root of this trap.}}

Seven of the angels who fell, came down and had relations with the daughters of men, which produced *the Giants*. These seven mentioned below are responsible for man knowing the deceiving evil teachings that encompasses many things plus the intricacies of *the Zodiac*. Here is the reading of this chapter from the *Ethiopian* Book of Enoch:

VERSE 1: Moreover Azazyel (one of the seven) taught men to make swords, knives, shields, breastplates, the fabrications of mirrors, and the workmanship of bracelets and ornaments, the use of paint, the beautifying of the eyebrows, (makeup) the use of stones of every valuable and select kind (jewelry) and all sorts of dyes, so that the world became altered.

VERSE 2: Impiety increased; fornication multiplied; and they transgressed and corrupted all their ways.

VERSE 3: "Amazarak" (another angel) taught all the sorcerers, and dividers of roots;

VERSE 4: "Armers" (another angel) taught the solution of sorcery;

VERSE 5: "Barkayal" (another angel) taught the observers of the stars. (*astrology*)

VERSE 6: "Akibeel" (another angel) taught the signs; (*the Zodiac*)

VERSE 7: "Tamiel" (another angel) taught astronomy;

VERSE 8: And "Asaradel" (another angel) taught the motion of the moon. (*serpentine*)

VERSE 9: And men, being destroyed, cried out; and their voices reached to heaven.

(All these things mentioned above many of us use in our daily lives, not knowing their beginnings. They came on the foundation of the teachings of the Fallen Angels to deceive man long before the true teaching came from the Son of God, Jesus Christ. So how much harder then is it to believe the truth? Yet, it was promised to us: *search for the truth with all your heart and mind and soul and with your whole strength~~ and you will find it*!)

{{SPECIAL NOTE: The above information is so important for our understanding that an actual curse was put on *The Book of Enoch* by a certain rabbi in the second century, so Jews would not have access to it, or reflect on its very importance. The rabbi's name was Rabbi Simeon ben Jochai. My question was & remains: was he the embodiment of yet another fallen angel, knowing the root of this very evil and trying to hide it from the people by *falsely* putting a curse on it? That's what it looks like to me based on the suggested data in this research!}}

THE SIGNS OF THE ZODIAC

1) PISCES: This means *fish* and in Greek (ichthudion) is a "little fish." (Mikeos) is of "little rank or station" or (low rank in position.) *Catch* in Greek (harpazo) is "to snatch or catch away." (Agreuo) in Greek is to "take by hunting." (Piazo) is "to capture." (Zogreo) is "to take alive."

So we have little fish (whom I associate with *the Grays*) of low rank in position, out hunting to capture, and snatch (alive) people chosen as abductees. If we look at the word *toil*, in general it is a "snare, an entrapment" and in (archaic) means "a net for trapping;" the Latin (tela) = web. (A net is used to capture alive.) 'Toil' in Greek in reference to capture as above, in symbolism is (basanizo) or "to put to the test," & "to examine by torture."

To *test* in general is "to evaluate and to determine a quality form; to test or check the condition of;" see 'exact.' The word *exact* (in relative meaning) is "to obtain by or as if by force."

POTENTIAL SCENARIO AS ENVISIONED BY RICHARD: The abductee is on the table. The reason for the examination is to seek out specific qualities that each person can contribute, regarding either tissue or DNA. *Obtain* here means "how this evaluation is conducted" (by surgical instruments,) i.e., "to examine by torture." *Torture* in Greek (tumpanizo) is "to beat" and *beat* in Greek (dero) is from the root (der) — 'skin' or primarily "to flay." *Flay* in general is "to strip off the skin or outer covering of" (as in 'scoop marks?') {{It is true, based on my research, that abductees who have undergone regressive hypnosis have found an *"unexplained"* piece of their outer skin missing on some part of their body; the culprits of these procedures are invariably *the Grays,* which is well known in the data surrounding the subject of Ufology. This usually takes the form of a "scoop mark" which looks like a small crater in the skin; a picture of just such a mark appears in Raymond Fowler's book, *THE WATCHERS II,* where he displays the *scoop mark* from his own leg, on the calf portion."}}

2) LIBRA: *Scales* in general is a plate-like covering that forms around fish and reptiles. 'Scale' also is a progressive classification as of rank & size. 'Scale' in Greek (lepis) from (lepo) means "to peel" which is "to strip or cut away" (enforcing the word 'obtain' earlier as of using surgical instruments above "to cut — to flay skin — to receive the so-called 'scoop marks.')

Regarding 'scales' in the zodiac, a sign shows the scales that are symbolic of the fish and reptiles, (i.e., *the Grays & the Reptilians.* **The Grays** have the <u>lower</u> rank as per (micros) mentioned earlier from the Greek; *the Reptilians* have a <u>higher</u> rank & size, under the word 'scale.') Another meaning of the word 'scale' here is "to weigh" which means "to evaluate" or "to choose carefully" as mentioned earlier regarding the citation "putting to the test & examining by torture." *Weigh* also means "to burden" which in Greek (baros) is "a pressing." The word *press* in Greek is (thlibo) & says to see the word 'afflict,' which in Greek is (kakopatheo) from (kakos) and means "evil."

THE CURS-ED NET

(So it seems that the test & examination become an infliction of evil!) *Evil* in Greek stands for (kakos) meaning "whatever is evil in character," "in distinction," (wherever the distinction is observable;) see the word 'base.' (The distinction of the evil characters that are observed here are *the Grays & Reptilians* in character as aliens but in reality as portrayed by fallen angels and their legion of helpers.)

The word *base* in Greek (agenes) is "of low birth" — "a negative race." (*The Grays & Reptilians* were a **created race of hybrids** (the descriptions of *low birth* and (by the usage of the word *negative, reflects* here that it is indicating to be a **false race** "not created or brought forth by God!") The word 'evil' in Greek (pomperos) also is defined as "what is evil in influence and effect, malignant." (They deceive you by the effect of influence through their appearance, and with malignant birth, theirs are a **cancerous seed** sown by & through implants.)

3) CANCER: This sign is symbolized by the *crab* and is indicative of a shellfish. This word is symbolic of "little shellfish" that is a little fish (**Grays**) with a shell. *Shell* represents the evil in character (***a costume shell***) or living tissue costume worn (while possessed by Fallen Angels.)

Cancer is "any malignant neoplasm" (an abnormal growth.) *Hybrids* reflect a pathological condition characterized by malignant neoplasm. They are shells of living tissue being grown through implants by Fallen Angels, portraying the very ('aliens') they are creating. It is to **deceive mankind** that 'aliens' are shown to exist & also have the ability to interact with man and act out their deception as real as is possible. All of this contributes to the final agenda. The 'scales' would represent having two malignant growths: *the Grays & the Reptilians*! (The shellfish are shells created for and as costumes of living tissue, representing symbolically both fish & reptiles.

Crab also has a meaning in general of "to interfere with or ruin." *Ruin* is a physical disintegration. In Greek 'ruin' is (rhegma) which is akin to (rhegnumi) "to break." *Break* in Greek (parabasis) is "a transgression," and 'break' metaphorically (ekklao) "off" which is "of branches." *Branch* (klados) from (klao) is "broken off for grafting." *Graft* (enkentrizo) is "to graft in" (kentrizo) which means

206

THE CURS-ED NET

"an insertion." *Engrafted* (emphutos) is an adjective derived from (emphuo) which means "to implant."

Implantations of the female fetus eventually bears the hybrid fruit: the Grays (fish) & *Reptilians* (reptiles) as living tissue **worker drone** costumes to be possessed by Fallen Angels.

4) AQUARIUS: *Water* in Hebrew is (mayim).) Gen. 1:7 reflects "the waters above and below…" In Exodus 20:4, "the expanse of the heavens…" as space atmosphere. (This seems to be symbolic of the **scales** as both fish & reptile swim in water, but *the Grays & Reptilian* come from **_another type of water_**: the expanse of space as they travel through **_their_** water!) {{Think of the expanse of space as the ocean of the universe, and the galaxies as island continents, and then the symbolism is aptly complete.}}

From *Vine's*, *water* is also used figuratively as of "oppression & affliction." (Mayim) symbolized both danger & distress. The word is used to picture something impetuous, violent and overwhelming. (An impetuous *imp* is "a small demon" or "mischievous child" while [obsolete] means "a graft" as to implant; also, Middle English is (impe,) where [scion, sprig,] as offspring.) Continuing from *over-whelming* it reads: terrors take hold of him (the terror of forceful sights) as waters, a tempest stealth him away (abduct) in the night; see the word 'amaze.'

Before we review 'amaze,' let us look at *tempest* in Greek; it is (thuella) which is a "whirlwind" — akin to (thuo) is "to slay." A whirlwind, a rapidly moving force is an apt description of (A UFO!) 'Tempest' in Latin is (tempesta,) variant of Latin (tempestas < tempus, or "time."

Amazement in Greek is (ekstasis) which, according to *Vine's*, is "a reference to the mind, or an alteration of the normal condition, a state of fear, being transported out of your natural state as in falling into a trance." (This involves the above-mentioned **_tempest with 'missing time'_**.) A *trance* is what you are put in, through the use of the rod or "goad" which was discussed previously. In *Vine's*, 'trance' is "ordinary consciousness & perception of natural circum stances being withheld, while the soul is susceptible to whatever they choose to *emotionally* implant into your mind." Through certain

THE CURS-ED NET

impulses to your brain, they also strike with *paralysis*, the inability to move. All this is done through this trance.

5) SCORPIO: *Scorpion* in Greek is (skorpios) which means "to scatter." This in Greek is (skorpizo) and (diaspeiro) "to scatter abroad;" also we have (speiro) which is "to sow seeds."

'Scatter' in general is "to cause to disperse," "to occur at widely spaced intervals," & "to separate and go in different directions." *Abroad* in general reflects "being in circulation, covering a large area, widely." *Sow* in general is "to scatter (seed) or to impregnate (a growing medium) with seed; to disseminate." *Impregnate* in general is "to fertilize." *Disseminate* in general is "to scatter widely, as in sowing seed, to cover."

This whole process can involve the abduction of females, covering the Earth, and implanting them, (where females are the growing medium.) Impregnated abductees are chosen all over the planet. Scattering could also involve UFOs that have the ability to separate and go in different directions.

6) VIRGO: *Virgin* (zool) "is an animal (female) that has not copulated, & also could be an insect that produces fertilized eggs without copulating" (i.e., joining together.) Incidentally, **Grays** have been known to be called insect-looking aliens. {{The best evidence of this is from Raymond Fowler's book, ***THE ALLAGASH ABDUCTION***, where the beings that allegedly abducted the four men out of a canoe and transported them to some type of *sphere-like UFO*, did indeed, when one of the Weiner brothers drew a picture of it, it looked like some type of walking-talking ***insectoid***, similar to a grasshopper, although their method of communication was through some sort of "mind melding;" cf. book for pictures & explanations into this most bizarre case, as noted in *UFO* & OTHER BOOK & ARTICLE REFERENCES.}}

Through implantation, a woman becomes pregnant without prior intercourse, or what could be described as a *virgin pregnancy!*" The female, through the implantation becomes "pregnant," yet she is still a virgin while not knowing that after about **eight weeks or so,** the fetus is taken. The insects (mentioned above) symbolize *the Grays* who impregnate the female without copulating. {{This also seemed to have happened to Kim Carlsberg, as was indicated in her

THE CURS-ED NET

book, ***BEYOND MY WILDEST DREAMS***," which was discussed previously.}}

If we look at the word *clone*, it states "an organism descended asexually from a single ancestor, & is a replica of the DNA sequence." The female is implanted with DNA mixed with a male's sperm. The DNA here is that of the hybrid *Gray* as they are cloned; they then become the **ancestors.** {{A very bizarre series of conversations occurred between Karla Turner and her *alien* interfacing entities (that reminded her of insects, especially the "mother" dream she had [p.18 of ***INTO THE FRINGE***,] as well as other visions of "gray shadow-like people about five foot tall" who said that they were her *ancestors*; elsewhere, on pages 205 & 218 of Karla's same book, her *roots* come up again that deal with pockets of information that were put inside of her (for future use) and they informed her that they — too — were her *ancestors.* Karla died of breast cancer by 1997, so whatever "pockets" of secrets locked inside of her, (to my knowledge) have not surfaced as or yet.}}

Now *asexual* is "having no evident sex organs – sexless" (as *the Grays* are!) This also relates to reproduction without the union of male & female gametes, as in binary fission. Earlier we explained the meaning of the word virgin as hybrids that are being cloned from each other, by their DNA being implanted into the female human. The female remains a virgin, yet was impregnated and the insect (*Grays*) implantation process is the fertilized egg without copulation.

7) ARIES: *Ram* in Hebrew is ('ayil.) Many passages use ('ayil) as a figure for despots (rulers) or ***mighty men*** as in the famous **Genesis 6:4.** The '*mighty men'* mentioned here, refer to the **sons of God** who were the **angels that fell** (or were thrown down) from their first estate (Jude 1:6.) Not all Fallen Angels are bound in the abyss; many are allowed to work with Satan in this world. {{This has actually been documented in *The Book of Jubilees,* chapter X, keeping in mind that (like *The Book of Enoch,*) it is not considered a canonical book.}}

In *The Book of Job*, (1:6 & 2:1,) the phrase, *the sons of God*, are used for angelic or non-human beings. *Mighty* has a meaning of "great power, skill, & strength in size, degree or extent." The word *skill* here shows that they are very good in what they do with art

THE CURS-ED NET

of proficiency, experience, technique & ability. These attributes are adapted to their evil character to obtain their goal for which <u>we</u> are the guinea pigs, so to speak.

Remember the *despots* above meaning "ruler as in despotism," and is a "governmental system in which this ruler exercises absolute power — a state so ruled." Territorial and political units (constellations?) composed of a federation under a government would be an apt description.

'Despots' in Greek is "a master." 'Ruler' in Greek (**archon**) is "a chief or prince," & is translated *rulers* (plural.) (So it seems that we have here by the use of the word *Aries (Ram)* — a reference to a body — a government of Fallen Angels with one specific ruler, who seems to rule a territory consisting of units [i.e., constituents who make up a whole, such as the constellations of the zodiac, for example.] The specific ruler here is none other than *Satan* himself!)

The word *Prince* above (archon) is mentioned in the title: "the prince of the power of the air" (Eph. 2:2.) This title is no coincidence; it states that he, *Satan*, is the **ruler of the air**. (In Greek [aer] signifies "the atmosphere," & in Latin (sphere) while ouranos denotes the heaven, which also refers to the "aerial heavens," or space. So this Latin 'sphere' as just indicated could well be connected to *the Zodiac* which itself is made up of the northern & southern hemispheres.) {{Richard seems to be saying that Satan, then, is, in fact, the ruler of *the Zodiac* (as we understand the symbolism,) as part of his "ruler-ship" as the designated *prince of the air* alluded to in Paul's epistle to the Ephesians; therefore, if true, the *curs*-ed net is being tightened and focused on in such a way as to clearly put forth a thesis about Satan's full *NET*work of operations, which, if correct, would project as one of its functions the **ensnaring of mankind as part of its "catch,"** ~~ **perhaps!** After all, in this same epistle, (6:12) there is a highly characterized description of this very ordered hierarchy of evil.}}

The word *master* mentioned earlier with the Greek (didaskalos) means "a teacher;" see Jude 5, NIV, where the title is referred to as "the doom of the false teachers." Those who have left their first estate — (these Fallen Angels,) are those false teachers mentioned in Jude! 'Master' also in Greek is (kurios) — "a lord;" see the word 'dominion.' *Ruler* in Hebrew says "to rule" (masal) which is "to rule, reign, to have dominion." (So I believe these Fallen Angels are inhabiting the **twelve constellations** which make up the **Zodiac**, but only the top-ranking ones, where each constellation has a specific Fallen Angel as its ruler, and includes Satan as the chief ruler over all.) {{If we were to view Richard's construct as a *perception* "of space" and not merely a "place per se," I think we could grasp the importance of why the Bible is warning us not to be swayed or seduced (trapped) into either honoring or serving the sun or moon or ANY star (Deut. 4:19;) we must remember that constellations (groups of stars where dot connecting gives ***impressions*** of men or animals (like Sagittarius — the archer, or Taurus — the bull,) are just that — perceptions! These *perceptions* however, were taught to men by these same aforementioned Fallen Angels (as per 1 Enoch 8,) and therefore would be symbolically more accurately cast as a *fisherman's lure* to trap unwary souls/spirits into the NET OF OBLIVION — and eventual death, but the symbolism is no less real. As St. Peter had warned in his epistle: Satan does go about like a roaring lion, looking for those of whom he could devour! THE BOTTOM LINE: Regardless of how you deal with Richard's ideas, they should be taken seriously. I will have a final comment about this Deuteronomy citation at the end of the final chapter.

Finishing up with THE RAM, Richard offers one more observation:}}

The word *sphere* has the meaning of "the sky, appearing as a hemisphere to an observer." It also means "an area of power, control & influence, or in short – a domain to surround or encompass." {{Is this what THE *CURS'*-ED NET is doing or trying to do to us all?!?}}

8) TAURUS: *The Bull* represents a male, strong & fearsome, a beast often used as symbols. In Hebrew, *bullock* (par) means "young bulls," (that we have linked to the Fallen Angels or evil spirits.) In Psalm 22:12, the word is used to describe "fierce, strong enemies." {{This would be Ps. 21:13 in the *Catholic* Bible.}}

Enemy in Greek (echthros) is akin to (echthos) reflecting the idea of "hate" & associated with (ektos) or "outside" (as in atmosphere or space.) In the active sense, it denotes *hostile*, a noun used here signifying an "enemy" or "adversary," and is said *of the devil* as in Matt. 13:39, as well as Luke 10:19; it is also used of *men* opposed to Christ, as in Matt 13:25 & Mark 12:36. (If we look at Jude 12, these false teachers, the Fallen Angels as alluded to before, they are used figuratively as men! {{Even in my own *Confraternity Catholic Bible,*" in a <u>footnote</u> regarding Jude 8, these same *men* are "understood as referring to the (evil) angels."}}

(We have *The Bull* as strong, fierce, and represented as young males, (Fallen Angels who came from the outside not of this Earth, being hostile, and associated with Satan.) *The Bull,* I believe, represents the Fallen Angels — evil spirits who make up the body of the Beast!) {{This, of course, would be *The Living Beast* that encompasses the whole of THE *CURS*-ED NET, which would be the '*NET*work' of SATAN, INCORPORATED!}}

THE TAURUS CONNECTION

[This *sign* is reviewed by co-author LeBeau:]

{{Another solar system within the constellation of Taurus is Aldebaran {{and known as *"follower of the Pleiades."*}} Similar to the Pleiades (also in Taurus,) it plays a part in the *ET SAGA* as expressed by author Dr. Michael Salla. Writing in Volume Three of *The UNIVERSAL SEDUCTION,* subtitled, *Piercing the Veils of Deception,* by collective author Angelico Tapestra, Salla claims that the Nazis had an occult connection with an ET group from Aldebaran via the *Vril Society*, which was allegedly *channeling messages* from this star system; this society actually (according to Salla) were planning to develop a craft that could make physical contact with the civilization there. Back on Earth, another Nazi group called the *Thule Society* claimed to be *communicating* with an advanced human race with Nordic features from an ancient Earth civilization that inhabited subterranean territories that were accessible from the Polar Regions and other secluded areas around the planet. According to Salla, Admiral Byrd ran into a group of subterranean Nordics, who said that their land was called ARIANNI. Of course the close relationship to the word 'aryan' or arian' meaning non-Jewish or Caucasian, related to Nordic, revolving around the gods of the Nazi occult, seem too coincidental to be coincidence;

THE CURS-ED NET

another tidbit revolves around the word 'ari' which, in the Gnostic tradition means LION TRADITION and since Satan is associated with a *roaring lion*, and since *el'* means a god, then *ariel* would translate as ___the lion god___...so for a "race of Nordics" to tell Byrd that their land is called the Arianni, gives more meaning to who Byrd may have really met ~ not ETs, but *Satan Inc.*.

Continuing on, as I read this series of disclosures in this essay called, *Foundations for Globally Managing Extraterrestrial Affairs*,, from Dr. Salla (who has a PhD in Government from the University of Queensland, Australia, as well as an MA in Philosophy from the University of Melbourne, Australia, and is an author of a book plus seventy article, chapters and book reviews on peace, ethnic conflict and conflict resolution,) it became obvious to me that even though Dr. Salla is presenting the ET disclosures in a historical framework where the mighty powers of the world, including THE U.S., BRITAIN, RUSSIA, CHINA AND FRANCE, have recognized that Nazi Germany had *occult contact* with "ETs" prior to WW II, they were so disturbed by the potential of the Nazis, that they sent Admiral Byrd to Antarctica (1946-47) to eliminate the final Nazi threat, but could not do so because of their connection to this same ET force, from *allegedly* Aldebaran, etc., and had gotten a fundamentally sophisticated group of flying machines (UFOs) that could function in a way as to keep Byrd's forces at bay! [According to Salla's information, Byrd had a forces of some 4700 men, including ships and an aircraft carrier, but within eight weeks of engagement in and around Antarctica, he had to turn back; Chilean journalists had been given certain information by Byrd himself, but needless to say, these anecdotal stories were buried in the annals of history because of the reasons given by Dr. Salla in his essay.]

If you read *this* essay carefully, you will be **able to substitute** *demonic forces* for **ET** FORCES, if, for no other reason, the *only* way the Nazis had of contacting these evil forces were through *occult contact*! [CLUE?] The situation had not been resolved by the end of this 2003 essay published report, and I dare say, *will not* until the dynamics of *The Book of Revelation* has been fully played out! It should not be surprising that these connections came about

THE CURS-ED NET

due to "psychic expeditions" to places like Tibet, Antarctica, South America, & Iraq, both by the Vril & Thule occult societies (193.)

What the help we were told we were given (spoken by famous rocket scientist Herman Oberth, where he mentioned that it was given by "peoples of other worlds," could very well have been entities from other dimensions (thrown down from their first estate!) This would be a perfect segue *from* Ufology *to* Demonology given the circumstances involved in the **connections** and also given the areas mentioned, i.e., Aldebaran, or an area within the constellation of Taurus — one of the signs of the zodiac that had been condemned by the Bible. The subterranean areas of the Earth would also fit very well the plight of the fallen angels, as per *The Book of Enoch*, so none of Salla's revelations are contradictory to the overall thesis as presented in this present essay of THE *CURS*-ED NET. (We just interpret the data differently! In fact, when I was working with the now deceased Colman Von Keviczky in the 1970s & 1980s regarding the potential world threat to humanity (vis-à-vis the UFO problem,) since he was a military man who had a close connection with Herman Oberth, he could only see the problem as *a potential invasion from the "GALACTIC FORCES" as he so labeled them in his writings and lectures worldwide*. I do not think either factored in just how important *The Book of Enoch* would eventually become in relation to the *fuller understanding of* what constituted the REAL THREAT facing humanity!

As Dr. Salla reported, eventually the U.S. was involved with this *psychic channeling* where a certain Dan Sherman had made contact and had gotten information through similar types of activities; cf. *ABOVE BLACK,* by Sherman for details of this interesting connection.}}

9) GEMINI as *the Twins*: In Greek mythology, Castor & Pollux (Latin) were the sons of Zeus & Leda. They were protectors for the sailors. The Greek word translated as "the Twin Brothers" which are reflected above as Castor & Pollux, and from the KJV, (dioskourois) from (dios) as (kouroi) — the "sons of Zeus." The 'dioscuri' were identified with the constellation GEMINI, the 3rd sign of the Zodiac. They are the two brightest stars in the constellation. According to

ACTS 14:12-13 & 19:35, in Greek mythology, Zeus {{Jupiter in Latin) was the ruler of heaven and the father of the other gods.

(I believe that Zeus is symbolic of Satan and the sons here are symbolic of the sons of the evil one (Satan) as in Matt. 13:38, and the devil of ACTS 13:10. Those who follow Satan as the leader of the Fallen Angels & evil spirits __*become*__ the sons of Zeus also by their very fellowship and allegiance to him.)

{{Richard makes a good point, and since *Astrology honors these gods - –* and tries to get us *to serve them* (by our very participation or recognition of astrology,) it seems apparent that this *lure* is very cleverly disguised, yet very deadly to those who take the bait! And who was the *one doing the fishing,* (when it came to this bait,) by teaching the Astrologers? Cf. again 1 Enoch 8:5, and look for a Fallen Angel called *Barkayal!*}}

10) LEO: *The Lion* in general is "fierce or ferocious." In Greek (leon) is both a title for Satan while indicating allusions of great features, majesty, strength, and indicative of royalty, for both its courage & cruelty. {{I cannot help wondering why The British Empire uses THE LION as its symbol of arms? Is it just coincidence or is there a darker, more sinister linkage? An interesting book that links governmental powers to the dark-side can be found in Jim Marrs's book called, *Rule by SECRECY.*}}

'Lion' acts as an (indirect) reference to the Fallen ones who inhabit these constellations ~~ {{if only symbolically, as alluded to before; however, even if where they inhabit is a 'place' of higher frequency/lower dimension, it is still an area that somehow can access our present reality — therefore giving these beings an *interdimensional ability*, which itself would answer some very perplexing questions in Ufology as well as color in some of the codes seeded in the *Holy Scripture*. To put it succinctly: How *high* is the boundary of their less dense ethereal air? How *low are the bonds of their prison abyss*?}} This 'Lion' must refer to the qualities of their character, but also symbolizes Satan as their chief ruler. {{Again, is it merely coincidence that the very symbol chosen for a part of the Zodiac is exactly the term St. Peter used to describe Satan, and what his function is as noted previously? *Absolutely not!*}}

THE CURS-ED NET

Fierce means "violent nature, terrible;" *ferocious* is "savage and unrelenting." *Strength* (as in having supernatural power) *is* their source of power. *Courage, cruelty & majesty* are all symbolic of those who inhabit **the Zodiac** *where dwells* the Fallen Angels and Satan. {{One may view *this* Zodiac as a very large part of a very dark *NET*work.}}

11) CAPRICORN: **The Horn** in general has a meaning of "either ends of a crescent moon" (which in itself reflects the meaning of a limited circle such as a hemisphere.) The two ends refer to the northern and southern hemispheres. This marks out a **large portion** of the Fallen Angels' **second** estate, as far as we can determine.

'Horn' also is "to join without being invited; to intrude." *Intrude* means "to force in; to enter as improper or unwanted element." In Latin it is "to thrust in." *Thrust* is "to force on an unwilling recipient;" (archaic) is "to pierce." *Pierce* in Greek (nusso) is "to inflict severe or deadly wounds." While (peripeiro) in Greek is used metaphorically of torturing the soul (1 Tim. 6:10,) *torture* in Greek (tumpanizo) means "to beat" & in Greek (tupto) from the root "tup" is "to smite, strike." Now *smite* in Greek sums it up by (patasso), since (metaphorically) it reflects "judgment & also ___the infliction of a disease by an angel ___with plagues to be inflicted." *Plague* is "a (curse;)" please refer back to **the flying scroll,** which emphasizes this curse in scripture.

12) SAGITTARIUS: **Archer** in general is "one that shoots with a bow & arrow." A *bow* is "a bent, curved or arched object." The word **arch** means chief— highest or ruler. The *ruler* in Greek (**archon**) is translated as "rulers." (We see a reference to this in II Enoch 4 [*The Book of the Secrets of Enoch,,*] with the angels ruling the stars.) Does this mean that there are angels as rulers or part of a counsel of sorts, which rule the Zodiac or sections of constellations? In Rev. 6:2, the white horse's rider holds a bow and is given a crown. This rider, in my opinion as cited below, refers to the **antichrist**. So this sign of Sagittarius could also very much represent the **_coming of_** the Antichrist. 'Sagittarius' from the Latin (sagitta) besides meaning arrow, also "refers to the Antichrist himself, who during the second part of the Tribulation period, becomes a world ruler as in the above (archon) for *ruler."*

HOW the ORION CONSTELLATION FITS within *THE NET:*

The Symbolism of Orion's "Club, Sword & Shield" within Holy Scripture

{{INTRODUCTION: As a Ufologist, reading & studying about the UFO & related phenomena for the last few decades, I was frankly puzzled why only certain constellations seemed to be singled out as to the **_home_** of the alleged ETs, and Orion, along with the Pleiades & Zeta Reticulum, seemed to take top billing. Why had **The Holy Bible** cited & seemingly singled out these very same constellations or parts thereof, especially giving mention to Orion & the Pleiades, as cited in the previous sections? Shortly, I will give specific references to this otherwise coincidental phenomenon, especially as it relates to the brightest star group in Orion, called **_Rigel._** Richard will confine himself to what can be gleaned from the prophets Job & Amos, below.

A NOTE ABOUT ORION: This constellation, according to the aforementioned **_THE STARS_** astronomical reference book, indeed pictures Orion as a hunter with the above-mentioned **_club, sword & shield_**, which Richard will analyze via his key word approach below. Why is Orion important, since it is **not** one of the constellations of the Zodiac? According to author, H.A. Rey, Orion dominates the southern sky, with its famous **_BELT_**; one other author, in particular, by the name of Robert Bauval, has tried to show that this **_belt of three stars_** is exactly aligned to the formation of the Great Pyramid and its two companion pyramids, (which may or may not be an intriguing side note.) I will briefly touch on Bauval's idea, "THE MYSTERY OF ORION" in my final comments at the end of this present work, based on a video presentation I saw relating to Bauval's ideas.

In any event, **_Orion_** has more bright stars than any other constellation (five) and two of the first magnitude, including Betelgeuse & the aforementioned Rigel, which is *lodged* on the right foot of Orion. This star, Rigel, is 33 times the diameter of our Sun & 20,000 times as luminous, (as per author H.A.Rey,) and this is the particular star we will address shortly, since it is connected with Ufological events and the "beings" that are alleged to hail from there.

THE MYTH SURROUNDING ORION: To understand this myth, we must first discuss the Serpent Holder:

It is allegedly the 13th sign of the Zodiac (***Ophiuchus***) but more importantly, figures in with the myth of Orion. The right arm of this constellation figure (as Voodoo doctor) has the *Serpent's head,* while the left arm holds the dangling *Serpent's tail.* The Serpent Holder **does reach into** the zodiac, yet it is not traditionally counted among the zodiacal figures. As H.A. Rey had noted on page 52 of his book, to speak of the Serpent Holder as a doctor is not a mere whim. The figure is thought to represent Asklepios, Greek god of medicine who can be traced back to the Egyptian *Imhotep* (about 2900 B.C.,) who himself was an eminent physician & architect. As Ray further notes, the Serpent Holder is the only person in the zodiac that represents an historical person.

Asklepios never lost a patient by death. This alarmed Hades, god of the Dead, who feared unemployment, and when Asklepios tried to revive Orion who had been killed by a scorpion, Hades prevailed on his brother Zeus to liquidate Asklepios with a thunderbolt. In recognition of his merits, however, Asklepios was put into the sky as a constellation, together with the scorpion ~~ but far away from Orion to avoid further trouble. Since then, Orion & Scorpion never meet, being on opposite sides of the sky.

Other areas also contain *the Grays* ~~ one made famous in the Betty & Barnie Hill story of the early 1960s regarding Zeta Reticulum; George Andrews seems to concentrate on yet another group of *Grays,* also from the Orion constellation, but from the star system *Rigel.*] In any event, the dots of these inter-related constellations and stars and even planets for that matter (which hold such sway in Ufology, now may take on a more ominous note if looked upon with the eyes of demonic awareness, i.e., *the dynamics of leaving one's estate for another under circumstances that were – not so ideal, to say the least!* The Bible, therefore, may indeed be giving us "coded clues" about this dynamic if we can fit the pieces together carefully.}}

THE BIBLICAL KEY QUOTES FOR THIS SECTION:

"He (God) made the Bear and Orion, the Pleiades and the constellations of the south" (Job 9:9.)

"Have you (Job) fitted a curb to the Pleiades, or loosened the bonds of Orion?

Can you bring forth the Mazzaroth in their season, or guide the Bear with its train" (Job 38:31-32)

THE KEY WORD ANALYSIS OF RICHARD:

Club in general is "a heavy stick thick at one end." It also means "to strike or beat." As per *Nelson's Bible Diet*, a variation of the club is a staff used by shepherds also known as a maul, a heavy long-handled hammer. A *shepherd* is "one who herds, or a herdsman;" *herd* means "to gather or keep," and is also "an owner." 'Herd' in Hebrew is (baqar) which means "herd; cattle."

A shepherd uses a staff; *staff* in Greek is (rhabdos;) see rod. *Rod* (rhabdizo) has the meaning of "to beat;" see 'smite.' 'Rod' as (rhabdos) is "a staff." A 'rod' in general is "a straight piece, bar – a stick – a staff or wand." (Look at the word **goad** that in general is a **long, pointed stick**. {{Does this sound familiar?}}

'Goad' in Greek is (kentron) from (kenteo) "to prick" which denotes "a sting." *Prick* in Greek is (katanusso) which primarily means "to strike or stun." *To strike* (as in 1 Enoch 68:18) is **the stroke of the embryo** — as in **the Bite of the Serpent**! *Stun* in general is "to render senseless by or as if by a blow, to stupefy."

Stupefy is "to amaze." *Senseless* is "unconscious." *Amaze* in Greek is (ekstasis) which in essence means "to put into a TRANCE." (So if people are abducted by using the rod/goad, so must be the cattle rendered unconscious before mutilation.) {{Although I agree with Richard about the abduction of people in general, I am not at all certain that all cattle are rendered unconscious while being mutilated, since there is a theory that it may be easier to drain them of blood while they are still conscious while the blood is pumped out of them; this however, is only a theory since as far as I know, no one knows for sure how this gruesome process is fully executed. It would be more *humane* to render the animals unconscious, but then again, we may not be dealing with humane entities to begin with

THE CURS-ED NET

— if, in fact, they may be demonic, **who may actually relish the infliction** of as much torture and pain as possible upon their unwitting victims.}}

We have the word 'beat', and earlier it was shown in Greek to be (dero) from the root (der) — "skin," "to flay" — "to beat" and "to smite." *Beat* also as (tupto) from the root (tup) =- "a blow" — to smite, strike (a stroke.) 'Beat' (rhabdizo) is "to beat with a rod" (the staff as a goad!) Club is symbolic of a staff used by a shepherd, and a staff is symbolic of the rod/goad used by the herdsman.

The word 'blow' mentioned above can be connected to the word *plague* that in Hebrew means "a blow." In Latin it also is "a blow or wound." 'Plague' in general is a widespread "affliction, a disease." In Greek (katara) it means "a curse." Look at the word 'smite' earlier mentioned in Greek as (patasso) and metaphorically, it reflects the infliction of a disease by an angel. (This plague could **very well be** the mutilation of cattle for purposes that had been covered earlier *as to the* overall discussion of the nourishment for the hybrids.)

Curse in Greek (katathema) by (metonymy) is "an accursed thing," where the object is being part of the curse such as the plague (mutilations;) check out Zacharia 5:1, where the *flying scroll* (where the cigar-shaped object **is** the curse as the object being *part of* the curse.)

The word 'beat' penned earlier, in Greek has a meaning of "skin." *Skin* in Greek (askos) is "a leather bottle;" see leathern. *Leathern* in Greek is (dermatinos) which is "skin" from (derma) & "skin — hide beasts" (such as cattle.) 'Skin' in general has a meaning of "to remove." *Flay* from the word "beat" in general is to "strip off" (hide.) *Strip* is "to remove, deprive, to remove parts from." The word 'smite' penned earlier, has a meaning in Greek of (sphazo) "to slay" & *slay* (apokteino) is "to kill" (the cattle) and (anaireo) "to take away" (the parts) and (analisko) "to consume" (to eat.)

THE SECOND SYMBOL: THE SHIELD

Shield in general is "a broad piece of armor for protection, & a protective device or structure." *Zool* (as a species of animal such as reptiles, etc.,) "is characteristic of a particular group, such as those with (a protective plate or similar, hard outer covering;) a shute."

A *shute* is "an external plate or scale" which is Latin (scutum) for "shield."

Scale is "a plate-like covering of fishes & reptiles" (such as the signs, *Grays & Reptilians.*) *Device* in general has a meaning of "a decorative design or pattern, as used in embroidery." In Latin it is "to divide." *Divide* in Greek (aphorizo) is "to mark off by boundaries or limits." *Limit* in general means "the point, edge or line beyond which something cannot or may not proceed; a specific area, a confinement," — and in Latin "border."

Shield represents "the area or boundary as a **circle** (the Zodiac?) *Limit* in Greek directs us to see "define." *Define* is (horizo) & in English "horizon," or "to mark out the boundaries of a place." *Horizon* in general means "the intersection of the earth & sky."

The Northern & Southern Hemispheres are the limited circles of the Zodiac + Orion & The Bear — with the Pleiades (as the 'horn cluster of stars' from the constellation of TAURUS **the Bull** as indicated before.) In other words — Orion — The Bear & the Pleiades are the symbolic "stake-out" areas of the *Reptilians & Grays* working together.

{{The question before us is as follows: Was this then the reason why these areas were mentioned or **coded** in The Bible — to warn us of the danger lurking in these specific said areas by entities that were not human, but in fact, demonic? Was this, in fact, part of the **Second Estate** Jude referred to where these very beings were thrown down, and now while in prison (as *wandering stars & wild waves*) as characterized by St. Jude, wish to also capture & imprison mankind as their **own** prey? Is this the reason why so many animals & men of the Zodiac reflect **predatory characteristics** such as the Lion — the Bull — the Scorpion – and the hunters with clubs and shields and swords? As we take a hard look at these symbols, both in Ufology & in Holy Scripture, this may well be the case! Although I will discuss this in more detail later, the abductors within the literature of Ufology also behave in a **predatory manner**, regardless of what they say, or what some Ufologists dismiss their so-called *"foibles"* as — " for the alleged good & growth of humankind." **This is hogwash**! It has all the earmarks of a *spin* put on the UFO phenomenon that needs to be exposed and corrected!}}

THE CURS-ED NET

Structure is "made up of parts held together in a particular way." The arrangement of parts involves constructing; for instance; *structural* is "relating to or having structure, or affecting structure." (Morphologically) it relates to "changing forms." (Morphosis) is the manner in which an organism or any of its parts changes form. *Shield*, as mentioned in *Nelson's Bible Diet*, says that in Biblical times, shields came in all different sizes & shapes.

(So it seems we have a "structural" shield that is symbolically the structure and comes in many sizes & shapes. It is confined to a boundary, travels throughout this limited territorial area (vibration-space,) and can also change shapes [as in UFOs.])

We look at the word *embroidery*, and from the word 'device' in general, it means "ornamentation." Then we look at the word *pattern*, and we see "an artistic work." In the word *design*, we see a "graphic form" where the word 'graphics' in general is "the making of drawings in accordance with the rules of mathematics." (So we could deduce that **shields** also stand for something that resembles graphic designs, such as **crop circles**!)

{{I see this analogy as follows: a hunter's job is to seize its prey, no matter how it goes about doing this; if the *crop circles* are indeed a part of the ploy of **allurement**, (a distraction to keep the prey from realizing it is being hunted,) then I would agree with Richard, i.e., that the shield *deflects* the possibility of its prey becoming wise to the real agenda – **_capture & eventual death_**! In this aforementioned phenomenon, I also see that many people have looked upon these designed circles as some sort of messages by our *space brothers* from afar, coming to 'enlighten' mankind, or at least help us out of our current woes, which so far has failed to materialize. If this truly is just another false façade of the Fallen Angels, etc., then the **deflecting shield** has served the hunter well!

In geo-politics, we see a similar phenomenon with the notion of **false flags**, where researchers like Alex Jones continually try to show (the American people, at least,) that the real terrorists of 9/11 were none other than **the elite shadow government** who try to deflect their devious activity of *an inside job* by blaming the terrorists hiding in caves thousands of miles away for pulling off very sophisticated activity and "fooling" and outwitting the mightiest government in

THE CURS-ED NET

the world with four separate attacks upon our property in just a few hours . Not only Alex Jones, but many other researchers, including author Dr. David Griffin, would say: NO WAY! THE REAL ENEMY LIES WITHIN! For more on this, read Griffin's book, *THE NEW PEARL HARBOR*, in order to appreciate the phenomenon of a *real* **false flag**!

If, in fact, the *shadow government* is part & parcel of the coming **New World Order**, (a phrase that seems to be taking on a comprehensive meaning as we see our precious **sovereignty** being dismantled (in this country alone,) they also may be part & parcel of the *curs*-ed net. Never underestimate the wiles of Satan, and how many have already been lured into his diabolical trap, with the promise of wealth & women beyond their wildest dreams. Keep in mind the very encouraging words of Jesus: MY GRACE IS SUFFICIENT FOR THEE! So prayer and fasting may indeed be the ingredients for a mighty *turn around,* if you feel that you may have been (with subtlety) sucked into this web. Whatever you do, do not underestimate the real enemy in this world.}}

THE THIRD SYMBOL: THE SWORD

Sword in Hebrew (harab) is a verb "to smite down or slaughter." *To slaughter* in Hebrew is (zabah) "to slaughter, sacrifice." (Zabah) is also used as a term for "slaughter for eating." 'Sword' in Greek (rhomphaia, can be used 'metaphorically' as the instrument of anguish or judgment. *Anguish* in Greek is (thlipsis;) see 'affliction.' *Affliction* (kakoucheo) is from (kakos) as "evil" & (echo) "to have" & in the passive voice "to suffer ill" or to "evil entreat." The Greek word (sunkakouchei) means "to be evil entreated with." 'Evil' (kakos) is "whatever is evil in character" (such as the 'façade aliens.') (Poneros) is akin to (ponos) meaning "labor or toil, and denotes evil that causes labor, or a malignant evil."

Entreat in Greek (chraomai) means "to use either well or ill;" *well* in Greek (kalos) means "finely" & *finely* (telor) means "to an end." (Kakos) as *bad* means "to use badly" & (poneros) is connected with labor. *Labor* in Greek (kopos) is "a strike" akin to (koptp) "to strike" or laborious toil & trouble. *Toil* in Greek (kopiano) means "to be weary" & *weary* (kopiao) & (kopos) together mean "a beating

THE CURS-ED NET

toil — violent." (A violent labor [as in the *strike* of 1 Enoch 68:18] that was postulated in **the Bite of the Serpent** portion of the book actually describes the abduction and implantation of the embryo/fetus a la the Fallen Angels.)

'Toil' (basanizo) is "to put to the test." (A procedure for evaluation concerns the looking for qualities in something, including a series of physical responses, to determine the availability of specific needs.) Then we have "to examine by torture;" see 'vex.' (A test examination would be one of probing, using "instruments" as mentioned earlier, with **sword** (metaphorically) as being an instrument of anguish.)

Continuing with the word *trouble*, we see that in Greek (tarasso) used metaphorically means "of the soul and the spirit." Following up on the word *vex,* in Greek (ochleo) it is "trouble" & in the passive voice we find that it is "being troubled by evil spirits." Based on this **key word** search and connecting the dots, we can pose the question: are the evil spirits **truly** the ones who are examining the abductees? This research is strongly suggesting that it **is the evil spirits** or Fallen Angels in evil character (**façade shells**) manifesting as *the Grays & Reptilians.!*

When these same Fallen Angels &/or evil spirits examine males &females, *scoop marks* (flays) are found, which literally means that DNA & tissue are being taken. By taking men's sperm they could somehow be making {{copies of}} human beings for the purpose of trying to come into the possession of a human soul/spirit or (clones) with a soul/spirit. There appears to be implants found in bodies located in and around areas of the needed DNA & tissue. Could this be the 'stuff' needed for cloning? It seems that the essence of human beings is being taken.

{{Please review the disturbing story of Ted Rice, as cited by Karla Turner from her book, *MASQUERADE OF ANGELS*, that deals with an evil attempt at **soul transfer** by some demonic force working on Ted's body (from his perspective as told to hypno~therapist Barbara Bartholic), with a possible clone involved; it can be found in the 24th chapter (p.243) of the 1994 edition from KELT WORKS PRODUCTIONS, Roland, Arkansas. It is a **must read** if one is to address some of the darker dynamics surrounding

THE CURS-ED NET

the "alien" abduction phenomenon. [An incident concerning the death of Ted's grandmother is also very disturbing, especially since it may have involved the work of the devil.]

Richard ends this chapter by reminding us of Amos 5:8, where God created both Orion & the Pleiades. If you recall, these symbolically represent the *cubs* of **the Bear** — or as Richard suggests, the **hybrids** (*Grays & Reptilians*) who will be needed for the work force to do the job required in gathering the people/cattle and other biological materials for the **hidden agenda** of **the *curs*-ed net!**}}

{{Comment: As a Ufologist, who has waded through many a book on the different theories surrounding the dynamics of the UFO & alien abduction phenomenon, I took particular notice of the constellation of **Orion**. It appears that it contains a star called *Rigel*, which according to one UFO author, George Andrews, plays a significant role in spawning beings who seem to have a particular attraction to earth beings. In his book, ***EXTRA-TERRESTRIAL FRIENDS AND FOES,*** Andrews makes the following remarks concerning these beings, starting on page 142 of his book; below are some of the highlights and a portrait of these malevolent humanoids:

1) These *Rigelian* humanoids are seen as short *Grays* (over four foot tall) with large heads (resembling embryos.) Note Richard's characterization of same when he dealt with the *scorpion* concept in the earlier part of the book.

2) Their solar system revolves around Rigel, some 800 light years from Earth.

3) They {allegedly} have a problem with their sebaceous glands, making digesting food difficult. This FRONT spells trouble for humans & cattle! It is ***a front*** because I think this story (myth) is a true cover to make it look like *the Grays* are ETs, and they need a "convincing" storyline, but just like their craving for strawberry ice cream, (as was suggested in a 1988 TV program about the *alleged truth* of the "aliens" called, *"UFO COVER-UP?...LIVE!,"* this façade falls flat, and upon deaf ears to the spiritually discerning individual; consult Andrews' book for the details.

4) This problem was generated from a previous nuclear war in a solar system "far far away." This is *yet another* fairy tale story, so like the movie **STAR WARS**, you will just have to read the book;

THE CURS-ED NET

however, just to see how the dark forces massage us with real science fiction posing as alleged truths, I will *share* some of the outline highlights.

5) They made an alleged secret deal with both Hitler & our own government in the good old USA. The deal concerned the taking and mutilating of cattle to help solve their gland problem. [Andrews thinks that our government is deluded into thinking that the "technology" given by these *Grays* will enable us to gain military superiority over the Russians, and although this tall tale may have seemed plausible to some ~~ even before the break-up of the Soviet Union, the government soon found out that it was part of a major deception.] Of course, if the government was smart enough to realize who or what they were **really** dealing with (*Grays* as *Demons*,) then they would not have believed them to begin with — assuming there is any veracity to the story to begin with, which, in my opinion, there isn't! The outgrowth of this horrible deal ostensibly was the getting of both 'Stealth Bomber' & 'Star War' technology. [Andrews is dubious — even in 1993 — that we really got anything of real value that really would have gained us superiority over the Russians or anybody else; it just would not be in the interests of these fiendish individuals, (who, as demons,) would like to keep humanity at each other's throats *ad infinitum*, which they have done from the beginning (as we have determined to be sometime after THE GREAT FLOOD.)

6) If they had to, the *Rigelians* have the ability to throw this planet off its axis.

7) According to the author, they manipulate us through our "laziness & ignorance." (143) I, for one, could only add our lack of spiritual non-discernment as our key character flaw, plus our collective greed (especially within the military) for superior technology, regardless of how it is achieved, which, unfortunately became manifest during the disclosures of *Project Paper-Clip*, thus allowing the evil of fascist Nazism to invade the collective intelligence community after WW II.

8) The *Rigelians*' pawns, (the CIA & former Nazi scientists,) developed the AIDS virus, so as to exterminate portions of the population, considered to be *undesirable*. This seems to be a real-life

concern of NEW WORLD ORDER researchers, who (despite one's belief in either *Rigelians or demons*,) the evidence points to these latter types as actually doing this to certain human beings, (acting through *their minions* like rogue elements of the CIA, for instance; this was initially documented by Dr. Robert Strecker, now deceased how these elements covertly infected the Blacks of South Africa with the AIDS virus under the cover of the smallpox vaccine. In the light of #7 above, it is also not surprising how man's inhumanity to man can be manifested when *certain men* have forsaken their true spiritual root *to follow the whisperings and urgings of the dark side.* One of the major themes of the Holy Bible is that we, as a race, are in the testing grounds for spiritual advancement, by demonstrating to the one true God that we *truly are children of God,* and not the sons of the Evil One.

9) In any event, the survivors of the above-cited horror show would "accept open control by the *Rigelians.*" (143) The discerning reader will note that the end game of *the Grays & Reptilians* — as demons & Fallen Angels — is no less insidious, if you believe in a soul/spirit that they also wish to destroy so you will not live happily ever after in God's spiritual kingdom. This deadly game also seems to posit (that somehow) they may avoid the awful punishment due them by some type of "end run" via their devilish scheming, so they will avoid or somehow forestall their inevitable end.

There are other insidious groups (as well as 'space brothers' who are here to help man, as Andrews relates *ad nauseam*, but it is my heart-felt feeling that once the reader puts two & two together, connecting the dots of this ET *travesty*, and breaks through the web of the paranormal smoke & mirrors, he or she will AWAKEN to the realization that the ET phenomenon & our "space buddies" combine to present a _**big fat facade**_, leading us away from the truth of the matter as delineated in this three-part thesis!

HOW JUDE 13 REFLECTS THE SYMBOLISM OF THE ZODIAC

{{INTRODUCTION. I personally think that this is a **short but marvelous** analysis by Richard regarding one of the shortest — if not the shortest of all of scripture: the epistle of St. Jude. I remember

THE CURS-ED NET

when I was in graduate school, and we had to dissect a difficult poem, and no matter how much we dug into it, the professor always was able to add some insight so we could appreciate and marvel at how the poet was expressing such beautiful concepts in so few words!

If you think about what Jude is **coding** to us (at least from my point of view, since he seemed to have intimate knowledge of some copy of *The Book of Enoch,* similar to other evangelists,) it almost reads like a scriptural poem with its **wandering stars & wild waves**, etc. It also — and not so surprisingly — sums up the whole of The *Curs*-ed Net thesis. Richard does a good job in showing how this is so. Pay attention to the unraveling of this most amazing coded book about the fallen false teachers — the wild waves as UFOs, plus the plight of pregnant abducted women — the sea as outer space — the wandering stars as both irregular and deceitful — the movement of the waves as the unceasing roll of the constellations seemingly revolving around our Earth as if they were made for our pleasure — but acting as a LIVING BEAST — and spawning other living beasts as hybrids!

These *'marvelous' traveling creatures* are putting on a carnival show: take a ticket and be ready to be put in a trance — a *trance* — where if we are not careful, we will lose our way to our real home somewhere in God's domain of frequency & vibration. BEWARE! And now some remarks by Richard:}}

This Jude 13 should add some extra punch to the meanings & symbolism of the twelve signs within the Zodiac!

THE FALSE TEACHERS — FALLEN ANGELS

JUDE 13 (NIV) "They are wild waves of the sea, foaming up their shame; wandering stars, for whom blackest darkness has been reserved forever."

As per *Vine's*:

Wild in Greek (agrios) is "not domestic" (but could we say: non-human or not of this earth?) yet it is "strange, fierce." Jude 13 metaphorically shows "it is used in the papyri as of a malignant wound." *Malignant,* as shown earlier, is a cancerous pathological condition — a growth, both abnormal and a pernicious spreading evil. {{This would be in keeping with the symbolism of the *Living Beast as an*

Evil Living Net that is expanding (via the hybrid phenomenon we see to this very day!)}} *Wound* in Greek (plege) is "a blow, a stroke." (Again, we refer you to meditate on 68:18 within Enoch, since it **is** the bite of the serpent as well as the strike of the embryo *verse*.)

Above is symbolic of the evil organism implanted within the female abductee, which not only *physically wounds* but also *spiritually wounds*.

We now go to the word *wave,* where in general, may symbolize some of the characteristics used by these Fallen Angels while referring to the UFO phenomenon. 'Wave' means "to move back & forth, up & down, and in the air, being a curved shape outline or pattern, with a sudden great rise." *Rise* also contributes to the image of "to ascend in intensity and speed, to appear above the horizon, to come into existence, to appear at the surface of the water or the earth; emerge." (It also sounds like this very image could easily refer to UFOs!)

Yet there is one more meaning of the word 'wave' in Greek: it refers to the word *wild!* This is a malignant wound, where 'wave' in Greek is (kuma) from (kuo) which means "to be pregnant" (reflecting 'figuratively' in Jude 13.)

Pregnant with a malicious wound is another way of saying (implantation.) The word *sea* as in "wild waves of the sea" is the meaning of the Hebrew (yam.) The word refers to the body of water (as on earth's oceans,) but also refers to the sea as (sky, the heavens, & space!)

Foam symbolizes the following: in Greek (epophrizo) is used metaphorically in Jude 13 of the impious libertine; the metaphor is drawn from the refuse (horne) on the crest of the waves and cast upon the beach. ("Impious" was mentioned in *The Book of Enoch* as the evil spirits of the giants.)

Libertine is "one who defies established religious precepts," (i.e., the Fallen Angels who defied God's laws.) *Refuse* refers to "the cancerous evil organism (the hybrid")" which is produced." *Crest* has a meaning of a "projection on the head," (just as *the Grays* have a large projectile head.) It also means something that extends beyond a prevailing line, (such as a boundary or territory, perhaps?)

THE CURS-ED NET

The word *prevailing* is something that is "predominant" (which their big heads sure are!) The word *beach,* mentioned earlier, refers to "the earth," (as in evil spirits cast upon the earth.) *Wandering stars* are symbolic of the following: 'Wander' in Greek is (planao) for which we see the word deceit; also, (planets) means "a wanderer," and in English, planet is used metaphorically in Jude 13 as the evil teachers (Fallen Angels) mentioned as wandering stars.

THE BASIC CONCEPT: (The Fallen Angels are the aliens traveling or wandering throughout the sea (space) and *stars* are symbolic of angels, which, of course, we had mentioned before regarding what Enoch had directly alluded to in the *Ethiopian* version.)

'Stars,' also described in *Vine's,* could be symbolic of UFOs. (Judge for yourself!) Also mentioned in *Vine's* is the quote about the "wandering stars of Jude 13" (as if the stars, intended for light & guidance, became the means of deceit by irregular movement; furthermore, the stars in the sea (space) seem to move in all different ways. They even react peculiarly just as UFOs are seen to move; does this make it then a causal relationship? You be the judge!)

'Star' in Greek is (astron.) If we look up the word *zodiac*, it is also (astron.) The constellations of the zodiac move, and they also wander, so could Jude 13 also be referring to wandering stars as the constellations of the zodiac? Could 'waves' by their movement also be representative of these constellations' movements? (It seems plausible, from the presentation thus far, that this is so!)

We look again at the word 'wild' in Greek (therion) and in the plural as *wild beasts* (KJV as "beasts.") [Rev. 6:8.] (So could this be translated as wandering "traveling" beasts (creatures?) *Zodiac* in Greek (zoidiakos) = 'kuklos' as a (circle) of the zodiac < (zoidion,) or "small represented figure," (as the figures of the zodiac, but could also represent this beast!) The diminutive of (zoidion) is "**a living beast**." (So the word 'zodiac' represents a living being here;) see the word 'zoon.' *Zoon* in general is "an animal or creature developed from a fertilized egg." (WOW! Could this, then, refer to the **hybrids**? *The Grays* also are a small representative figure. Could this be the product of the fertilized eggs as the evil organisms implanted by the Fallen Angels spoken of in Jude 13?)

THE CURS-ED NET

We end this analysis by looking at the word *beast*, which in Greek is [zoon.] (Earlier, as represented by the word 'zodiac,') it denotes "a living being." (Therion) in Greek distinguishes it as "a wild beast," (as in the "wild waves" of Jude 13!)

'Wild waves' then could symbolize the beasts &/or beast (Satan,) with his beasts (as the Fallen Angels.) These same Fallen Angels in Jude 13 make up part of the Beast. Satan, therefore, is the head of the Beast, and (in keeping with the past thesis of this picture,) the evil spirits make up the remaining part of the body of this living Beast. It is truly a living creature, even though the 'beast' itself is symbolic, (thus operating in a dual fashion,) {{which is not uncommon in Biblical interpretations, where, for example, the 'Book of Revelation' itself, is an ongoing metaphor that stands for an underlying future reality, it seems to me.}}

The Zodiac, itself, represents this symbolic beast (as living creature,) reflected within the meanings **_decoded_** regarding the twelve signs of the zodiac. The "wild waves of the sea" are the traveling creatures (Fallen Angels) that inhabit the constellations of the zodiac, & make up the living beast who try to deceive us by showing themselves as aliens (as part and parcel of the UFO phenomenon.) THEY ARE NOT! {{Richard couldn't have said it any more succinctly! BRAVO!}}

END NOTES:

Nelson's New and Illustrated Bible Dictionary
Publisher: Thomas Nelson, Inc. ©1995

Vine's Complete Expository Dictionary of Old and
New Testament Words:
Publisher: Thomas Nelson, Inc. ©1996
Used by permission of Thomas Nelson, Inc.

CHAPTER NINETEEN:

Symbols of the Net's Beasts

(Other Symbolic Net Beasts)

{{Introduction: In PART ONE of THE *CURS*-ED NET (chapter eighteen,) Richard Stout analyzed many aspects of astrology, including the constellations of Orion, as well as the Pleiades, which itself is ensconced within Taurus (*the Bull*,) as one of the twelve signs of the zodiac. All of these concepts had been mentioned in **The Holy Bible**, and part of the analysis centered around how these very concepts were connected to the Fallen Angels, (including the evil spirits,) with Satan as the head of these very dark forces, who somehow were thrown down to their *Second Estate*, which also <u>**interfaces with**</u> our very reality. They interfere with our spiritual development by influencing us to become entrapped within their very *curs*-ed net.

This second part will focus in on two of the beasts mentioned in *The Book of Job*, namely the **Behemoth & Leviathan**. The major concepts that will be developed here include the following:
1) Using an analysis of selected verses in Job, chapter 40, the Behemoth will be looked upon as the symbolic combination of all the "earthbound" evil spirits who emanated from the original **Giants** of Gen 6:4.
2) The Leviathan (Job 41) will likewise symbolize all the other forces (including the Fallen Angels) whose domain is the sea

THE CURS-ED NET

(or really the expanse of outer space) and whose leader is Satan.

3) Your relationship with Jesus Christ will be a litmus test to see how these symbolic monsters can negatively impact on your life.

4) Many of these verses from both chapters, 40 & 41, will reinforce the concepts developed in chapter eighteen.}}

THE *BEHEMOTH* EXAMINED

The behemoth of Job 40 is one of two mysterious creatures mentioned in **The Holy Bible** that is symbolic of **_many_** living creatures that make up the body of which is called *THE BEAST*. The behemoth is symbolic of the **earthbound** creatures, namely, the evil spirits who once themselves were behemoths (the Giants) as related in the *Ethiopian* Book of Enoch (1 Enoch.) When the Giants passed, their spirits became **the unclean earthbound spirits** that make up part of the body of the living Beast. {{These are the very unclean spirits that are mentioned in the New Testament, of whom Jesus & His disciples had cast out.}} The other part of this living Beast body will be discussed in the section on the leviathan. Satan, of course, is in charge of *all* parts of the living Beast.

JOB, CHAPTER 40

VERSE 15: *"Look at the behemoth, which I made along with you and which feeds on grass like an ox."*

Behemoth in general is "something large in size & power." In Hebrew we have (behemot) which means "intensive," and is the pleural of (behema) for "beast." The expression, *like an ox* is only meant as to resemble an ox, but <u>not an ox</u> in appearance & form.

Ox in Greek is (tauros) & in Latin (taurus.) In Hebrews 9:13 & 10:4, the "bull" Paul refers to (may very well be the zodiac sign for TAURUS — *the Bull*.) The *bull* (in decoding the zodiac signs) stands for the **Beast**, the body of which plays a part here on earth as its habitat, and also belongs in the sky — the *Leviathan* space as the other part of the Beast. The evil spirits are that part of the body here on earth (behemoth) and the Fallen Angels are the part of the body of the Beast that lives in the heavens.

THE CURS-ED NET

As mentioned before, the evil spirits are the product of the Giants (1 Enoch 15:8,) which states the following: *"Now the giants, who have been born of spirit and of flesh, shall be called upon earth evil spirits, and on earth shall be their habitation. Evil spirits shall proceed from their flesh because they were created from above; from the holy watchers (now Fallen Angels) was their beginning and primary foundation. Evil spirits shall they be upon earth, and the spirits of the wicked shall they be called. The habitation of the spirits of heaven shall be in heaven; but upon earth shall be the habitation of terrestrial spirits, who are born on earth."*

Behemoth, the land beast, is <u>part</u> of the body of the whole beast, which contains the evil spirits. Evil spirits came from the giants (also Gen 6:4) are the 'nephilim' who themselves are (were) *behemoths* — a true symbolism!

Let's take a look at Enoch 15:2: *"Wherefore you have forsaken the lofty and holy heaven, which endures forever, and have lain with women; (you) have defiled yourselves with the daughters of men; (you) have taken to yourselves wives; (you) have acted like the sons of the earth, and have begotten an impious offspring?"*

Now looking at the word *impious*, we can see how symbolically it refers to the character of the beast here on earth, and what sort of agenda it may introduce. 'Impious' in general is "lacking reverence" (i.e., not holy or good.) *Imp* in general explains quite a bit involving their character & actions here on earth. Let's now take a look at some of the things that the evil spirits are involved in.

IMP

1) A small demon
2) As Obsolete — a "graft."
3) To furnish with wings (as a mode of transportation.)
4) In Middle English, we have the words (impe, scion, & sprig,) which mean offspring (of the giants;)
5) In Old English, we have (impa,) which is a "young shoot" (and could very well symbolize a **hybrid** or *Gray*.)
6) In Greek we have (cmphutos) which equals "grafted" < (emphuein,) "to implant" or "to make grow."

THE CURS-ED NET

The evil spirits that are living within the living tissue costumes (as hybrids) of the *Grays*, and interact with man, are also functioning to deceive man that *they exist as aliens*. The grafting implants embedded into female abductees actually create these costumes of the living tissue hybrids, which then are possessed by and controlled by the evil spirits. See how the meanings of the word "impious" (then "imp") opens up the UFO phenomenon picture [?])

As we progress into the next group of verses of Job 40, you will see how these meanings relate to the *impious* works of the evil spirits. The earthly beast — *the behemoth,* thus become part & parcel of the manifestation within the UFO phenomenon. As mentioned above, *imp* mentions being "furnished with wings," and is a mode of flight that you will see in the following verses.

VERSE 16: "*What strength he has in his loins, what power in the muscles of his belly.*"

(All through the above and next series of verses, we reflect upon the character and ability and uses that the beast as evil spirits possess.)

Strength in Greek is (dunamis) which means "strength" & (ischus) means "ability." (Kratos) is "force" and for the word 'might' it says to see 'dominion.'

Loin in Greek (osphus) is "the seat of generative power." *Generative* in general is here "having the ability to initiate, produce, procreate; of or relating to the production of offspring." In this sense, it relates to the production through implantation of the female abductees regarding *the Gray hybrids*, to produce [workers.] These are bodies to be lived in to complete a number of tasks — assigned to its ability.

(So it seems that the evil spirits, together with the Fallen Angels, work toward the same end: they probably **both possess** the *Gray & Reptilian* living tissue bodies for this task — a task which includes not only hybrids of this kind, but other creatures as well; there is also the possibility of cloning humans due to the fact that they abduct many people, **_only to flay the skin_** as in (scoop marks!) This latter process seems to be so to gather DNA tissue, and not for creating their kind of hybrids; rather it looks more like **human hybrid cloning!** This seems to make the most sense.

236

THE CURS-ED NET

{{THE QUESTION BEFORE OUR COURT of INQUIRY: Are they looking to somehow obtain a human soul/spirit for some use? Maybe it is to try an attempt to free itself of its habitats! Who really knows? At this point in the abduction phenomenon mix, we can only truly guess.

WHAT DO WE KNOW? It seems apparent (especially to anyone who has read the three parts of this thesis so far, that evil spirits do play **a big part** in the actions & ability to interact with man as *false aliens* for their own evil purpose(s). (To me, it seems obvious that there is **not** a collage of interacting groups working hand in claw for some grand political inter-galactic purpose; this *does not mesh* with the ambiance of THE HOLY BIBLE in any way; rather, if you take the demonic element seriously, it has its own inter-activeness that does make sense, especially if we overlay it with *The Book of Enoch*, noting how ambition and presumption have led to devastating consequences for *so highly created* beings! This looks like the **long & short** of it. To put it even more bluntly: we can fit the ET phenomenon into the **demonic** scenario, *but not the reverse*!}}

MORE *KEY WORDS* AS RICHARD CONTINUES BUILDING HIS CASE:

Power in Greek (dunamis) has different meanings, and seen via 'metonymy,' it reflects (angels) & (persons.) The word *dominion* (mentioned earlier,) comes from the word 'strength.' 'Dominion' in Greek (kueiotes) denotes "lordship," and (kurios) is "a lord." (There are authorities spoken about in the angelic order, including the epistles of Jude (8,) Ephesians & Colossians.) We are discussing a ruler here over the evil spirits (kurieuo) that means "to be lord over, ruler over." *Satan* holds the title of "the ruler of this world" as per John 12:31; 14:30; 16:11. His other name is *Beelzebub*, the ruler of the demons, as per Matt 9:34 & 12:24.

Muscles in general mean here "power" & "authority" (as in absolute power & authority.) *Belly* in general means "the stomach." *Stomach* in Greek is (stomachos,) properly a "mouth, an opening," akin to (stoma) "a mouth." The Hebrew *mouth* is (pch) and has a meaning of "utterance; order; command." *Utter* in Greek (aphiemi) has a meaning of "to send forth;" also (phthengomai) is "to utter

THE CURS-ED NET

a sound or voice" (as in **hauntings** or hearing ghostly voices or sounds; this also includes those who are possessed and speak by the evil spirit(s) within them.)

Satan also has the power through *command* to "send forth" these evil agencies upon mankind...as in...(a top general orders a command!)

'Utter' also means a reference to "mind influence." This evil knowledge will be expressed into our minds and conveyed through (the mouth) by speaking so that our minds understand something; it is a type of "spiritual gift" people mention that they have received through UFO encounters! (Since UFOs may very well represent the dark side, the knowledge conveyed is evil, so it is projected into the *receivers* **(as one of the three chosen types to assist in the evil agenda)** in order to deceive us, as per the analysis of Richard in the beginning part of the book.

Continuing with Job 40:17, "*His tail sways like a cedar; the sinews of his thighs are close knit.*"

Tail in Greek (oura) has the meaning of "the tail of an animal" (the beast) or (in this case being referenced to the tail of something of the beast [evil spirits] which is used by them.) 'Tail' means "the limitation of the inheritance of an estate," (or, in other words, the evil spirits of the giants, being earthbound, cannot leave the planet outside the atmosphere, so this is their limitation of inheritance because of who they are.)

Sways in general means here "to exert influence on or control over;" in (Archaic) it is "to rule or govern" & "to have dominion over."

THEIR INHERITED TERRITORY: *THE EARTH*

They have the power to sway all of those here on our earth *who are not truly seated in a relationship with Jesus Christ.* If you believe you have a good relationship with Jesus, and these evil things are troubling you, (via UFO experiences, etc.,) then you must look at this relationship within your heart and truly pray about it; something could be very wrong. It might not be the true relationship that you think it is. (I, Richard, have personally been through this before. If one knows that he or she is doing anything the Lord God *preaches*

238

against {{via **The Holy Bible,**}} then something both with God & His Son Jesus needs to be straightened out — and *the sooner the better!*)

The word *cedar* symbolizes the beast's evil powers as they are both lasting & stable, and are not depleted by the evil spirits' use. This power will last *until* the Lord Jesus Christ returns and destroys them! On a personal note, their power will cease over you when you personally accept your one true God and the Blessed Savior. Then these spirits will be dealt with for us since *we have no direct power over them.*

Sinews are "the strength or power of something." *Thighs* in Greek (meros) "are emblematic of their strength to tread upon their prey." *Emblematic* is that "the *thighs* stand for a symbolic emblem of their ability to overcome their prey," (i.e., all those who are **spiritually destitute!**)

THE CONCEPT OF *CLOSE-KNIT*

Close in Greek (atusso) means "to double up;" 'close' as an adverb (anchi) means "near." *Near* in Greek (anankaios) = "connected by bonds, intimate." *Bond* in Greek (desmios) relates "to binding" and denotes "a prisoner," (whether by *familiar spirits* within us as in the aforementioned **"receivers"** or by abduction bodily.) *Intimate* deals with **familiar spirits**, as per 1 Sam. 28:3,9 (KJV;) {{1 KINGS in Catholic version.}} *Knit* in Greek (sumbibazo) is "to cause to join or knit together."

Verse 18: "*His bones are tubes of bronze, his limbs like rods of iron.*"

Bones in Hebrew ('esem) is used as "bone; body; &/or substance; the plural of ('esem) sometimes signifies one's" whole being" or the "substance of a thing." 'Bone' in general is "a dense material, or a tissue which forms a skeleton, an anatomically distinct structure." *Anatomical* means "related to a structure." (Bone is symbolic of some sort of structure.) *Tubes* in general reflect "a hollow cylinder for fluids or a function as a passage, an organic structure having the shape or function of a tube." (This, then, is representative of a body or structure shaped like a cylinder of bronze [*metals.*]")

THE CURS-ED NET

Bronze in general contains "various alloys, such as copper & tin" and is also characterized as "a moderate yellowish to olive brown " which "gives the color and appearance of bronze." According to *Nelson's Bible Dictionary*, when bronze is mentioned in the Bible, it refers to either copper or bronze (1Cor. 13:11, Rev. 1:15, 2:18, 9:20.) So bronze, copper and brass all relate to each other, and can be used as the same metal.

Brass in Greek (chalkos) is primarily "copper," and became used for metals in general; later it was applied to "bronze." In the meaning (chalkolibanon,) it reflects "a white or shining copper or bronze." The word *shining* in Greek (phaino) means "to cause to appear" & "to give light." (Lampo) has the meaning of "shining as a torch," whereas (periastrpto) is "to flash around." (So now we have a body or structure, shaped like a cylinder, containing metal such as bronze, that gives off a very shining effect, as a light flashes around.)

Limbs in general = "jointed appendages," or "an extension or projecting part. *Appendage* in general is "something or a thing needed or attached to a large entity or structure." *Rods* in general reflect "bar metal," or material such as metal having a particular use." In Biblical times, it also meant "a line of descent, a branch of a tribe." (The line of descent reflects the behemoth beast as of the evil spirits, a product of the Fallen Angels & the daughters of men. The Giants were born — then died and subsequently their spirits which were descended from the Fallen Angels became the evil spirits **(symbolic of the Beast — *Behemoth!*)**

'Rods' also means something else: "rods of metal," where metal refers to the word *iron*. 'Iron' in general reflects the "iron shinny metal" as in Rev. 9:9; it is also "a magnetic or 'magnetiz-able' metallic element." *Magnetic* has the meaning of "relating to magnetism," or "operating by the means of magnetism," as well as "relating to the magnetic poles." 'Magnetization' is the process of making a substance (bone, for example,) temporarily or permanently magnetic as by the insertion within a magnetic field.

A *magnetic field* is "a condition found around a magnet or electric current, characterized by the existence of a detachable magnetic force at every point in the region and by the existence of magnetic poles" (north & south.) Electric current (electro-magnetism) in general is

240

THE CURS-ED NET

a "magnetism produced by electric charge in motion." (So now our structure (bone) has the ability and use of electro-magnetism.)

If we refer back to the word "iron" (as in Rev. 9:9,) in the NIV it states the following: "They had breastplates like breastplates of "iron" and the sound of their wings was of many horses and chariots rushing into battle (as in thunderous vibrations.)

Thunderous in general = "loud & unrestrained." *Vibration* in general has "a rhythmic sound, a sound resonating." *Electric-magnetic energy* (sound) is of a humming noise: ''the more energy the louder the hum!'' It is a resonating sound with vibrations. (People who have UFO encounters, tell of hearing a humming sound from time to time, which reflects the electro-magnetic energy.)

From what has been analyzed above, it seems that *breastplates* are symbols of the **locusts'** mode of transportation, which reflects the aliens (as) evil spirits & Fallen Angels' wings that are being covered by breastplates of iron — reflecting two halves of their craft [the UFO.] This is also a shining structure as well as a circular object of metal & flashing lights, with rods projecting out limbs of iron, used for landing gear.

{{Within the UFO phenomenon in 1964, there was solid empirical evidence of just such a mysterious craft that landed in Socorro, New Mexico, and seen by policeman, Lonnie Zamora; the then prestigious Allen Hynek actually came and measured the depressions of the landing gear a few days from when Zamora saw the UFO blast off over his head, the UFO having a bluish flame behind what was described as an egg-shaped craft with an orange bottom and strange writing on it. The case has never been explained, except in the mind of the now deceased debunker, Phil Klass, but, of course, **if the occupants were demonic in nature,** what barometer would have been used to so explain it? It is very difficult for a spiritually inclined Ufologist to score any points in this rather hedonistic secular society that we presently inhabit. If you wish to see the details of this fascinating case, go to Michael Hesemann's *UFOs: The SECRET HISTORY*.}}

VERSE 21: "*Under the lotus plants he lies, hidden among the reeds in the marsh.*"

THE CURS-ED NET

Under in Greek is (katotero) meaning "below" & "beneath." *Lotus*; is general is "an aquatic plant." *Aquatic* in general has the meaning of "relating to or being in water, or living or growing in or on the water," (and if a structure, one that can go below the water.) Regarding the expression *lies hidden*, 'lies' in general has a meaning here of "a haunt or hiding place." (A haunt is to inhabit, visit, or appear to; to recur or visit often.) 'Hidden' in general is to be "concealed" or "to keep out of sight, secret." (This structure's *cylinder* [circular object] lies below the water, a place inhabited or most often visited.)

Reeds describe "various tall perennial grasses." *Marsh* reflects "soft, wet, low-lying areas, where the land is marked by grassy vegetation, and often a transition between water & land;" (therefore it is giving the impression of a circular structure which leaves its mark [print] in the swamps or marsh land.)

VERSE 22: "*The lotuses conceal him in their shadow (these are the beast as evil spirits within their structure;) the poplars by the stream surround him.*"

Stream is "a bed of water which is flowing; a swampy or marshy area of a stream-like area." (Both the water plants & the trees help to conceal the structure within the marshy land.)

VERSE 24: "*Can anyone capture him by the eyes or trap him and pierce his nose?*" This, of course, is the mighty structure – **the UFO** — that ostensibly is impregnable!)

Capture in general is "to gain possession of or control of, to seize." *Eyes* in general here is of "external visible portions, together with associated structures;" "an opening, a loop or window of some sort." (These structures have been seen with holes and windows of sorts.) {{Just such a craft with six window-like holes was actually spotted by airplane pilot Clarence S. Chiles (along with co-pilot John B. Whitted,) who were traveling in an Eastern Airlines DC-3 over Montgomery, Alabama, on July 24, 1948. This was described as a one hundred foot long cigar-shaped object that was twice the diameter of a B-29, with no protruding surfaces. It gave off a bluish glow with a red-orange flame as an "exhaust." This *windowed* UFO was also showcased in Hesemann's book, cited above. NOTE: *It is either extra-terrestrial or demonic, since no one had the tech-*

THE CURS-ED NET

nology in 1948 to fly such vehicles outside our atmosphere, traveling as a rocket, with ostensible sentient life aboard.}}

Trap is "a sealing off, to confine, seal off from escape." *Pierce* is "to cut, penetrate, make a hole in, or enter or penetrate into." *Nose* in general is "a forward part of something, the forward end of or protruding part of a structure." (Does anyone have the ability to seize it? Are we able to possess this structure by hooking or taking hold of any visible openings on its body? Can we seal it off from flight or movement? Can we cut into it or penetrate it by the use of any type of tools? Can we pierce its nose? Can we hurt or damage the structure? **NO!** *Man has not the ability to do this*!) {{Maybe our own government knows all of this, and the reason they really keep all of this *UFO stuff secret* is because they themselves have seen the powers of the *powers of the air*, and have themselves been seduced by the **lustful lures** of so-called advanced technology, given by these "alien demons" so that these same "alien-demons" can go about their tasks of trapping unsuspecting souls with their stealthy <u>*and*</u> *curs*-ed net.}}

THE LEVIATHAN of SEA & SPACE: SYMBOLIC *BEAST #2*

{{The information to be analyzed will be confined to *The Book of Job.* chapter 41, while exploring the **symbolism** that Richard deduced via his analysis, incorporating verses 12 through 34. This symbolism will be drawn from Richard's usual *key word* approach, which will compliment & supplement the symbolism after the citing of each verse.

This analysis starts with a note concerning verse #3. This concerns the *Leviathan*, referred to as <u>*he*</u>. This beast is <u>part</u> of the overall symbolism of the full <u>*Living Beast*</u> that incorporates the full land, sea & space, where the *Behemoth* represented the *land portion* only. Verses 12 through 32 will show the comprehensive range of the full beast, which will incorporate the UFO & DEMONIC ABDUCTION PHENOMENON in all its metaphorical glory   & as penned through the understanding of God's obedient servant Job.}}

This <u>*he*</u> of verse 3 in general is used to refer to a male animal, (the same animal beast that contains the evil Fallen Angels, evil spirits, & includes Satan, so per force, it is metaphorical in nature!

THE CURS-ED NET

JOB 41:12 reads as follows:

"I will not fail to speak of his limbs, his strength and his graceful form."

THE SYMBOLISM: The limbs of the beast are his extensions — Fallen Angels doing certain jobs, while evil spirits are doing other jobs. The groups are all making up the body of the beast, of which Satan is the head.

Limbs mentions small demons (evil spirits or *the Grays.*) Some of the jobs include the following:

1) Grafting
2) Implanting
3) Growing offspring
4) Wings, as a mode of transportation (UFOs.) These wings carry the Fallen Angels "as aliens" throughout their estate or territory. It is their "strength" — their authority, a government, a principality of high-ranking angels. The *force* they use is in abducting people, and as **herdsmen**, abduct cattle for their parts.

The *feature & form* are "specified shapes, outward appearance, a manufactured structure (wings-UFOs,) that have the ability to change shapes." {{Of course, this later trait has been observed throughout the Ufological literature, and would lend credence to the supernatural characteristics of these beings.}} The Greek meaning in general is "morphosis" which is "the manner in which an organism or any of its parts changes form." The Greek (morphosis) = "the process of forming." [THIS ENDS VERSE 12.]

SOME HIGHLIGHTED WORDS & PHRASES FROM VERSE 12:

Limbs (plural) in general is one regarded as an extension, a member of a representative of a larger body or group. (Informally) it "is an **impish** child." (*Imp* in general has a meaning of three things, all of which were discussed in the previous section under Job, chapter 40. The *limb* ("astron") is "the circumferential edge of the apparent disk of a celestial body." *Circumferential'* has three aspects:

1) it is the boundary line of a circle.

244

THE CURS-ED NET

2) It is the boundary line of an area.
3) The length of such a boundary. In Latin it is "to carry around."
   If you check the word "wings" above, as to furnish with, it
   would be a means to carry around!)

Strength had been noted before; *power* (exousia) denotes
"freedom of action," as well as "authority;" see also 'principality'
(arche) 'rule.' *Ability* in Greek (dunamis) is "power in action." *Force*
in Greek (harpazo) is "to snatch away" & "carry off by force," (as
in seizing & abducting.) The word (diarpazo) = "to plunder," which
is "to rob of goods by force, property stolen." (This would be reflective of taking cattle by the herdsman.)

Dominion from strength, in Greek (kuriotes) denotes "lordship"
& "power," whether angelic or human. (Kurieuo) is "to be lord over,
rule over, have dominion over." *Principality* in Greek is "governmental rule" & "is used of super mundane beings who exercise
rule." Cf. the evil angels of Rom. 8:38; also, in Col. 2:15.) (Supre) =
"above" & (mundanel) "is relating to this world." (This would mean
then that the beings are above this world.) In Jude 6, it signifies
this fallen estate for the Fallen Angels, having "their own" power
which had been assigned to them by God, which they left, aspiring
to prohibited conditions.

VERSE 12 Continuing with *Form + Graceful*

Graceful in general shows "grace or characteristic of movement."
This characteristic is a distinctive feature. *Feature* is "distinct parts,
an overall appearance." In (Archaic) it is "an outward appearance,
form or shape." In Latin (factura) is "a working or making up." The
word *distinct* is "readily distinguishable from all other things, easily
perceived by the senses."

VERSE 13: "*Who can strip off his outer coat? Who would
approach him with a bridle?*"

SYMBOLISM: This stripping concerns the unveiling of the
deceptive outer coat or mantle, overspread by colors (bends) in the
covering that allow for many different shapes. They also have the
ability to travel from one place to another at the speed of light. They
can move through a medium (which entails a portal.) *Transient* is "a
passing with time." The object being sent to its destination through

THE CURS-ED NET

a passage is to their specific home territory within their *now* second estate. The message says that if you think that (in any way) man can control this beast (the evil spirits — the Fallen Angels & Satan,) ***think again***! God is saying in this verse (13) that He is — and is alone — the ***only power*** that can have dominion over the beast. It is only through a ***true relationship*** with Jesus Christ (as stated before,) that the beast can be restrained!

SELECTED KEY WORD HIGHLIGHTS FROM VERSE 13:

The outer cloak is a *traveling cloak,* or a cloak of transport, so it can travel from place to place, movement or passage (such as dimensions.) The stripping of the outer cloak or covering would expose the *Grays & Reptilians* to what they really are: evil spirits!

In Greek, the meaning of a *covering* as in (epe) & (Kalupto) is "upo" "to cover" which implies wickedness & deceit. (Plane) renders deceit as "wandering" (as in wandering stars!) & (phrenapatao) means "to deceive in one's mind." (So we have a traveling cloak of protection "which is deceiving in appearance," & a *mantle* that also has a meaning of "being overspread by colors," (as UFOs are.) There is also a meaning of fold or pair of folds of a body wall that lines a shell. (*Fold* = "a bend" which accounts for the many shapes of UFOs, with the shell being the cloak or outer coat!)

The word *travel* also has a meaning of "being transmitted, a light" (as in the speed of light?) Now the word *transmit* in general is "to send from one place to another," and in (physics,) "to propagate through a medium." It also has the meaning of the word "passage" (which is the act or process of passing, especially a movement (travel) from one place to another, across a corridor — *transition!*)

Let's look at the word 'transit' in (Middle English) which is transite < & Latin = (transitus;) see 'transient.' *Transient* has a meaning of "passing with time." *Passage* is the medium spoken of above. *Send* is " to be conveyed by an intermediary to a destination." *Intermediary* is "that which occurs between the object sent and its destination." The passage as medium, then, would be the ***doors*** or the portal corridor. The object is transmitted at the speed of light through — to its destination.

VERSE 14: *"Who dares open the doors of his mouth, ringed about with his fearsome teeth?"*

SYMBOLISM: Who would not be afraid of the beast? Who would be bold before the appearance of him? (His representatives take the forms of UFOs, ghosts, "mothman," hauntings, etc.) When the jaws (doors) of his mouth open and let these evil things out, they create a very dangerous & evil situation, a confrontation that you would be wise in not embracing.

SELECTED KEY WORD HIGHLIGHTS FROM VERSE 14:

The *doors,* in Greek (tolmao,) have the sense of not dreading or having fear of, being bold! Yet 'jaws' in general has a meaning of a dangerous situation or confrontation. *Mouth* is "the body opening through which an animal takes in food (the devouring beast,) remembering that "Satan walks about like a lion seeking whom he may devour" (1 Peter 5:8.) 'Mouth' in Greek (epistomizo) is "to bridle" (V.13) earlier, and is used metaphorically as "stopping the mouth, putting to silence."

Out of the mouth of the beast comes true evil, deceit, torment, inflictions, terror, etc., while __he__, **the beast**, is looking to devour YOU — thereby keeping you away from God! The beast will teach you his ways, and not God's ways.

THE SCOPE OF THE TERRITORY OF THE
FEARLESS LEVIATHAN

'Mouth' is also symbolic of the area of his domain where evil spirits and Fallen Angels all make up the beast as their habitation & estate with Satan. (This, then, would be the earth and the "sea," (open space) the twelve constellations of the zodiac (as enumerated in the previous chapter,) plus the Bear & Orion (as one of its two cubs, where the other is part of one of the zodiac constellations,) and this **WHOLE AREA BOUNDARY** is symbolic of the Beast's mouth (or *areas of operation!*) The *teeth* symbolically represent the inhabitants of the beast's mouth within its territory. It is something that injures or destroys with force

VERSE 15: "His back has rows of shields tightly sealed together."

SYMBOLISM: *Back* in Greek (notoc) signifies "to bend, curve." *Bend* in general is "to assume an angular shape, and to force to assume a different direction or shape, according to one's own purpose." (For the special purpose of each UFO encounter, you will see a different action played out most of the time (as) actions, shapes or light shows in order to suit their Fallen Angels' purpose for evil & deceit toward the end they are moving to. Each encounter is personal. {{I can personally attest to the "packaging" effect, where, if you were to have a series of **paranormal** sequences, all of which seem to jive with one another – *WATCH OUT!* It could be a "packaging" both very personal & very deceptive, (so much so) that you would swear it was on the level, when, in fact, it is really a spiritual *sting*! Remember that UFO encounters & paranormal happenings are really two tricks in & from the same trickster — the same ball of wax — so *BEWARE!*}}

Rows in general is "a series of objects (at times UFOs together,) or next to each other." *Series* in general is "a group of objects related linearly, with varying successive differences in form or configuration, (i.e., able to change shapes, where there are many different sizes indeed!) *Shields* in general is "a protective device or structure (usually round) and is also a structure of plates or mesh, or an arrangement of such. *Plates* are that which are of a plate-like part or structure such as that covering some reptiles; see scales. *Scales* are small plate-like structures that are the coverings of fish and reptiles. (So shields could also be symbolic of the fish (*Grays*) & the reptiles (*Reptilians*) mentioned in the twelve signs of the zodiac section.)

'Shield' in Greek (thureos) formerly meant "a stone for closing the entrance of a cave." (How about the doors of the beast's mouth?) The entrance is a stone (portal) and the door to the habitat of the Bear, Orion, & the Pleiades (as the <u>horn of stars</u> of Taurus – *the Bull* within the zodiac.). The Bear & its cubs (cave) above represent that from which the shields (UFOs) come from! 'Shield' also has a Greek meaning reflective of "then a shield oblong & large" where the symbolism is of a cigar-shaped object! {{It was a sixty foot-long long cigar-shaped object that my own father saw casually drifting up the Hudson River in New York in 1925; what was it doing there? My father knew aircraft, and it certainly was not either a blimp or a

THE CURS-ED NET

zeppelin. Could it have been from **the Bear**, or one of its cubs, Orion &/or the Pleiades? Based on the information presented thus far, it may not be such a bad guess!}}

VERSE 16: "...each is so close to the next that no air can pass between."

KEY WORDS & SYMBOLISM: *Air* in Greek (aer) signifies "the atmosphere," and (ouranos) denotes "the heavens." It is a word derived from the root meaning "to cover or encompass." (In other words, the shields (UFOs) have the earth & sky encompassed so well that the atmosphere being so large cannot hide you! There is no place that they cannot find you — especially if they choose to! The air (as atmosphere) is so well covered by these UFO shields, that when needed, nothing could slip by between them. {{Anyone who had seen the documented story of Alexander the Great on "THE HISTORY CHANNEL" over the last few years, as part of ancient UFO presentations, could not help but visualize these **shields** in the sky (as the ancients called these circular flying vehicles,) actually *helping him* in one of his campaigns against an enemy, since it was so difficult to storm a particularly well-built garrison while he was in the Middle East. This also adds another level of concern about UFOs as to not only knowing what is going on "down here," but also the reason why "they" are aiding and abetting certain individuals. [Why would an ET race from the planet 'Zeonphobia' care what happens during our tribal squabbles?] From an extra-terrestrial sense, this story (that I have seen chronicled from Alexander's own historian,) does not make particular sense, but from Richard's point of view it would make eminent sense, since the demonic forces have a <u>**vested interest**</u> in us right from the start! For those readers interested in just such accounts of *flying shields*, which — by the way — both helped Alexander against his campaign vs. the Phoenicians at Tyros, and also *thwarted his advance* while he & his Macedonians were crossing the river Jaxartes on the Indian border, go to the aforementioned Hesemann book (p.241 for such details.}}

VERSE 17: "They are joined fast to one another."

KEY WORDS & COMMENTS: *Join* in Greek (kollao) generally has the meaning of "to write," "to be joined with," or "to yoke together" as in (su n zeugnumi.) *Yoke* in Greek (zugos) from a meta-

249

THE CURS-ED NET

phorical point of view, means "of submission to authority of bond service to masters." (Those who operate the *shields* (UFOs) {{and probably connected to the same "flying shields" that Alexander encountered,}} are united to a cause as an army joined fast together under submission to yet higher authority — their *Satanic* masters!) {{Perhaps Alexander was **thwarted** from going into India because *the higher masters [from "ON HIGH"]* issued orders like "so far you can go and no further since it would upset the whole diabolical plan being prepared as a trap for mankind!" Of course this is just speculation on my part, but it certainly seems *very peculiar* on the face of it.}}

CONTINUATION OF VERSE 17: "They cling together and cannot be parted."

(This means that they are loyal to and follow their masters, who would be represented by the spiritual wicked hierarchy. {{Remember Ephesians 6:12, and you will perceive the comprehensive sweep being presented by Richard as St. Paul understood it, and stated so well back in the first century of our current age.}} They are part of the whole, and cannot be separated from that whole (of *the Beast!*)

VERSE 18: "His snorting throws out flashes of light."

His (The Beast's) *snorting* is symbolic of the appearance of light (as "intense") flashes of light, (which is being breathed forcefully!) *Breath* in Greek (emphusao) means "upon," (or, in other words, to all these they wish to attract.) 'Breathe' in general is "to make apparent." *Apparent* is "to be readily seen, visible, or appearing as such."

(The *life* of the shields UFOs & occupants Fallen Angels who have given life to these shields by operating them, this 'life' therefore means "breath" symbolically, making the shields [UFOs] give off intense flashes of this same light.) {{What is extraordinary is that there may very well be an **inter-relationship** between "machine" and the operator of that machine (like a key in a lock) so that the "machine" cannot be operated by *just anyone*. This concept was brought forth by David Adair in a lecture that I had seen a few years ago; it could also explain why our government (secretly) had such a problem in understanding how the retrieved "saucers" really operated, (using the Roswell incident as a prime example,) unless it could

250

THE CURS-ED NET

be connected to a type of "mind melding" with the same "saucer." Obviously, if this dynamic turns out eventually to be, or, in fact, *most likely demonic* as we have been suggesting all along, it would — per force — bring the discussion (of the core understanding of Ufology) into an entirely different realm of understanding! If (any) *secret* government made an agreement with these demonic forces, then they may have been introduced (via the key of "mind melding,") so as to even operate these demonic vehicles. Of course, this is only speculation, but given what has already been provided in *the Bite of the Serpent* portion of this treatise, including this third part on the *demonic net of astrology and related subjects,* (thanks to the tireless labor of Richard,) it is not beyond the realm of possibility.}}

Flashes in general is "to give off light or to be lighted in sudden or intermittent bursts; to appear or occur suddenly; to move or proceed rapidly; to make known or signal by flashing lights; to display ostentatiously." It also means "to flaunt, a sudden intense display of light." (I think we just described a UFO!) *Light* in Greek is (phos) which is akin to (phao) meaning "to give light." (It is from the root pha — and phan — & metaphorically as "reaching the mind." The flashes of light also (colors) have a trance-like effect on your mind.)

Another word (kaio) is Greek for *to burn.* (Many UFO encounters have had people being literally burned by heat &/or radiation.) {{One of the most tragic and well- documented cases on record entails a man who touched a UFO, only to suffer eventually from radiation poisoning. It is a lengthy story yet well documented, and may offer some insight as to our present discussion, so I will quote the details at length, and then connect it to yet another portion of Enoch!

The man in question was Stephen Michalak. This case was seen on TV (via *SIGHTINGS*, etc.,) but I am indebted for the details of this dramatic story from Timothy Good's classic 1988 book, *ABOVE TOP SECRET*, where the author goes into the extraordinary details, starting on page 195. Stephen had the encounter near Falcon Lake, in Canada & near the Ontario border. It was May 20, 1967. There were two objects, but the object that landed, actually changed colors from red to gray and finally "hot stainless steel," and surrounded by a golden glow. As Stephen touched the cigar-shaped object, which was 35 feet in diameter and 12 foot high, he saw a purple light flooded out of the upper openings of the craft.

As he sketches the craft, he felt warm waves of air and the smell of **sulphur** also radiated from the craft. The door then opened, and he could here two human-like voices, one higher pitched than the other. Thinking that it must have been an American experimental craft, he went through a series of six languages that he uttered into the door, but got no response. He pushed down his tinted green lenses on his goggles, and peered into the opening. He saw many lights, some in patterns and flashing in random sequence. The door closed, and as he examined the outside of the craft, he found that the glove he was wearing to inspect it had burned and melted! He was facing an exhaust vent when suddenly a blast of hot air struck his chest! It set both his shirt and vest on fire, causing him severe pain. He ripped the clothes off him as the object left. He later suffered from headaches and nausea.

He was examined by 27 doctors, one of whom noted that Stephen got a radiation dosage of between 100-200 roentgens, and luckily, (because he was only exposed for a short time,) did not receive a lethal dose! As the case gained notoriety, the Canadian government became less than enamored with releasing the full contents of the details of the Michalak case, and according to Mr. Timothy Good, the complete case was never fully disclosed up to the time of the publication of the book in 1988.

I personally get the strange feeling that these beings inhabiting this craft were *demonic Fallen Angels* or somehow connected to Satan's *NET*work. The sulphur portion of the story reminded me of the sulphur pits that these same unfortunates were subjected to, a la *The Book of Enoch*; you may check Enoch 66:6 wherein lies the valley of the angels who seduced (man,) and were buried under the soil mixed with *sulphu*r and the waters [Richard Laurence translation.]}}

NOW WE CONTINUE ONWARD WITH THE *KEY WORD* ANALYSIS OF VERSE 18, from chapter 41 of Job:

(Erchomai) is another Greek word with the meaning of 'light.' From this we get (pipto) *lightning* that means "to fall," and rendered "to strike;" see 'smite.' *Smite* in Greek (patasso) means "to strike,"

THE CURS-ED NET

and (metaphorically,) of judgment. It also has the connotation of an affliction of **disease by an angel** (as in Fallen Angel.) 'Smite' (plesso) is akin to (plege) which means "a plague, a wound;" also (rhapizo) which is "to strike with a rod of light, "a goad," (and this is the **very** instrument that these evil beings put you into a trance with, as mentioned before.)

Plague is (mastix) which means "a whip scourge," and (metaphorically) is of a disease. A *scourge* is a wide spread affliction (abductions?) where the word *curse* means "of a source or cause of 'evil' — a scourge." (Refer again to the **Flying Scroll** of Zacharia 5:1for the details.)

VERSE 18 (continued): "…his eyes are like the rays of dawn."

Eyes as in the Greek (ophthlmos) are akin to (opsis) which conveys the idea of "sight, signifying here penetration." *Penetration* in general is "a process of piercing the act of entering to establish influence over or to gain information; an attack (to strike) as in influence over another." (The aliens *as* Fallen Angels have the ability to enter your mind, control you through influence while under trance, which is symbolized by the "good-old" goad or rod!) *Eye* in Hebrew (ayin) is also used figuratively as "mental & spiritual abilities, acts & statements." *Spiritual* (Fallen Angels) have the "abilities", including the power to perform or to do something spiritual — but the power is supernatural power!

Acts means that these (alien Fallen Angels) have a "process of doing, performing, & playing a part or role as a character. They behave in a manner suitable for the role." {{Remember that everything they do is a *facade* — a deceitful cover for something else, and why [?] — *because* you are the fish & they are the fishermen! You are the hunted & they are the hunters! There is a curious use of this same terminology in the *Book of Jeremiah 16:16-18.where* man had turned from worshipping the one true God to useless false gods, (which we contend are these same Fallen Angels, etc.,) so God punished these same foolish men by **sending them fishermen & hunters** (the Fallen Angels' entourage as depicted in the zodiac [?]) to avenge the just anger of God. I found the remark curious — but apt!}}

Statement is the "act of declaring something to create a certain impression." (Would this be the **UFO façade sideshow**?) Let's look at the word *evil* in Greek (kakos) which stands for "whatever is evil in character!" We also have the word (poneros) that is "what is evil in influence & effect." *Rays* in general here is "to send out" as rays (which would be the supernatural influence that can penetrate our minds, just like the rays of light penetrate our eyes like the dawn.

VERSE 19: "Firebrands stream from his mouth; sparks of fire shoot out."

Fire in general is "to cause to burn, to arouse emotions" (physical) & "to generate an electrical impulse." *To arouse emotions* is "to awaken, to stir up;" 'emotion' is an intense mental state, or agitation; in Latin, it means "to move" (where to move as in 'abduction' and to generate stimulation through electrical impulses by the use of the goad or "rod.") The impulse is how the trance is induced. *Brand* in general is "a trademark or identification indicating identity or ownership, which is burned on the hide (skin) of an animal or (person.)" {{As an investigator, I personally have seen these "branding marks," especially the little red triangle shapes embossed on the abdomen of at least one female who herself has indicated some type of **the bite of the serpent,** since she also had connected the event with the observations of UFOs. I have also heard of other cases on TV regarding UFO abduction discussions, and it crops up in the Ufological literature on occasion.}} So 'firebrand' symbolizes a mark or brand burned into the skin, which could refer to someone's ownership, possibly of the burned-in skin marks on "alien" abductees.) {{It must be a frightening thought for some female to feel she has been so branded by entities that may not be benevolent. As our thesis is unfolding, I hope that these same "bitten" people will take solace in the saving grace of Jesus Christ, who came so that we all shall not perish, but have life everlasting. This IS serious business!}}

Stream in general is a "flow, a steady flow, to put forth or give off." *Mouth* in general is "an opening;" also "to utter." (A flow of utterances, i.e., evil teachings & influences, which become "fire branded" into our minds like a **remembrance** as in an earlier statement, is an evil false knowledge through a **negative spiritual** encounter.) *Utter* means "to send forth," and has the symbolism of the words "rays of light." *Speaks* in general is "a flash of light, a glistening of metal, and also a quality or feeling with latent potential; it has the meaning also 'of a seed.'" *Latent* is "present & potential but not evident or active," (i.e., something present but not known of.) 'Pathol' is a dormant or hidden stage (as in the implanted organism,) & 'biol' is underdeveloped but capable of normal growth under the proper conditions.

(My understanding of this is that the implanted organism is being under-developed but capable of normal growth, as long as it is implanted into a human female that then makes it the "proper conditions!") The last meaning of 'latent' in line is (psychological) which itself means "present in the unconscious mind but not consciously expressed." Under hypnosis, the abductee recalls the event that took place; it remains present in the unconscious mind but cannot be consciously expressed. The Latin expression is "to lie hidden." So the whole of the abduction event is kept hidden in the unconscious and only through hypnosis can it be revealed, i.e., that which is not consciously expressed!

Fire in Greek (pur) means "both of a fire or judgment, and as symbol of danger & destruction." *Shoot* in general has the idea of "uttering forcefully, or sending forth; also covering (as in territory.)" In a hunting game, the (abductees) begin to grow or produce (hybrids) and then put forth new growth, germinate, and engage in hunting (covering territory for the prey: *US!*)

Out in general means "away," "out of a normal position, from inside to outside." (The lighted shields (UFOs) are traveling outside their habitat to hunt for their prey — the abductees!)

VERSE 20: "Smoke pours from his nostrils as from a boiling pot over a fire of reeds."

(Literally, it is smoke, but it is symbolic of itself, not of its chemical make-up, but of its color. *Smoke* in general has the meaning of color as of "a pale gray to a dark gray.") This color of gray I believe to be symbolic of the evil agencies, which are deceiving us as aliens (*the Grays*) but they are of the Fallen Angels.

Pour in general has the meaning of "sending forth" or "proceeding in numbers." 'Pour' in Greek (ekcheo) means "to pour out," & (ek)

THE CURS-ED NET

"out" is used also as divine wrath, as in Rev. 16,1-4,8,10,12 & 17. *Nostrils* in general is of (two) external openings of the nose; in Old English (OE) we have (nosthyal) = nose, & (thyrl) = hole. *Hole* in Greek (pholeos) means "a den or hole," while (ope) is "caves" KJV; see 'cave.' (NOTE: A den or cave is usually home to a bear & its cubs; symbolically, therefore, it could relate to the Bear, Orion, & the Pleiades' constellations, where the Pleiades is a portion of Taurus.) *Boiling* (as) from a boiling pot here, is in relation to "the smoke pouring from his nostrils," (with) "the pot boiling & the steam rising." 'Boiling' means here "an agitated swirling mass." *Agitated* is "moving with sudden force (power) and violence." *Violence* in Greek (hormema) is a "rush" & 'rysh' in Greek (hormao) is akin to (horme;) see 'assault;' also (trecho) which is "to run" and is translated "rushing" (to war as in Rev. 9:9.)

'Swirling' in general is "to move in a whirling motion," (such as a whirlwind symbolism?) *Pot* in general has five meanings:

1) It is made of pottery, glass or metal
2) It is a round vessel.
3) A container with contents (as symbolic of a UFO and its occupants.)
4) An artistic decorative vessel of any shape.
5) Something such as a chimney pot, (as could be envisioned by a pipe shape or cigar-shaped object.)

Fire in general is "that which releases heat and light, luminosity or brilliance, (just as a UFO does.)" (I believe that this verse related to a judgment, the coming assault of UFOs & their occupants, which we have seen demonstrated as *the Grays & Reptilians*. The smoke is not only gray in color, but reflects as the smoke mentioned in Rev. 9:9 of the abyss where the locusts come from. The abyss is the holding place of many fallen angels, so it would make sense that the locusts are the *Gray* fallen ones — symbolized here as a coming invasion! This is, in fact, a judgment where the cigar-shaped object is being mentioned with the pot, and therefore relates to the ***curse of the flying scroll,*** as per Zacharia 5:1. Fire is symbolic of the brilliance & heat being generated, the same type of heat that UFOs

THE CURS-ED NET

emit! Swirling, as a whirlwind, could relate to other objects of a round shape rotating.)

VERSE 21: "His breath sets coals ablaze, and flames dart from his mouth."

Breath in Greek (pneuma) means "spirit" & 'spirit' (pnoe) is akin to (pueo) which is "to blow." It literally signifies the "breath of life," & (in this case,) the life of the Beast simulated through the Fallen Angels as giving life to the crafts [UFOs] as we "give life" to our vehicles; it operates in the same manner, so breath is symbolic of the Fallen Angels operating the "blazing coals" (or illuminated objects.)

Ablaze in general means "radiant with bright colors, (just as UFOs flash.)" *Flames* in Greek (phlox) is akin to the Latin's (fulgeo,) which is "to shine," & is used apart from (pur,) which is the "fire" of 2Thess 1:8, where the fire is to be understood as the instrument of divine judgment. *Dart* in general is "a sudden rapid movement, to move suddenly & rapidly." *Mouth* is (symbolic for the Beast's domain,) where the evil agencies inhabit; basically the mouth here "represents space, atmosphere, where the blazing coals come to administer judgment."

VERSE 22: "Strength resides in his neck, dismay goes before him."

Strength in Greek (ischus) is "ability," & (kratos) means "force, mighty." 'Strength' in Hebrew is (hayil) which reflects "property, capability, influence." *Power* is the "ability to effect or produce something."

Resides in general is "to live in a place, to exist." *Neck* in Greek (trachelos) is (metaphorically) "putting a yoke upon." *Yoke* (zugos) also (metaphorically) denotes "a submission to authority with (the power to control.)" *Dismay* is to "destroy the courage or resolution of by exciting dread or apprehension — a sudden or complete loss of courage in the face of trouble or danger." In Latin it is "to deprive of power." (So the Beast has the force, power, and ability plus the numbers to produce the effect upon (his prey: *US*!) He does this through the use of supernatural usage, by (the sight of UFOs) and in general, exciting dread upon us so as to incapacitate us into submission.)

THE CURS-ED NET

VERSE 23: "The folds of his flesh are tightly joined. They are firm and immovable."

Folds (GM) are "the sheep of the flock." *Sheep* as in the Greek (probaton) — metaphorically — means "of those who belong." *Flesh* in Hebrew (basar) is the "male sex organ." This is symbolic of the creation of creatures by the Beast (as in Satan & the Fallen Angels.) (Basar) also means the "meaty part plus the 'skin of men'." The words "meaty parts of animals" (as in Deut. 14:8 & Gen. 41:2,) speaks of cows as "fat of flesh" & (basar) often means the "edible part" of the animals. (Could this be referencing the edible parts useful of mutilated cattle, etc. [?] Could the 'skin' of men be the "scoop marks" noted in Ufology [?] Could DNA tissue help create human clones [?])

{{If **The Holy Bible** has coded other aspects of the UFO and demonic abduction phenomenon (as demonstrated in this three-part series heretofore,) why not in the answers to the above three questions, which, in may respects, our present day reality would wish to bury into the files of simple anomalous activity, and leave it at that. This subject is **too important** to leave to idle speculation or worse — misinterpreted or spin controlled data.}}

Flock above in Hebrew (so'n) relates to "small cattle" and should be distinguished from (baqar) which is a "herd." "Small cattle" are small in stature, (similar to *the Grays*!) You see the word (so'n) in Hebrew as either "sons" or "son." *Cattle,* as in hybrid herds, could be symbolic of the sons of the Beast! 'Cattle' in Hebrew ('cleph) has three meanings, and one of them is the word "groups." *Group* in general has a meaning of "a class or collection of related entities or objects." *Related* is "the way or person is connected to another by blood (as a parent to a child or a beast to a herd.)" *Entity* is "of existence, being" and in Latin, "to be."

Continuing with verse 23, they "are tightly joined" where *joined* in general is "the connection with, a close association, or relationship with." *Relationship* is "of being related, a connection by blood." *Firm* in Greek (bebaios) is "steadfast & secure." (All of these hybrid clones, etc., created by the (Beast as Satan) & the Fallen Angels via the process such as implantation create a bond of sorts between them. The herds, 'sheep,' folds of his flesh the beast's, are tightly joined by

258

relationship, brought into existence to do a job, with loyalty to their creator, and are firm & immovable in this sense; if we were to allude to a military term, there are no "AWOLS!")

The word *immovable* means "unalterable, unyielding in principal, purposeful, with adherence to their cause; they are incapable of being moved emotionally since there are no emotions within these hybrid clones." {{This is not only formidable but frightening; one may think of a "Manchurian Candidate" mind-controlled type of person — now "shelled" in human form or other facades, and ready, willing and able to perform tasks for its immoral leader — Satan! At least since WW II, our very own intelligence services have been so dabbling in this dark arena in order to come up with the perfect spy/&/or assassin; cf. Gordon Thomas's excellent introduction into this dark area by reading *JOURNEY INTO MADNESS*. Have the alphabet agencies & general intelligence services in any way joined hands with the *claw of Satan's realm*? The evidence within the New World Order research would seem to point in that direction.}}

VERSE 24: "His chest is hard as rock, hard as a lower millstone."

Chest in general is the (thorax) & 'breastplate' in Greek is (thorax.) The *breast* denotes "a breastplate consisting of two parts, and protecting the body on both sides from the neck to the middle" (Rev. 9:9.) (Breastplate is a piece of armor that covers the Beast.) The Beast's breastplate is as hard as rock. In Greek, *hard* (porois) denotes "a hardening, a covering. (Symbolic here is breastplates [chest] where two pieces as hard as rock are protecting the Beast (the collective Fallen Angels) as an outer covering. Could the body armor worn by *the Grays* or the covering for the UFOs be of the same type of shell?)

Millstone is the Greek (mulos) that is a "handmill," consisting of two circular stones, one above, & the other, the lower millstone fixed! 'Millstone' serves as storage containers (as one of its meanings,) as per Exodus 7:19. (The storage container of the occupants, which are circular and have two halves like rock protective coverings, one up and one down: could this not be descriptive of a UFO?)

THE CURS-ED NET

Fixed in general means "secure — a stable form — an unmovable and stable platform." *Form* is "the shape & structure of an object, as an outward appearance. " (The lower millstone, the circular half, is fixed, while the top one rotates.) *Circular* also is just not a "saucer," but can mean "the shape of a cylinder" (as in "cigar-shaped!")

NOW SKIPPING TO VERSE 26: "The sword that reaches him has no effect, nor does the spear or the dart or the javelin."

Sword in Hebrew (hereb,) represent "an implement that can be or is being used in war; the exact shape of the implement however, is not specified by this word." (Sword is symbolic by modern weapons, and of no particular shape.) *Spear* is "a long shaft with a pointed end." (It is symbolic for modern-day rockets, missals, etc.) *Dart* is a slender pointed missal (small) as those used on jets, etc. *Javelin* is a light spear thrown by the hand. (It is symbolic of hand-fixed rockets or projectiles.) Of course, *none* of these modern day weapons can harm the vehicles of the Beast (i.e., the UFOs!)

VERSE 27: "Iron he treats like straw and bronze like rotted wood."

Iron in general is "of great hardness, strength, firmness; it is inflexible & unyielding." *Treat* in general is "to regard and handle in a certain way; to subject to a process, an action or a change, especially a chemical or physical process." *Straw* is "a stalk of threshed grain." (It is easily broken, bent, cut, etc.) It is very manageable. *Rotten* has the idea of "being in a state of decay, decomposed." *Decay* (in Biology) is "to break down into component parts, rotted matter." *Bronze* is general means "various alloys of copper & tin and traces of other metals" (as discussed previously.) 'Rotted' wood is "that which crumbles & breaks apart into small pieces." *Treats* are "a process of handling metals in a certain way, & a way to change iron (steel) by a chemical or physical process."

VERSE 28: "Arrows do not make him flee; sling-stones are like chaff to him."

Arrow are "thin shafts with a pointed head at one end; it is also flight stabilized" (as in modern day missals.) *Sling-stones* are "slingshots for flinging small stones" {{like the one David flung at Goliath.}} (It is symbolic for small to heavy weapons' fire.) *Chaff* is "finely cut straw or hay; trivial or worthless matter." (These weapons

THE CURS-ED NET

do not harm or hurt the Beast at all! It is like hay being tossed at him.)

VERSE 29: "A club seems to him but a piece of straw, he laughs at the rattling of the lance."

Obviously, this is one very strong Beast, since a club is one very strong weapon, {{and certainly not to be ignored by the "average Joe," yet, as we have seen by the various descriptions in the ongoing verses – *this Beast* is not your average Joe!}} *Lance* is a cavalry lance (sword) as in (rattling the saber) so to speak!

VERSE 30: "His undersides are jagged potsherds leaving a trail in the mud like a threshing sledge."

Undersides (in the plural) are "the bottoms or the sides that are less desirable." *Jagged* is "marked by irregular projections & indentations." *Potsherds* relate to "a pottery fragment or fragments." *Pottery* has a meaning of "the craft or work of the potter" (as the Beast,) {{just like God is the potter of men as in Jeremiah chapter 18.}} The bottoms of the fragments or sides less desirable are marked by 'irregular projections' (contrary to rule, accepted order or general practice;) these are the parts that extend outward, the image of a geometric shape. *Fragments* (small parts) with irregular & projective geometric shapes leave a "trail" (the traces of a hunting track, or a mark or trace left behind by something,) that resembles exactly what a UFO does when it leaves its landing spot. {{This is exactly what transpired in the 1964 Socorro, New Mexico UFO that we had mentioned previously, leaving well-defined circular imprints in the New Mexican desert, reflecting a fairly heavy unorthodox vehicle, which was allegedly transgressing both our air and land space!}}

Mud = "soft earth." *Threshing* is "to beat the stems or husks of grain with a machine or flail; to separate the grains or seeds in this manner; to thresh grain." (UFOs have been known to leave their signature marks as landing impressions of heat & weight in the soft earth, the tall grass or wheat fields!) {{From what I have come to understand, the 'signature marks or designs' in the *crop circles* may be due to some unknown energy force directed from above to below, but done with mighty intelligence and elegant artwork and precision, *and certainly not by some bungling fools* who are good with a stake & some pressing device that bends and breaks the wheat, etc. The

THE CURS-ED NET

real circles do not break, but rather bend, while being subjected to intense heat that can cause a chemical change in the wheat (perhaps supernatural in nature,) but in any event not the simplistic fruit of superficial minds thrust on the public by the mass myopic media.}}

Sledge is "a type of vehicle used as a sled, and symbolically as a vehicle for transportation." (One could say — just as UFOs are vehicles transporting their goods, whether occupant abductees and other goods.)

VERSE 31: "He makes the depths churn like a boiling caldron and stirs up the sea like a pot of ointment."

Depths = a deep part or place & often used in the plural. *Churn* is "to agitate or stir, as in (waves churning in the storm.)" *Boiling* is "to change from liquid to vapor, and to be stirred up, to vaporize by the application of heat; a swirling mass of liquid." *Caldron* is "a large vessel used for boiling (the sea depths) being agitated or stirred." *Sea* is "the expanse of water in the ocean." *Stir-up* is "to pass an implement through (a liquid) in circular motion, so as to mix the contents, as to introduce an ingredient," for instance.

Pot = a container. 'Pot' in Greek (xestes) is in Latin "liquid measure," as (sextarius.) *Measure* in Greek is ("metron") and is "that which is used for measuring — of a vessel." (Meros) is a part of. (Prosanaperoo) is "to fill up by adding to, to supply fully." *Ointment* is "a viscous or semi-solid substance used on the skin;" in Latin, see 'unguent.' *Unguent* is "a salve for healing or soothing." In Latin = "anoint." *Viscous* is "having a relatively high resistance to flow (as in being able to resist the drag forces of water.)" *Resistance* then is "an instance of resisting; a force tending to oppose or retard motion." *Anoint,* from the Hebrew (masah,) indicates "anointing" in the sense of a special setting apart for a function. 'Anoint' in Greek (aleipho) is a general term used for an anointing of any kind; for example, for physical refreshment. *Physical* is relating to the body, while *body* is "relating to a material thing; it also relates to matter or energy." *Refreshments* are something such as food. *Function* is something related to another, and dependent on it for its existence. In Latin we have performance — the way in which something operates, functions or performs; in Latin — to furnish.

THE CURS-ED NET

(This past verse is talking about the **underwater UFOs**, and includes the stirring up of the water – the churning as they travel undersea, & like a boiling caldron, it means the objects are emitting high heat, and glowing in the same process while evaporating all the water around it as it moves rapidly through the water [without any drag.] As the object moves along, it is emitting heat. This is done (because at the same time,) the ointment used on the skin is symbolic for that which is needed for the UFO's body to function. It is a process for providing *"food"* (physical) for the object (energy.) Power is provided by the flowing water of dams; so also (analogously) the movement of the object through the water is generating its energy supply.)

VERSE 32: "Behind him he leaves a glistening wake.' One would think the deep had white hair."

Glistening is "to shine by reflection with sparking luster, a lustrous shine." *Wake* is "a visible track of turbulence left by something through the water; a condition left behind." *Condition* is "a mode or state." *Mode* is "a manner or way of doing something, a method or given condition of functioning." *Spate* is "the condition of a physical system — a condition of being with regard to circumstances."

NOW FOR THE PHRASE "WHITE HAIR":

White is "the maximum lightness," whereas *hairs* are pigmented filaments; therefore, the expression means (white pigmented filaments.) *Pigment* is "a substance used as coloring, & mixed with water." *Filament* is "an incandescent wire emitting visible light to shine brilliantly, as a result of being heated. In effect, it is white water colored by a substance that shines."

The object is being heated so as to boil water. The object is shining; it gives off a whitish shiny color, with a trail of white phosphorous (or literally is phosphorus.) Let's look at *phosphorus.* It is "a highly reactive element (substance) existing in three allotropic forms: white, red & black." The (white) is as "white hair." Phosphorus in Greek is (phaj) for light, and in Latin, it means "morning star." (As you may know, this was a title for Satan himself!)

263

THE CURS-ED NET

{{This ends the citations Richard wanted to make regarding the *all-important* verses (relating to *the Living Beast – Satan,*) as was depicted by Job in his two chapters — 40 & 41 within **The Holy Bible.** In the final chapter of this present work, both co-authors will express their overall views concerning the UFO phenomenon, the abduction phenomenon, and how both are *an intricate part* to the cover-up of the *negative spiritual net,* propagated by *wicked spiritual forces from ON HIGH.* What you can *now* do about it will also be examined.}}

END NOTES:

Nelson's New and Illustrated Bible Dictionary
Publisher: Thomas Nelson, Inc. ©1995
Used by permission of Thomas Nelson, Inc.

CHAPTER TWENTY:

Conclusions of the Co-authors
FINAL REFLECTIONS BY RICHARD, AS PER THE *KEY IDEAS* OF PSALM 91

{{Introduction: Richard has decided to end this three-part series with one of the most beautiful and important psalms ever penned, *to give a certain solace to the spiritually weary, plus a sense of faith & hope where there only looks like dark despair. There is also a warning to those who think themselves powerful within the* **curs-ed net** — *that their days and nights are* **very** *numbered!* This is the psalm that Satan knows well, since he quoted part of it to Jesus, the Son of God Himself, before Jesus started His very mission to reconcile men to God the Father, so **the fallen ones** know that their days & nights are numbered! After Richard finishes his key word analysis, I will have some final reflections on the whole of the three-part thesis.}}

In closing, I leave you with Psalm 91 (of the NIV,) that states that one is *to have trust in God* through all troubles, especially those we cannot control. ONLY HE CAN STOP IT! Through our trust in Him & His Son, the Savior, Jesus Christ, He will do battle against those evil forces that we have no control over. As you read the key verses within this psalm, you will see how this trust will comfort you, and especially within verses 5 & 6, which, I believe, deals with the UFO phenomenon, orchestrated by evil forces of Fallen Angels. I will analyze these verses (using the NIV,) to show you that with

THE CURS-ED NET

trust in Him, plus having a **true relationship** with His Son Jesus, you will not have to fear this portion of evil that descends down upon the whole world, *hunting* for prey of those they can abduct, using this very prey for their own benefit (and certainly not yours!) GOD *promises* to stop this evil in your life if it is there now. He will also prevent it from happening again! Please read the following verses of PSALM 91 — not with your mind — but *with your heart!*

VERSE 1: *"He who dwells in the shelter of the Most High will rest in the shadow of the almighty."*

VERSE 2: *"I will say of the Lord, 'He is my refuge and my fortress, my God in whom I trust."*

VERSE 3: *"Surely he will save you from the fowler's snares and from the deadly pestilence."*

VERSE 4: *"He will cover you with his feathers, and under his wings you will find refuge; his faithfulness will be your shield and rampart. "*

(With faith in Him and a *true relationship* with His Son Jesus Christ, He will protect you from the following, as cited in verses 5 & 6. He (God) is stating it is so!)

VERSE 5 *"You will not fear the terror of night, nor the arrow that flies by day."*

Terror in Greek (phobetron) is "that which causes fright, a terror." It is translated "terrors" in Luke 21:11, and in the RV (KJV) "fearful sights;" note, for (ptoesis) see 'amazement.' Now Luke 21:11 states: "There will be great earthquakes, famines and pestilences in various places, and fearful sights and great signs from heaven."

Heaven in Greek (ouranos) is used in the New Testament as the "aerial heavens" — where *aerial* means "of, in the air, living in the air, sky & atmosphere." (These terrors, fearful sights from the sky, from the atmosphere & space *are none other than UFOs*! *Night* is (literally) "the hours of darkness;" symbolically *darkness* in Greek (skotos) has a meaning of " the evil powers that dominate the world" (Luke 22:53.) At the end of the verse, Christ is speaking "when darkness reigns" during these very hours of darkness.

(In Eph. 3:10, NIV,) according to the *Bible Note Life & Spirit,* the "rulers & authorities in the heavenly realms" (including the sky

THE CURS-ED NET

& atmosphere,) refer to the ruling powers of darkness in the spiritual realm.

In Eph. 6:12-NIV, it states: "For our struggle is not against flesh and blood, but against the rulers, against the authorities, against the powers (also another word which is symbolic of angels,) of this dark world and against the spiritual forces of evil in heavenly realms." (This terror by night from the heavenly realms our sky and atmosphere, including space, is *not referring to aliens* but rather to Fallen Angels **in character as** aliens.)

The arrow is symbolic of the vehicle seen in flight, in the sky that appears. If we look at the word *dart* in Greek (belos,) it denotes "a missile, an arrow, javelin, etc., but also in Eph. 6:16, it is referred to as *fiery*." "It mentions the flaming arrow of the evil one" (i.e., Satan.) *Flame* in Greek (phlox) is "to shine." *Shine* in Greek is (phaino) and means "to cause to appear" or (that which appears;) also, the word (lampo) means "to shine as a torch" while (stilbo) means "to glisten." (Perilampo) is "to shine around," & (periastrapto) has the meaning of "to flash around, to shine round about."

(UFOs suddenly appear; they shine like a torch, glisten and shine round (the whole of the object,) and then flash around meaning "light flashing from them.") *To fly* depicts "the act or process of flight." *Day* here in general means the following: "the hours of sunlight," but also "the 24 hour period during which earth completes one rotation on its axis — (meaning that this terror not only hits as night or day, **but** the whole of the 24 hour period!)

PSALM 91: VERSE 6: "*...nor the pestilence that stalks in the darkness, nor the plague that destroys at midday.*"

Pestilence in Greek (loimos) has the meaning of "any deadly infectious malady." In general, it is "a disease pernicious, evil influence or agent." *Evil* in Greek (kakos) is "whatever is evil in character" (such as the Fallen Angels and their 'alien' *Grays & Reptilians*;) also, "what is evil in influence & effect, malignant" (like an evil power that affects a person — and malignant as a cancerous disease as in "the implantation of an evil organisms," and is the power which affects all of its victims , such as those subjected to the "trance" by goad!)

267

ASTROLOGERS: *PHONE CALLS TO SATAN!*

Another meaning of the word *evil* is (poneros) which is akin to (ponos) and denotes "evil that causes labor, a malignant evil; toil." The word *influence* (in Astrology) is "a factor determining one's tendencies & characteristics believed to be caused by the positions of the stars & planets at the time of one's birth" (as per the zodiac, which reflects an evil influence!) *Toil* in Greek (kopiao) means "to labor" (here as to be pregnant.) (Basanizo) means "to put to the test" (i.e., look for certain qualities a person has to offer,) then "to examine by torture" (by probing with instruments that those abductees — chosen as *donors* for future implantation, as well as DNA material for cloning.)

This *is* the evil disease!

Stalk = "to track prey," or "to pursue by stealth" (as UFOs do. This was mentioned in the decoding of the zodiac signs as being hunted "for abductions.") *Darkness* is literally "the night." *Plague* is "a widespread affliction" (which is exactly what the UFO phenomenon is — since it is world-wide, and seen in every country of our globe.) 'Plague' in Greek (mastix) is "a scourge" & 'scourge' means "curse" in general; if one were to look up the word **curse**, it has the same meaning as the word **scourge**. (If you refer back to chapter twelve. you will notice a *curse* of a cigar-shaped object that represents abductions of a demonic kind that have been occurring approximately three to five thousand years ago until this very time! This curse involves UFOs *abducting* people. It is a curse against mankind for his sins, which reflect transgressions against God.)

Destroys in Greek (apollumi) refers "to perish" as of spiritual destitution, from (luo) which is reflected in 1 John 3:8, regarding "the works of the devil." (This, of course, is destitution – *without God* — and *without His Son as your savior*, Jesus Christ!) A spiritual perishing through a curse is a disease by the Fallen Angels. *Midday* means "the middle" & *middle* "begins at neither one extreme or the other," or (in other words,) **anytime** of the day within the 24 hour period of each day!) {{Jesus had warned us that we *know not the day nor the hour,* **so be vigilant always**!}}

SO, these attacks can happen at anytime & anywhere, but if you have faith & trust in God as reflected in Psalm 91, then you have a true relationship with God's Son, Jesus Christ. You will then – *not fear this curse* — the curse that comes upon those who are spiritually destitute! Accept the Lord Jesus Christ as your savior, *as I did* — with a true heart, not out of fear, but rather, with *a true wanting*! *True* is "of giving thanks always and living your life wholly in Jesus." God has emotions too, and we should always give thanks and include Him in our lives. If we act appropriately, He will protect you against all these evil forces.

RICHARD'S TESTIMONIAL REPEATED!

As He protected me after that night, having prayed to God the Father because I was so overwhelmed with these evil forces (as UFO agencies,) I cried out to Him for His Son Jesus, and as soon as I did, He lifted a heavy weight out of my chest, which today I know now to have been evil spirits!

This evil that was in me may very well dwell in anyone who gets so wrapped-up with UFOs, hauntings, and so forth, and although may not have experienced what I have exactly, may have experienced varying levels of these troubles. I strongly feel that it will somehow catch up with you as you allow yourself to go deeper down this road.

I, personally, have **not** been troubled now for over fifteen years, and through Jesus Christ, I am at peace! It is through Him, who sent His Holy Spirit that I now can **bear witness** and share this with you! Please do not allow yourself to suffer through life without Jesus, the Father, and the Holy Spirit. As it says in the Good Book: Jesus Christ **is** the way, the truth and the life (as per *The Gospel of John.*)

REFLECTIONS of *Byron LeBeau:*

"And when you look up in the heavens and behold the sun or the moon or any star among the heavenly hosts, do not be led astray into adoring them and serving them." [Deut. 4:19]

For those who take **The Holy Bible** seriously, it becomes pretty clear that the above quote reflects part of the thesis for which Richard labored these many past months, ending with a fuller understanding of what we have framed as **the *curs*-ed net. _Any_** star that we can see (and we can see roughly about 2000 on any given night, were

THE CURS-ED NET

used to connect certain dots that led to the *adoring & serving* of the fallen portion of the heavenly hosts, i.e., the Fallen Angels of which *The Book of Enoch* has thrown a mighty light on in the course of this thesis. Why was this warning given in the *Book of Deuteronomy* to begin with? According to Enoch, it was the Fallen Angels that taught mankind about these very stars, both in astronomy & astrology! (CF. chapter 8 of *Enoch*.)

To see just how real this *curs-ed net* really is, EXHIBIT A will be drawn from the work of one, Robert Bauval. This man was featured in a TV documentary called, "THE MYSTERY OF ORION," which was televised in 1995 by *The Learning Channel*. The ostensible purpose of this program was to explore the whys & wherefores behind the shafts in *The Great Pyramid*, which actually pointed to a certain key constellation (Orion) and bright star (Sirius,) both of which played a mighty drama in Egyptology, which, according to Bauval, **immortalized** Orion & Sirius — not for what they were, but for what they represented. I will quickly go through this mystery "solved," before we go to the bigger picture:

According to Bauval, (working with Graham Hancock,) they came to the conclusion that *The Great Pyramid* was not built by the Egyptians, but rather an advanced civilization that preceded the Egyptian one. Their evidence was based on the incredible knowledge ensconced in this pyramid, by mentioning that its directional points were exactly aligned to the cardinal points of the Earth, and it was even built to scale — (according to author Graham Hancock) of one to 43,000, reflecting the mathematical scale of the northern hemisphere, or in other words, whoever built *The Great Pyramid* knew a great deal (supernatural type of knowledge) of the pyramid in relation to the Earth and our galaxy, so this pyramid, in particular, acts as a type of monument to this knowledge. [Neither Hancock nor Bauval brought up *The Book of Enoch* in their discussion about this great knowledge, but, as alluded to before in the 8th chapter of 1 ENOCH, an explanation is provided as to how man knew so much about these incredibly built monuments in relationship to a certain star and constellation, and memorialized it in stone (and according to Robert Bauval,) this was done to reflect what the heavens looked like approximately 10,500 B.C.

THE CURS-ED NET

What was it immortalizing? Bauval found that the shaft leading out of the 'King's Chamber' of **The Great Pyramid** actually pointed to the belt of the constellation **Orion** as it would have looked circa. 10,500 B.C.; likewise, the shaft coming out of the 'Queen's Chamber' pointed to the star **Sirius**. *Orion* represented the high **god of resurrection** (according to the myth of the Egyptians,) and Sirius represented "his consort" — *Isis* — as the **queen of the heavens**. [You may recall, I had previously penned a warning from Jeremiah 7:18-21, where the holy prophet warned the Jews of his day, *not to honor* the so-called 'queen of heaven' — who was referred to as *Ishtar* (the Egyptians' *Isis*,) since it would anger the living Lord & God who took such great offense at having strange gods before Him! So whoever built (or was responsible for the construction of **this pyramid**, was slapping the living Lord God in the face, by incorporating an *honor* for these same lower gods, (whom I see as part of the Fallen Angels' hierarchy.)

To me, this is a **crucial** understanding; according to this program, the Egyptian pharaoh had one major goal: that when he died, his spirit would co-join with Osiris of Orion, (becoming "a star,") [wandering?] and therefore becoming one with him, which is a blasphemous mockery of Jesus' wish that we all become one with the true Father (as per *The Gospel of John*, 17:21-22.) If you can connect these dots in this same manner, the architects (**archons** as alluded to by St. Paul,) behind the construction of **The Great Pyramid**, may not only be veiled in mystery, but more dangerously, veiled in deception, a lure to attract, but within is a *hook to capture*!

EXHIBIT B: Angel vs. Angler

While I was thinking about this **curs-ed net,** and how the symbols revolve around hunting and trapping, and how the Fallen Angels were once upon a time — good angels, I looked at the word **angel**, and saw that by inverting two of the letters and adding an "r," it made an angel an *angler* or *fisherman*. A fisherman catches things by stealth, by presenting a lure, but unbeknownst to the fish who fails to see the hook, he becomes trapped, and eventually "soul-food" for the fisherman. I thought to myself: is not this what the Fallen Angels' function is toward man, hunting him or her until he

THE CURS-ED NET

or she falls into the trap! As Richard pointed out in chapters 17 & 18, the zodiac represents just such imagery. Coincidence? *I do not think so*! Did not the prophet Jeremiah warn the fallen away Jews that God would send "hunters" & "fishermen" to prey on them for the honoring of false gods? (CF. Jeremiah 16:16-18.)

EXHIBIT C: *THE BIG PICTURE*

If *The Book of Enoch* is correct, and there were two falls of the angels (the **Watchers** over men,) the first fall due to **presumption** as per chapter 67, and the second due to **lust** as per chapter 68, then mankind has been immersed in the same "net" where the angels (as **anglers**) are co-inhabitants — only we do not ordinarily see them in their proper form!

This is (according to Richard & myself,) where these hunter/fishermen have been given free reign to **_test man to the limits_**.' In my own past writings, I call this process **"necessary fertilizer,"** where — by overcoming these "angelic" obstacles, man grows from a **bud to a blossom**,' and although we cannot earn heaven, per se, are given enough grace (**if** we rely on the Father & His Son, Jesus Christ,) so that we will — *truly* — become one with Him, and live happily in peace with the Father forever; cf. Romans, chapter nine, for an explanation of this key idea. This *is* my belief, and the writings of Enoch, as well as that echoed through the prophets Joel, Zacharia, Isaiah, Jeremiah, Daniel, and the author of *The Book of Revelation* have **all** been telling us likewise, if we would but heed the warnings. [These ideas were reviewed thoroughly in PART II of this very book.]

EXHIBIT D: WE HAVE ALL WE NEED TO SUCCEED!

In **The Holy Bible** it says: "My grace is sufficient for thee." What comforting words. In the first epistle of John, chapter four, it states that the God within you is more powerful than the god of this world. Richard poured out his heart by examining the key parts to Psalm 91, where we are specifically shown how those who rely on the Father will not be harmed by the powers of darkness. The Beast, represented by the metaphors of Behemoth & Leviathan, which would ordinarily bring people to their collective knees due to the might of such a powerful force arrayed against them — a force of supernatural abilities — (as analogously was depicted in the science fiction movie, **WAR OF THE WORLDS**, where only a miracle would *and did* save them,) so too the Father (throughout the Bible) had pleaded with His *stiff-necked people* to rely on Him and *Him alone*...but they wouldst not — and so, as related by the prophets, they suffered the consequences of relying on their false gods of wood and stone, being led down *collective rabbit holes*, to the allurements of promise, *but in reality (not fiction)* became the prison of spiritual destitution!

Other than the LAST WORD of Richard (below,) this ends the thesis that was subtitled: *A Biblical Reality of the UFO & Abduction Phenomenon.* My hope is that seriously mature Christians will take the information presented, using it in such a way that they will never be fooled by the allurements of Satan, Inc. These have been writings of warnings yet *writings of hope.* The world is full of mysteries, but by using spiritual discernment, we will always be able to see the hook within the lure, and may peace come to *all men of good will*!

THE LAST WORD

God's Word is the only TRUE AUTHORITY mentioned throughout the Bible. We believe in His Word by faith through His beloved Son, Jesus Christ. Even for those who do not have this faith know in their hearts God's Word bares truth. The Bible is very explicit in dealing with all of the facts pertaining to Satan, the fallen angels and evil spirits and all of their attributes, activities, evilness and interaction with mankind. Many verses are warnings to us by God to turn away from their evil.

The Curs-ed Net was inspired through the Holy Spirit and written to disclose much more information on Satan's evil activities that have taken place with mankind throughout the centuries and continues to move forward full steam. This information was found by digging deeper into God's Word into coded **key words** located within chapters and verses throughout various books of the Old Testament and New Testament. Another contributor was the *Ethiopian* Book of Enoch that included vast amounts of information within its inspired writings. Together, these books and their key

THE CURS-ED NET

word meanings deal with **<u>new exposed truths</u>** about Satan's evil past and present activities.

God's Word disseminates to us the truth about their evil characteristics because it is the ONLY TRUE SOURCE of authority on these matters. There are similarities found through the coded meanings from the key words and addressed with the subject matter held within the foundational writings and cataloging over the years from the witnesses involved with UFO sightings and abduction events. This has brought forth information on the "aliens'" activities and attributes to be studied with this book, which should only reflect the similarities of the two; Satan's activities and the "aliens'" active agendas are too perfect in nature and seem to fall together – to the degree that they – *are one and the same.*

One needs only to study closely *The Curs-ed Net*, which reflects the testimonies from good and respectable people who, from all walks of life, have bravely come forth over the years to disclose their encounters by which this information on the so-called alien activity can be seen for what it really is. Take some of their testimonies and compare it to the Word of God on Satan and the evil ones for which God's Word is TRUE AUTHORITY. Make the comparison for yourselves and see. You cannot just dismiss either of them; it is all *too perfect.* We've been in the dark for too long now and it is time to see at last *some light.* And to quote the Bible:

John 12:46 (Christ speaking)

"I have come into the world as a light, so that no one who believes in me should stay in darkness."

-Richard Stout

REFERENCES:

American Heritage College Dictionary 3rd. Edition
Publisher: Houghton Mifflin Co.   Year: 2001
Author: American Heritage

Holman Bible Dictionary
Publisher: Holman Bible Publishers   Year: 1991
General Editor: Trent C. Butler, PH.D.

King James Version
Publisher: Thomas Nelson, Inc.   Year: 1985

Nelson's New and Illustrated Bible Dictionary
Publisher: Thomas Nelson, Inc.   Year: 1995

New International Version
Publisher: Zondervan   Year: 2002

New King James Version
Publisher: Thomas Nelson, Inc.   Year: 1982

Vine's Complete Expository Dictionary of Old and
New Testament Words:
Publisher: Thomas Nelson, Inc.   Year: 1996
Author: W.E. Vine, Merrill F. Unger, William White, Jr.

THE CURS-ED NET

Willmington's Guide to the Bible
Publisher: Tyndale House Publisher's, Inc.   Year: 1984
Author: Harold L. Willmington

Other References:

Forbidden Mysteries of Enoch
Publisher: Summit University Press   Year: 1984
Author: Elizabeth Clare Prophet

Bible quotations are taken from

New International Version
Publisher: Zondervan   Year: 2002

New King James Version
Publisher: Thomas Nelson, Inc.   Year: 1982

King James Version
Publisher: Thomas Nelson, Inc.   Year: 1985

UFO & OTHER BOOK & ARTICLE REFERENCES

Andrews, George, *Extraterrestrial Friends and Foes,* published by IllumiNet Press, Lilburn, GA 30226, 1993.

Carlsberg, Kim, *BEYOND MY WILDEST DREAMS,* BEAR & COMPANY, Sante Fe, New Mexico, 1995.

Druffel. Ann, *Techniques for Resisting Alien Abductions, FATE MAGAZINE, a Llewellyn publication. (November, 1993.)*

Fernandez, Dr. Joauim & Fina D'Armada, *HEAVENLY LIGHTS,* Eccenova Editions, Victoria, BC, 2005.

Fort, Charles, *The Books of Charles Fort, Henry Holt publisher, New York, 1941.*

Fowler, Raymond, *The Allagash Abductions,* Wild Flower Press, Tigard, OR, 1993.

THE WATCHERS II, Wild Flower Press, Tigard, OR, 1994.

Good, Timothy, *Above Top Secret,* published by William Morrow & Company, N.Y., N.Y., 10016, 1988.

Haley, Leah, *LOST WAS THE KEY, Greenleaf Publications, Tuscaloosa, AL, 1993.*

Heiser, Dr. Michael, *THE FAÇADE,* XLIBRIS Publications, Philadelphia, PA, 2000.

Hesemann, Michael, *UFOs: SECRET HISTORY,* Marlowe & Company, N.Y., N.Y., 1998.

Hopkins, Budd, *WITNESSED,* POCKET BOOKS, N.Y., N.Y., 1996.

Jacobs, Dr. David M., *SECRET LIFE,* FIRESIDE Publications, division of Simon & Schuster, N.Y., N.Y., 1992.

Littrell, Helen & Jean Bilodeaux, *Raechel's Eyes,* Wild Flower Press, Columbus, NC 2005.

Lewis, David Allen & Robert Shreckhise, *UFO: End-Time Delusion,* New Leaf Press, Green Forest, Arkansas, 1991.

Lorgen, Eve, *THE LOVE BITE,* Elogos & HHC Prtess, Bonsall, CA, 1999.

Marrs, Jim, *ALIEN AGENDA,* HarperPaperbacks, a Division of HarperCollins Publishers, N.Y., N.Y., 1997. *Rule by SECRECY,* HarperCollins Publishers, N.Y., N.Y., 2000.

THE CURS-ED NET

Rey, H.A., *THE STARS,* HOUGHTON MIFFLIN COMPANY, Boston, MA, 1962.

Salisbury, Frank B., *The UTAH UFO display: a biologist's report,* Devin-Adair Co., Old Greenwich, Connecticut, 1974.

Salla, Dr. Michael, "FOUNDATIONS FOR GLOBALLY MANAGING EXTRATERRESTRIAL AFFAIRS," (2003,) included in *THE UNIVERSAL SEDUCTION, Volume Three:* Piercing the Veils of Deception, by Angelico Tapestra, in association with Global Book Publishers, distributed through BookSurge.com.

Sherman, Dan, *ABOVE BLACK,* OneTeam Publishing, Wilsonville, OR, 2001.

Thomas, Gordon, *Journey into Madness,* Bantam Books, New York, 1989.

Thompson, Richard, *ALIEN IDENTITIES,* Govardhan Hill Inc., San Diego, CA, 1993.

Turner, Dr. Karla, *Into the Fringe,* published by Berkeley Books, N.Y., N.Y 10016, 1992. *Masquerade of Angels,* published by KELT WORKS, Roland, Arkansas 72135, 1994.

THE CURS-ED NET

INTERNET REFERENCES

Chapter One:

Bartley, James, **ALIEN ABDUCTIONS IN THE 21st CENTURY, 2004:**
http://www.alienlovebite.com/bartley4.htm

Chapter Three:

Turner, Dr. Karla, **ABDUCTIONS IN A GINGERBREAD HOUSE,** donated by James Vandale:
http://www.reptilianagenda.com/research/r100799a.shtml

Chapter Five:

Amorth, Fr. Gabtiele, Vatican exorcist Amorth speaks on Satan's smoke:
http://www.speroforum.com/site/article.asp?id=2879

Chapter Eight:

Crop Circle Theories
http://www.crystalinks.com/croptheories.html

LeBeau, Byron, FATIMA: FRANK FACTS vs. ILLUSIVE FICTION, [book review] of *HEAVENLY LIGHTS, written by co-authors* Dr. Joaquim Fernandez & Fina D'Armada:
http://theuniversalseduction.
com/bookreviews/fatima-frank-facts-vs-illusive-fiction

THE CURS-ED NET

Chapter Twelve:

Unruh, J. Timothy, **The Present Day UFO-ALIEN ABDUCTION PHENOMENON:**
http://www.ldolphin.org/unruh/alien/aliens.html

Winn, Craig, from chapter two (*"Enduring Love,"*) *as part of website,* **YADA YAHWEH website,** (which includes an examination of the numbers 15 & 30.)
http://yadayahweh.com/Yada_Yahweh_Going_Astray_Chesed.
YHWH

Winn, Craig, [From BOOK III of *Yada Yahweh*, SALVATION located at: CH. 6, also called "Salvation."]
http://yadayahweh.com/Yada_Yahweh_Salvation_Yasha.YHWH

Gan, Rev. Richard, *SATAN'S SEED*
(as reviewed by Byron LeBeau):
http://inspectorblebeau.pbwiki.com/SATANS-SEED-Explored

LeBeau, Byron, A highlight review of Stephen Quayle's important book, **GENESIS 6 GIANTS:**
http://inspectorblebeau.pbwiki.
com/GIANTS-IN-THE-MIDDLE-EAST-AND-ELSEWHERE

Chapter Seventeen:

LeBeau Testimonial
I invite anyone to visit my poem, *"RELIANCE"* for my reflection on this very sensitive subject, where I started to understand the *serpent's subtle ways.* Go to the Internet web page located at http://
inspectorblebeau.pbwiki.com/RELIANCE

THE CURS-ED NET

Chapter Eighteen:

Tolkien, J.R.R., *THE SILMARILLION, as discussed on this website,* **THE WORLD OF MR. TOLKIEN:**
http://www.indepthinfo.com/tolkien/sil.shtml

LeBeau, Byron, discussing a book review of Paul Laviolette's book, **EARTH UNDER FIRE:**
http://inspectorblebeau.pbwiki.
com/COSMOLOGY-THE-BIBLE-AND-WORLD-MYTHS

LeBeau, Byron: Citations taken from Texe Marrs' **MYSTERY MARK of the NEW AGE,** published by Crossway Books, Westchester, Ill., 1988.]
http://inspectorblebeau.pbwiki.
com/CONSTELLATIONS-and-ZODIAC-FACADES-for-SATAN

LaVergne, TN USA
07 September 2010
196146LV00004B/70/A